A MacBrayne Memoir

Brian Patton

ISBN 978-0-9564288-0-6

First published in Great Britain in 2009 by Brian Patton
Second impression 2010

Printed and bound by
Martins the Printers Limited
Seaview Works, Spittal
Berwick-upon-Tweed, TD15 1RS
www.martins-the-printers.com

Set in 10/12 Minion and 8.5/10.2 Gill Sans
Design by www.simprimstudio.com

Contents

Front cover.

In May 1964, *Lochearn* approaches the new pier at Craignure, while, along with her sister, she was standing in for the much-delayed car ferry *Columba*. Despite valiant efforts on the part of the crews, there were problems and all were glad to see the new ship arrive in July. (Author)

An unidentified MacBrayne crew member, in the early years of the 20th century.
(By kind permission of the Mull Museum)

Frontispiece.

The MacBrayne houseflag flying at the bow of *King George V* off the east coast of Mull.

Back cover.

Despite their success with the AEC Q-type in the 1930s, MacBraynes took some time to decide in the 1950s that, at least in urban service, the future lay with the underfloor engine. In 1953 the Company acquired a batch of three AEC Regal 3 buses, with Roe bodywork, of completely traditional appearance, all of which were used on local services from Fort William. No.27 is seen under the balcony of the pier in the 1960s and, rebodied in 1961, lasted until the break-up of the bus fleet in 1970. For comparison two AEC Regal 4 underfloor-engined vehicles were bought at the same time. (Malcolm King)

Introduction

A JUNE MORNING IN 1945. We had gone on to Rothesay pier to meet my grandmother coming down form Glasgow by the MacBrayne steamer. The war in Europe had been over for just a month and the railway steamers had acknowledged this by yellow funnels, but their hulls were still grey and streaked with rust, their saloon windows boarded up. From Craigmore came the first faint drumming that normally heralded *Lochfyne*'s arrival in the bay, then around the corner came a ship unlike any that I had ever seen – could this vessel indeed be the grey *Lochfyne* that I had come to know over the last few years. The black hull gleamed in the morning sun, the white paint of the upperworks shone, the varnish of the woodwork sparkled and the whole was topped by the two smart red and black funnels. Yes, she was still rather squat and she still thumped and vibrated, but this was a ship of a beauty that I had never seen before. Of course my grandfather had told me of the colours of the Clyde in the old days, when he talked of *Grenadier* and *Columba*, and had promised me that, when the war was over, I would see those for myself, but, although I believed him, somehow I had never expected colour so vivid and I now knew for certain that the war was indeed over. The next year brought *King George V* to the Clyde, elegant as well as colourful, and 1947 saw *Saint Columba* sweep into Rothesay again – and indeed, as had been promised, she did have three red and black funnels, just like the *Queen Mary*. (I had had doubts on that point – only big liners had three funnels – but was too fond of my grandfather to say so.) And from then on, I could not and cannot imagine a more fitting colour scheme for ships whose business is in the waters of the west of Scotland.

Sixty-four years on from that June morning, the same colours – with the addition of red lions on yellow discs on the funnels – still sparkle, despite attempts along the way to replace them by something nearer to consultants' tastes, and, incredibly the ships now carry their names also in what in Bute in 1945 was known as "the old tongue", a tongue which, I was once told, would be "of no use to you". And once again the ships are controlled in Scotland. The changes have been remarkable. There are of course those who, usually from the comfort of an office, would introduce the "benefits of competition" and ensure "value for money", just as there were in the 1920s and 1960s. Watching the pier staff and ship's crew coax the present *Bute* in to Wemyss Bay on a stormy December night, sailing across a wild Sound of Sleat as the only passenger on *Lochmor* and seeing *Hebrides* coming safely into Tarbert in the teeth of a force 11 gale, I would suggest that we already have excellent value for money.

It seems only a short time since I first saw the red lions adorn the funnels of *King George V* as she crossed to the North Pier on another June morning, but it is now thirty-six years since David MacBrayne Ltd effectively came to the end of its independent existence and became a part of Caledonian MacBrayne. It was, as the members of the commission of 1919 remarked, a unique organisation, with nothing comparable to it in Britain. It was a pity that a Transport Act (1968) which was intended to co-ordinate transport, actually had the opposite effect as far as the MacBrayne's road services were concerned. Within three years the bus system had gone and, although the goods services remained into the 1980s, these were ultimately dismantled by a Westminster government obsessed by the concept of privatisation and with no mandate in Scotland. Memories fade and it seemed that it was time to try to capture something of this organisation before they were lost for ever. There have been plenty of books on the Company, but there is still a place for the story from the angle of its people – crews, passengers, shore staff, bus and lorry drivers – to tell people what it was like to be part of "MacBraynes".

It would be easy to follow the example of the writer of the MacBrayne guides and cast a romantic glow over the Company and its workings. That would be a false impression. There is nothing romantic about Tarbert at 3am on a dark winter's morning, and very little even at 6.45. There were clearly times too when people had problems with workmates or managers. Nonetheless, after listening to so many people who worked for the Company, it can be said that on the whole people enjoyed their time with MacBraynes and took pride in being part of a service with a remit like few others. In many cases it was a job for life and at the end of that working life, it was usual to look back with satisfaction, on a job well done.

It seemed that there were also topics in the history of the Company which had not been thoroughly explored and, working as far as possible from original records, I have attempted to shed light on some of these. The records are incomplete and probably we shall never know exactly why things happened as they did, but some issues have been clarified.

The result is the present book. It is in no sense a complete history of the Company, nor does it set out to cover every port served and every ship used. It is not intended to provide a factual record of the ships and road vehicles, as these have been amply covered elsewhere. Details of these books are given in the bibliography at the end of the book. Except where necessary to continue a story, or to use some suitable photographs, the book finishes with the creation of Caledonian MacBrayne in 1973.

I have used the 12-hour clock, except in the two cases involving naval service, in which it seemed more appropriate to use the 24-hour clock. Likewise I have used imperial measurements and pre-decimal denominations of money, as both seemed more suitable for this present work.

The translations from Gaelic are entirely my own. I hope that native speakers of the language will look on them kindly.

I have tried in every case to ascertain copyright on material and photographs, but in some cases this has proved to be impossible. It will be appreciated that many of the photographs used are old and, in some cases, damaged and thus not of high quality. It is now possible, using modern techniques of digital imaging, to improve such views to present-day standards, and to a certain extent this has been done, but it seemed that it would be wrong to improve these to look like images of 2009 and more fitting to leave them as they were.

Acknowledgements

It would not have been possible to prepare this book without the generous help extended to me by so many people throughout the highlands and islands, who have not only provided information, documents and photographs but have welcomed me into their homes with a warm hospitality and, on more than one occasion, ferried me back to base when I missed the bus. If any name has been omitted, it is only because there have been so many to remember.

Charles Aitchison, Glasgow, Malcolm Black, Connel, Nick Chaytor, Robert Hale Ltd, London, Mrs Meg Douglas, Tobermory, John Gallacher, Oban, Alastair G Gunn, Edinburgh, Ricky Henderson, Tobermory, Donald Hodgson, Tarbert, Harris, Martin Jenkins, Online Video Archive, Walton-on-Thames, Malcolm King, Leeds, Rev. Archie Lamont, Taynuilt, Mrs E Letley, London, Murdoch Livingstone, Sandwick, Lewis, Bill Lucas, Stornoway, Mrs D MacDonald, Shawbost, Lewis, Miss Jay MacDonald, Barcaldine, Douglas MacDonald, Oban, Ronnie MacIntyre, Oban, Mrs K MacIver, Stornoway, Catherine Mackay, John MacLennan and other staff, Stornoway Port Authority, Donnie MacKinnon, Isleornsay, Louis MacRae, Portree, Duncan MacTaggart, Oban, James Mitchell, Ardrishaig, Alasdair Munro and Mrs A Munro, Inverness, Alan Oxley, the Omnibus Society, Ms E Richmond-Watson, Harper-Collins Ltd, Miss I Robertson, Teangue, Iain Robertson, Tobermory, Norman Robertson, London, Frank Walton, Oban, Iain Quinn, Glasgow.

I have also been grateful to the following staff in archive offices and other offices and libraries, who have gone to considerable trouble to find material and make it available to me.

Agyll and Bute Archives, Lochgilphead. Ms J Davenport and Ms Marina Campbell.

Caledonian MacBrayne, Gourock. Alan Redhead and colleagues.

Centre for Business Studies, University of Glasgow. Ms C Leslie.

Glasgow University Archives staff.

University of St Andrews, Department of Special Collections. Ms Pam Cranston and other staff. Apart from photographs, the Department provided access to much MacBrayne material in the collection of R N W Smith and also kindly agreed to the use of postcards by Valentine of Dundee in my own collection

The Mitchell Library, Glasgow. Ms M Beaton, Mrs E Ryan and other staff, in particular to the photographers, who performed miracles in providing images from the Langmuir Collection, including some of very poor quality.

The Mull Musuem, Tobermory. Mrs J Whittaker and Dr Bill.Clegg

Leabharlann na h'Eilean, Stornoway. Ms Mary Ferguson and colleagues

Library of the National Railway Museum, York. Ms Karen Baker, Lorna and other staff.

Staff of the National Library of Scotland, Edinburgh

Staff of the National Archives of Scotland, West Register House, Edinburgh

Staff of the Archives of the Free State of Saxony, Dresden. Frau Gisela Petrasch and colleagues.

Staff of Oban Public Library

Dualchas Heritage Service, Portree. Ms Alison Beaton

Highland Photographic Archive, Inverness. Ms Lesley Junor and Ms Catherine Niven

War and Peace Museum, Oban. Ms Jackie Penfold

National Maritime Museum, Greenwich. Ms Julie Cochrane,

The Information Service, BBC Scotland. David Stewart and Cat.

The *Oban Times*. Stella, Margaret, Ali and the Managing Director, for help and a warm welcome on many visits.

The Editor and staff of the *Stornoway Gazette*

Lastly I must thank Graham Campbell and the staff of Martin's print works in Berwick, who have made it possible to bring this into print, and Humphrey Weightman of Simprim Studio for graphic design and typography.

Brian Patton
Foulden, Berwickshire, Scotland TD15 1UL
25 July 2009

Author

Brian Patton was brought up in the west of Scotland and came to know its ships from a very early age. After graduating in History from the University of Glasgow, he moved to London and ultimately trained as a teacher of History and Economics. This led later into a guidance post with Royal National Institute for the Blind and then to that of Assistant Education Officer for Further and Higher Education. A desire to return to Scotland brought him back in 1991, since when he has written several books and many articles on transport topics, including Paris transport, modern trams and Scottish shipping.

GLASGOW AND HIGHLAND ROYAL MAIL STEAMERS.

THE

ROYAL ROUTE

·R·M·S·

R.M.S Columba

ROYAL MAIL

David MacBrayne.

1 The Royal Route

THE FIRST MONARCH TO TOUR THE WESTERN ISLES in modern times was not a member of the British royal family but King Friedrich August II of Saxony, who came to Scotland in the course of a fact-finding tour of British industry in 1844. The tour was recorded, in great detail, in a journal kept by his physician, Dr G G Carus, and even by 19th century standards, it would seem to have been a crowded schedule. Unfortunately Dr Carus did not record the number of people who accompanied the monarch, but from references to "carriages", it would seem that it must have been at least a dozen. They used their own carriages which were brought from Saxony, by train and ship. The tour seems to have been meticulously planned and, despite the tight schedule, went off without any serious hitches.

The royal party left Dresden on 22 May and landed in England four days later. They were in London from 1 to 20 June, where they attended a state banquet at Buckingham Palace, but apart from that period, not more than two consecutive nights were spent in any one place and very often only one. The next five weeks were spent visiting industrial installations and inspecting such developments as *Great Britain* at Bristol. Culture and recreation were not neglected, since there was a concert of the Handel Society and a regatta with the Royal Western Yacht Club. Having made a brief detour into Wales, the party went on to Scotland via the Lakes, and, after visiting Hamilton Palace and Glasgow, they set off for the highlands on 23 July. Probably to see Loch Lomond, they travelled by road via Balloch and Inveraray, where they spent one night, and they arrived in Oban on the evening of 24 July. Dr Carus was complimentary about the roads traversed, which he found to be made to a high standard.

On 25 July they made the trip from Oban to Staffa and Iona, on board *Brenda*, a paddle steamer built in 1836 and at that time owned by Messrs Thomson and McConnell. It was a beautiful day, reminding the doctor of Ossian's visionary world. They left Oban at 4.30am and en route were entertained by a blind Scottish fiddler who played, among other tunes, "My gloomy winter is gone" and "Rose's dream". Breakfast was served as they went up the Sound of Mull and Staffa was reached about 10am. The party was rowed into Fingal's cave and put ashore for a short while. When they came to re-embark, they found in attendance some of the Commissioners of Northern Lights, who had come to pay their respects. The ship proceeded to Iona, where they again landed and made some sketches of the island, but a mist descended and rather spoiled their visit. They went on by the south end of Mull, the ship now rolling a bit, despite which they enjoyed an excellent lunch, and Oban was reached again at 8pm. Cannon were fired in honour of the King's visit and a crowd of "very orderly people" welcomed him. The group now proceeded to an inn to partake of dinner, mine host having donned his kilt to mark the occasion.

This was not quite the end of a perfect day, since an hour later they were off again by steamer, with twelve other passengers, for Fort William. The ship's funnel sent showers of sparks in all directions and they arrived about midnight and went on by their carriages – which had been sent on by road – to Banavie. Here they briefly took some tea, the doctor remarking that, like much of the food in this region, it tasted of peat. They then tumbled into bed, but not before Dr Carus had recorded that it had been "the most considerable, magnificent and beautiful excursion of our whole journey".

King Friedrich August and his group, in which no ladies were included, were clearly men of some stamina, since they hoped to climb Ben Nevis on the following day. In the event, bad weather prevented this and they went instead to Loch Shiell (sic), where the views were "quite

Scotch". On the return leg, Dr Carus ventured to try riding on top of the coach and found that this perch afforded excellent views of the countryside, provided that one was not upset by the swaying motion. The mist continued on the next day, ruling out an ascent of the Ben, which they abandoned, to leave instead at 6am for Inverness, after some delay embarking the carriages. Unfortunately no details of the ship were given but the vessel most likely to have been used would have been Messrs Burns' *Inverness*, then on the Glasgow-Inverness through service. There were about 20 other passengers, including several pretty Englishwomen and some little girls. The latter whiled away the voyage by building castles with the footstools which were provided for the comfort of passengers, and in playing with a kitten. There was a break of 90 minutes at Fort Augustus, where the King went ashore and was offered a taste of "whiskey" by one of the locals. There was also a break at Foyers, where the party was ferried ashore to admire the falls, which reminded Dr Carus of the Reichenbach falls in Switzerland. Thereafter rain began to fall and they were glad to arrive in Inverness, where they stayed at the Caledonian Hotel. The return south was by road and no further sailings were involved. They returned to Germany via Leith and Hamburg and reached Dresden again on 9 August.

The translator of Dr Carus' account considered that it should serve as a model for all such tours of this kind and in many respects it did. The tight schedules, with many early starts, the interest shown in natural features, including geology and the emphasis on modern improvements were all to find an echo in the MacBrayne guide of later years.

In 1847 Queen Victoria visited the Clyde and went on to tour the west highlands, the first British monarch to do so. Her progress was rather more sedate than that of Friedrich August. She was of course accompanied by Prince Albert and they brought their two eldest children, the Princess Royal and the Prince of Wales, later Edward V11. Given the then-current unrest in Ireland, there were some fears about her reception, but in the event the crowds were rapturous in their acclamation of the royal party, who travelled in the royal yacht, the first *Victoria and Albert*. As Her Majesty was a notoriously bad sailor, she preferred to sail via the Crinan Canal, but the dimensions of the yacht precluded her from using it and the Queen had to travel on *Sunbeam*, one of the passenger barges belonging at that time to Messrs G and J Burns. Having visited the Duke of Argyll at Inveraray Castle on 18 August, she returned to Ardrishaig, to be greeted by ecstatic crowds, and, after passing under a floral arch, embarked on *Sunbeam* for her trip through the canal. The barge was pulled by three large, black horses, decked with red coats and adorned with silver trappings. The postillions also wore scarlet coats with silver riding caps. One of these was John MacTavish, who had cut his hand the day before and was therefore recognisable by his bandage. Her Majesty wore a blue and white striped silk dress, a white bonnet and carried a green parasol, with which she from time to time acknowledged the applause of the crowds lining the banks. In choosing this itinerary, the Queen gave that firm and its successors some very welcome publicity and thenceforth this route from lowland Scotland to the highlands and islands rejoiced in the title of "The Royal Route", a usage which continued until 1969. Curiously, a later king of Saxony, King Albert, visited Scotland in 1887 and sailed on *Ivanhoe* on the Clyde, but did not come to the west highlands. However, his patronage of their yacht-like ship encouraged the managers of the Frith (sic) of Clyde Steam Packet Company to market their Arran sailings as "The Royal Route", but this usage did not catch on.

In truth, although she admired the barge and commented on its smooth motion, the Queen found the passage tedious, but there was no need to let the public know what HM actually thought of her transit of the canal. As soon as they reached Crinan, the party boarded the royal yacht with all possible haste, and, for the time being, that was the end of the Queen's connexion with local shipping. Fortunately the weather obliged with a fine sunset over Jura and for the next few days the sea was like glass. The royal tourists went on via Oban bay and the Sound of Mull to visit Fingal's cave. Accounts of the trip written for English papers such as the Illustrated London News laid much stress on the "wild shores and deserted promentaries" (sic) and the grim and solitary aspect of ruined strongholds, such as Duart Castle. These were contrasted with the "peaceful objects of Queen Victoria" and the changes which had been wrought on the landscape in the name of orderly progress. When the royal barge was rowed into Fingal's cave, the oarsmen dipping their oars with great precision and the royal standard fluttering overhead, it must have seemed that the highlands and islands were now officially approved as a holiday destination for solidly respectable subjects of the Queen and writers of tourist guides in due course took their cue from these reports of her progress.

The Queen was soon followed by Marie Amélie, ex-Queen of the French who in 1851 came to Oban from Fort William, with her daughter-in-law the Duchess of Orléans, her children and servants. They were greeted by a salute from the battery and much cheering. They commandeered a good deal of the available hotel accommodation and it is not recorded what other visitors thought of this. In that year, *Dolphin*, in her first year with the Hutcheson fleet, sailed on alternate days to Fort William and to Iona and it would seem that she was the ship on which the royal party sailed.

In 1865, by which date *Iona* of 1864 was on the Ardrishaig service, the Glasgow departure was at 7am and a coach connexion left Ardrishaig for Oban at 1pm, going via Kilmartin and Melfort and arriving in Oban at 6.30pm. In the return direction, departure was at 7am with arrival at 12.45, in time to connect with *Iona* on her southbound run. The Ardrishaig-Oban fare was 12/- first class (presumably inside) and 10/- second class. The introduction of *Linnet* on the Crinan Canal in 1866 and the Crinan-Oban link, at that time generally provided by *Mountaineer*, not only brought a much earlier arrival in Oban but also a more comfortable journey and most tourists now used that route. It was probably also cheaper, since the Oban-Ardrishaig single fare (at a slightly later date) was only 9/6 or 5/- and returns were available at 14/6 and 8/6.

There was also a coach service from Oban to Inverarnan (north of Ardlui and reached by canal from Loch Lomond), then by loch steamer to Balloch and train to Glasgow; this trip took exactly twelve hours.

By 1878, the first leg of the tour, from Glasgow to Oban, via Ardrishaig and Crinan, gave a Glasgow departure at 7am, with a later train connexion via Greenock Princes Pier at 8.25. From Rothesay onwards, there was a good prospect of a race between *Columba* and *Lord Of The Isles*. Most tourists would have travelled cabin, although the crack was definitely better in steerage. At Ardrishaig, passengers for *Linnet* to Crinan were met by a gathering of local, often barefoot, boys, offering to carry their luggage and giving a wildly exaggerated account of the distance involved between the pier and the landing stage. One tourist, correctly, estimated that it was only "five minutes smart walk". Some of these boys would follow the ship when she set off, running along the banks and hoping to catch some of the pennies which tourists threw for them; as the tourists' aim was not always accurate, most of the coins ended up on the bed of the Canal. The little ship was remembered as being "better than Noah's ark in capacity for storing many and various into a small space", although, as her capacity was only 274 passengers, at busy periods, the horse-drawn barges were still used for some years to cope with the overflow. In the 1850s there was apparently a passenger tug boat on the Canal, which also took Royal Route travellers, although she does not seem to have belonged to Hutchesons. She had a roomy cabin, into which the ladies retired, while the male passengers sat on the semi-circular roof of this cabin, their feet resting on the gunwhale. In later years the Canal icebreaker *Conway* often had to be pressed into service to help *Linnet* cope with the crowds. In 1875 she was described as "elegantly fitted". Class distinctions were still maintained on *Linnet* and in one respect those in steerage, which was forward, had an advantage, since they could enjoy leaning over the rail and watching the sharp bow cut through the still waters of the canal. Her amenities were further improved in 1894 when a deckhouse was fitted and a bridge erected, to spare the helmsman the task of trying to steer the vessel when surrounded by chattering passengers. At Dunardry, a heard of cows waited to be milked by bare-legged lassies, just as *Linnet* came alongside and thirsty tourists could refresh themselves, at a price. The Cairnbaan Stores offered a variety of souvenirs and, later, post cards, *Linnet* probably being the subject of more post card views than any other ship in the fleet, not excluding *Columba*. There was also a piper, who, like many of to-day's buskers, had but three tunes in his repertoire

1.1 A very early view of *Iona* at Ardrishaig, 1864 (Glasgow University Archives)

1.2 Passengers on the deck of *Iona* in late Victorian times. (By courtesy of the Mitchell Library, Glasgow City Council)

1.3 The engine room of *Iona* . (By courtesy of the Mitchell Library, Glasgow City Council)

1.4 Donald Leitch, the "able but sometimes irritable" pilot of *Iona* in Victorian times. (By courtesy of the Mitchell Library, Glasgow City Council)Council)

1.5 Captain C MacDonald and Chief Engineer Robert Beattie on board *Iona* c1920. (By courtesy of the Mitchell Library, Glasgow City Council)

1.6 Passengers on their way to Islay or Jura crossed to West Loch Tarbert by road, to connect with *Pioneer* (1905) on her afternoon sailing. This view in August 1912 shows returning passengers from Islay boarding the brake at the West Loch pier to take them to meet *Columba* on her return trip. At that time, the fare for this short journey was 6d (2.5p) and some passengers have clearly decided that it is better to walk. (National Maritime Museum, Greenwich, London, neg. no.N30215).

1.7 These passengers did not travel light. Luggage is piled up on the West Loch pier, with *Pioneer* behind. The brakes did not convey luggage, which followed in a cart. (National Maritime Museum, Greenwich, London, neg.no. N30214).

1.8 Arrival at Port Ellen – "a lovely place for a holiday", according to the writer of this card posted in 1938. This must have been the start of the Glasgow Fair holidays and *Mountaineer* (1910) has been brought down from Oban to help *Pioneer* to cope with the crowds. Buses and saloon cars now provide onward transport on Islay. (Author's Collection)

1.9 The Royal Route in winter – *Grenadier* at Tarbert in 1920. (Glasgow University Archives))

1.10 The Royal Route in wartime. The early war-time livery of black hull and funnel and yellow saloons worn by *Lochnevis* at Wemyss Bay dates this picture to the early months of 1940. The saloon windows have not yet been boarded up, as was later the case. (By courtesy of the Mitchell Library, Glasgow City Council)

1.11 The ships sailed in all weathers. On 2 November 1960 *King George V* is mooring at Rothesay pier in a south-easterly gale, which was to preclude calls at Innellan and Dunoon. (Author)

1.12 The end of the Ardrishaig service. *Lochfyne* berthing at no.3 berth at Rothesay pier in August 1969, a few weeks before MacBraynes bowed out on the Clyde. A view taken from the gallery of the then-new pier building, which in the event was to have a very short life. (Alastair G Gunn)

1.13 Coaches await the arrival of *Columba* at Ardrishaig. The clock shows 12.47 and it would seem that she is slightly late. Some of the barefoot boys await the tourists. (By courtesy of the Mitchell Library, Glasgow City Council)

1.14 *Linnet* approaches her landing place at Ardrishaig, watched by some of the youthful luggage porters from a perch on the gangway. *Conway* is moored behind. (Author's Collection)

1.15 A view showing passengers aboard *Linnet* c1900. She is certainly crowded and one passenger (admidships) has decided to stand rather precariously outside the deck rail. (By courtesy of the Mitchell Library, Glasgow City Council))

– "*The Barren Rocks of Aden*", "*The Drunken Piper*" and "*The Green Hills of Tyrol*", the last being now better known as "*The Scottish Soldier*". Bairns and more bare-foot lassies sold heather nearby. It would seem that the natives of Knapdale had found quite a few ways to persuade the tourists to part with their holiday money and they were probably glad to reach Crinan.

Here another ship of the fleet was waiting, from 1879 to 1914 usually *Chevalier* and *Mountaineer* (1910) replaced her from 1919 to the end of the Canal service in 1929. There was no problem here in locating the point of departure of the steamer, since *Linnet* berthed right at the end of the Canal, just opposite the larger steamer. Of course piles of luggage had to be transhipped and in the early 1900s the crew were assisted in this by three blonde young men, who turned out to be the ship's band. They were from Saxony and therefore considered not to be dangerous. For tourists going north via Crinan, it was reassuring to know that "Immediately after starting (at 3pm), the dinner bell is rung for Cabin passengers" who must have indeed been hungry by this hour, if they had had nothing since breakfast on *Columba*. Apparently the dinner was "fit for a lord". Steerage or Third-Class passengers dined in the forecabin about half an hour afterwards; presumably the galley could not cope with serving meals to rich and poor at the same time Oban was reached at 4.50pm.

Nothing had been said to prepare the tourists for the scrum which awaited them on the North Pier when *Chevalier* arrived. This difficulty had first been observed in 1863 by the author of "The Journal of a Scotch Tour", who complained of the rush to secure hotels, of which the Caledonian (not the present hotel of that name) was "the oldest and best inn". By the 1890s a double line of hotel "boots" and the older licensed ("badge") porters dinned the ears of the travellers with the names of the various hotels. If any got past them, escape was only momentary, since there was also a lively little knot of lads and lassies, pushing cards into unwary hands and endlessly repeating "Private lodgings, Sir, private lodgings". Only the very brave escaped to select at leisure their own lodgings. Even then, they were still not immune from harassment. A party leaving their hotel at 7am to go on board *Mountaineer*, was assailed by the wailings of a "wandering female minstrel" intent on giving a rendering of "Whistle owre the lave o't".

Even after the Callander and Oban Railway opened its line, there were still plenty of tourists who preferred the Royal Route and this remained the case up to 1914, and to an extent on to 1939. The return fare from Glasgow, in 1898, of 20/- in cabin and 11/- in steerage also compared very well with the former coach fare of 12/- single in first class and 10/- in second (via Loch Lomond). A week-end return was also offered, at 18/- and 10/-. Tickets allowed break of journey at any place en route and were also available covering a wide range of circular tours. A cabin return from Glasgow to Gairloch, going via Crinan and returning via Loch Awe cost £3 in 1888.

Until 1914, there was a second sailing, by *Iona*, leaving Glasgow at 1.30pm and reaching Ardrishaig at 7.15pm, but of course it did not allow a continuation to Oban on the same day.

From a reading of the MacBrayne guide, it all sounded very straightforward, but there were times when things went wrong. On 18 July 1883 *Columba's* purser wired to the Company's Greenock agent to ask that a rope should be provided to hold back waiting passengers at Princes Pier. There seems to have been a fair degree of chaos and, he added hesitantly, "I am afraid that there were some mistakes about luggage". This was of course during the Glasgow Fair. An account of a trip when conditions were certainly not of the best appeared in the "*Gartnavel Gazette*" in January 1920 and is summarised here. It was written by someone who simply signed himself "Mac" and it may be assumed that he was a doctor. He had been with a party on a fishing trip somewhere in Knapdale and by the time only he and one other person were left, they became aware that a railway strike was in the offing. (This dates the trip to the summer of 1919.) They decided to leave on the following Tuesday and travelled by "mail motor" to Ardrishaig, where they boarded *Iona* at 1.30pm. Apart from a goodly number of passengers, 100 sheep were on board. The number of passengers increased at

1.16 *Conway* alongside Ardrishaig pier. (James Mitchell Collection)

1.19 Passengers on board *Chevalier* at Crinan in the 1890s. (By courtesy of the Mitchell Library, Glasgow City Council)

1.20 The saloon of *Chevalier*. She was fitted with electric light during an overhaul in 1919 and this view must date from then. (By courtesy of the Mitchell Library, Glasgow City Council)

each calling point and at Rothesay a "frightful" crowd awaited the ship. Not all managed to board and there was "weeping and wailing" as she finally cast off. Unfortunately the writer had gone forward into the steerage just before that point and now found himself trapped there, wedged against a very stout lady, in whose opinion the strikers were worse than the Germans. The weather had been good during the first part of the journey, but it deteriorated and when the steamer came out of Rothesay bay, she rolled quite heavily, further increasing the discomfort of her passengers. One man was a particular source of annoyance to his fellow travellers, since he had acquired a set of antlers – presumably a trophy – and these were now always in someone's way, no matter what he did with them. After another traveller had shouted at him "Here you, watch thae horns", he solved the problem by holding them aloft over his head ; in the gathering dusk, they gave him a distinctly eerie appearance. The writer was especially worried about the fate of his canvas hold-all, which was now buried beneath a pile of luggage, atop of which some passengers had found seats, but there was nothing he could do about it. At 9pm they reached Glasgow, where he was relieved to be reunited with his hold-all, which he found to be none the worse for the journey. He was glad to be home again.

In later years, the Glasgow-Ardrishaig/Tarbert and the summer-only Glasgow – Fort William coach services supplemented the Royal Route and a circular "Tour Argyll" was offered by steamer and "luxury motor coach" between Glasgow and Ardrishaig. The fare in 1933 was 12/-, allowing cabin travel on the steamer. There were then two through coach services daily (including Sunday) from Glasgow, with an additional one on Saturday, but oddly there were in summer three daily services in the reverse direction. The time to and from Ardrishaig was four and a quarter hours, only very slightly faster than the train and steamer journey and a good deal less comfortable.

After a break in Oban, tourists who wished to complete the Royal Route could sail on by steamer to Fort William or Corpach and thence to the Caledonian Canal.

1.21 Another occasion when things went wrong. In 1929 *Iona* had a breakdown in the Kyles of Bute and suffered the indignity of being towed away by tugs, that on the left herself a paddle steamer. (Courtesy of the University of St Andrews Library, RWN Smith collection, RNWS-14-114)

1.22 In 1932 the Company took delivery of four Maudslay ML6A buses, with Park Royal coachwork, seating 30. They seem to have been used on the Glasgow-Ardrishaig service and are remembered as being slow, noisy and not very adept at hill-climbing. Publicity claimed them as "luxury" coaches, but this was definitely stretching a point. In this view of no.53, something seems to have gone wrong, somewhere around the Rest and be Thankful. Luggage was stored on the rack on the roof and covered by a tarpaulin to protect it from the weather. By this date, hikers had become a feature of the west highland scene and one, apparently with an injured knee, can be seen of the left. This particular vehicle had a fairly short life, being scrapped in 1942, suggesting that even in war time, they were not valued members of the fleet. At that time, the bus and coach livery was crimson lake and off-white, with gold lining. (The Omnibus Society)

1.23 The classic MacBrayne bus, seen throughout the west highlands in the 1950s. There were 34 of these Maudslay Marathons, mostly with bodies by Park Royal, but some were bodied by Croft of Glasgow. There were also nine similar AEC Regals. They were sold off in the 1960ss and all but two were snapped up by smaller firms for further service. The least far-travelled were nos.21 and 143 whose new homes were with MacTavish of Arrochar, and the former is seen at Tarbet in a typical west highland downpour on 22 May 1965. It lasted until 1971 and no.143 until 1977. (Author)

1.24 By 1965 the Company's road services provided an overland alternative to the traditional Royal Route. In this scene at Crianlaraich station on 7 August 1965, no.44, an AEC Reliance with Duple Midland coachwork, is running through to Inverness, while, behind, another Reliance of the series 200-202 and another vehicle are bound for Fort William only. (Alastair G Gunn)

"This is not an ordinary voyage on which you are about to embark. You will find it easy to lay aside the ledgers and reckonings of everyday usage for the air is filled with the scent of clover and as the steamer beats away from a make-believe quay in to a fir-wood, you will hear the comments of wild pigeons. This water lane winds round more than the immediate physical corners. It would be no surprise to meet the Walrus and the Carpenter, the Jabberwock, the White Queen or Alice herself."

1.25 The paddle steamer *Lochness* at Fort Augustus . (Author's Collection)

Thus did the MacBrayne guide for 1939 introduce the tourist to the passage of the Caledonian Canal from Banavie to Inverness aboard the paddle steamer *Gondolier*. The use of the Caledonian Canal by ships of what became the MacBrayne fleet dated back to the 1830s, when the paddle steamers *Rob Roy* and *Inverness* were placed on it by a Mr William Young, who later sold out to Messrs Burns. The latter had *Culloden* – perhaps not the most tactful choice of name – built for the local service in the centenary year of the battle (1845) and in the next year *Cygnet* and *Lapwing*, were bought for a Glasgow-Inverness through service, via both Crinan and Caledonian Canals. On Loch Ness these were soon joined by the paddle steamer *Edinburgh Castle*, later, after a major rebuild, better known as *Glengarry*. But these were basically year-round ships, catering for local passengers and cargo rather than summer visitors, though the latter did begin to use them from 1850 onwards. The local Inverness – Fort Augustus service offered a year-round departure from the latter pier at 6.30am, arriving in Inverness at 9.30am and returning at 3.30pm (1905 timings). In July and August this was supplemented by a second service southbound at 11am and returning from Fort Augustus at 3.45pm, clearly aimed at the tourist market. The basic service was successively worked by *Glengarry* (from 1893) and two ships named *Lochness*; the first a paddle steamer (1885-1912) and the second a small screw vessel, formerly a "Clutha" on the River Clyde service.

By 1866 it was clear that something better was required for the growing tourist traffic and the result was *Gondolier*. Like all important tourist steamers of the time, she

1.26 *Glengarry* seems to have met her end in this view taken in 1919, but she was in fact being overhauled and was to continue on Loch Ness until 1927. (Glasgow University Archives)

1.27 The crew of *Glengarry*. (Highland Photographic Archive)

had oscillating engines, though in her case they were rather a miniature set. She was to become the only Hutcheson/MacBrayne steamer to carry the reigning monarch. In the event, the passage of the Crinan Canal on *Sunbeam* in 1847 was not to be the only time that the Queen travelled on part of the Route. In September 1873 she stayed for some days with Lord Abinger at Inverlochy Castle and on conclusion of that, she returned to Balmoral via Inverness. On 16 September, a day of generally fine weather, although with some mists around the mountain tops, the Queen and Princess Beatrice embarked on *Gondolier* at Banavie with her lady-in-waiting Jane Churchill, John Brown and other attendants. The Queen did not say much about the vessel, apart from the statement that she was built on the same principle as the one she had had on Loch Lomond[1]. She did, however, enthuse about the fine large cabin with many windows, in which 62 people could dine at one time. The mist prevented her from sketching the top of Ben Nevis and she settled down to watch the scenery at a lower level. Once again, as in 1847, she complained about the time spent going through the locks, and commented that, while the Caledonian Canal was no doubt a wonderful piece of engineering, travel by it was very tedious. However, she did find it "amusing" to watch the people on the banks going round and round as they opened the gates. At one place, a poor woman brought oatcakes and milk to the royal party. Just after mid-day, they went below to enjoy a hot luncheon, during which time *Gondolier* negotiated the locks at Fort Augustus. This allowed people on the banks to look down on the royal party, but the Queen philosophically noted that this was "unavoidable". A sharp shower fell while they dined but when they came back on deck, the weather was once again

1.28 *Glengarry* at Fort Augustus. At this period, she sailed without a mast. (University of Glasgow Archives)

1.29 *Gairlochy* entering Loch Ness. The card was posted by "Harriet" in Inverness on 4 September 1906, to an address in St James, London S.W. to say that "I think we leave here on Saturday but not certain". She was presumably a servant and servants had to travel when their employers decided. (Author's Collection)

1.30 Passengers on board *Gairlochy* 1919. (By courtesy of the Mitchell Library, Glasgow City Council)

1 The Queen had cruised on Loch Lomond aboard *Prince Consort* on 4 September 1869. Her grasp of naval architecture had, understandably, faltered slightly in comparing the two vessels, since on that ship the sponsons were carried from stem to stern and the deck saloons occupied the full width of the hull. On *Gondolier* the sponsons were much shorter and the saloons narrower than the hull, with alleyways round the sides. In both cases there were seats outside the saloons and it seems to have been this latter feature which confused Her Majesty.

fine and it continued thus until Dargarroch was reached, where, in a crush of people and carriages, they disembarked.

Curiously, although she spent her entire long life on the service for which she had been built, *Gondolier* did have a very brief career as a Clyde steamer. On 25 May 1875 Georgiana, Duchess of Argyll, died in London and, after a service in Westminster Abbey, her body was conveyed to Wemyss Bay pier by train, prior to a funeral in Kilmun. The mourners included the Marquis of Lorne, the Duke of Sutherland and Mr W E Gladstone. It is not know which ship carried the coffin and the funeral party, from Wemyss Bay, but after the internment, the party "re-embarked" at Kilmun on to *Gondolier*, which would suggest she had carried them on their outward journey also. Presumably she had been on the Clyde for overhaul and was chosen as her accommodation would offer a fitting standard of comfort to the ducal and royal party.

The timetable established in 1866 for the Caledonian Canal cruise did not vary for very many years, although in pre-1914 days it was given as a daily service and calls were made at rather more piers. A connecting service was given on the railway between Fort William and Banavie pier. The daily service of course required two ships and running opposite *Gondolier* until 1893 was *Glengarry*. She was by then over fifty years old, hardly a fit steamer for a crack tourist service and was replaced on it by *Gairlochy*, a slightly younger steamer which had originally run on the Clyde as *Sultan*. She was bought by MacBraynes in 1894 and fitted with deck saloons. However, in December 1919 she caught fire at Fort Augustus while working the mail service, and, as she was not replaced, the frequency of the cruise (and the connecting train) was reduced to thrice weekly in either direction. The timetable of the 1890s also featured a very early start from Inverness, at 7am, with an arrival in Banavie at 3pm. Going north the departure time was also rather earlier than in later years, but was a relatively civilised 9.30.

The 1898 guide book devoted almost 16 pages to this route. It began with a fairly detailed technical description of the Caledonian Canal and went on with the

1.31 The crew of *Gairlochy*. (By courtesy of the Mitchell Library, Glasgow City Council)

1.32 A view over the stern of *Gondolier*, as she leaves Loch Ness, c1904. Sheep have clearly taken precedence and these elegant Edwardian passengers are confined to a small part of the after deck. (By courtesy of the University of St Andrews Library, JEAS 28-a9)

1.33/4 Two views of the Inverness-Foyers bus service, showing first the tricky situations which could be encountered when roads were still narrow, and secondly the mail compartment being unloaded at Foyers. The bus, no.98, was another Bedford with Duple bodywork, but seating 20 and was bought in 1938. (The Omnibus Society)

1.35 Pre-1939, crews wore uniform gaiters, as seen in this view of another small Bedford, no.69 of 1935. (The Omnibus Society)

usual blend of natural features, large houses with the names of their owners and some slightly adapted history. The writer unbent enough to point out, at Inverlochy, the distillery from which came "Long John" whisky. Those who wanted a bit of exercise could leave the steamer at Kyltra (now Kytra) Locks about two miles north of Cullochy and walk along the canal bank to rejoin her at Fort Augustus. There was ample time for this, as she did not leave the latter point until 2.15pm, but of course walkers would have had to make sure that they were back on board in time for the second sitting of dinner. Cycles were not carried on the Canal steamers.

MacBraynes began bus services along Loch Ness in 1911/2, but the local steamer service continued until 1928, when it was withdrawn in one of the first economies instituted by the new management. Local pressure briefly forced its re-introduction in 1929 but, as road services could now provide a better and much cheaper service, it was finally withdrawn in that year. In 1933 there were three daily bus services each way between Fort Augustus and Inverness, via the west side of the Canal, and three between Foyers and Inverness via the east side, with an extra service on Saturday and two return services on Sunday. In the 1950s Alex Munro was a driver on the Foyers service, on which Bedfords were then used and on a Sunday evening run to Inverness, there was occasionally a passenger who was a piper and entertained his fellow-travellers (loudly) with a selection of Scottish airs. Alex also once had to act as midwife to a labrador who decided to give birth to three pups on the back seat of his bus – mother and family were all well by the time they arrived in Inverness. As elsewhere, bus crews delivered milk and meat and collected mail, from both local post offices and roadside letter boxes. As a gesture of goodwill, drivers would also collect medical prescriptions and deliver these to outlying homes. Children travelling alone were entrusted to their care. Unaccompanied items might include day-old chicks, eggs, milk, meat, small machinery and nuts and bolts to repair that of farms, and items for the DIY enthusiast. As on the Oban-Ardrishaig bus on a Saturday evening, passengers and crew had to suffer the attempts of out-of-tune singers. Anyone who in his confusion boarded the wrong bus would be recognised as an alien immediately and turned off and conductors became adept at ensuring that even the most befuddled passenger got off at the right place. On one journey into Inverness, a conductor was slightly surprised when an elderly lady boarded, carrying a large garden rake. She explained that her husband had just died and she was on the way to make arrangements with the undertaker. As she had not had a tape measure to hand, she had measured him with the handle of the rake – "He was quite tall – one and a half lengths".

By the 1930s it seemed that, despite the buses, *Gondolier* would go on for ever. She had in 1930 received one of the boilers from *Grenadier*, in 1935 she was given new steel saloons with large windows and in the following year a deck house was placed over the saloon companionway. The local train service to Banavie now consisted of one elderly ex-North British Railway six-wheel coach, hauled by an equally elderly goods engine, but a touch of distinction was conveyed by the polished metal rosette attached to its smokebox door[2]. In 1937 *Princess Louise* was transferred to Inverness to supplement the sailings of *Gondolier* by a daily cruise to Fort Augustus, leaving at 11am, and in the handbill for this, passengers were told that they might see the Loch Ness Monster. Obviously even this possibility did not generate enough traffic for this cruise to be repeated in other pre-war years. It was to be international politics that dictated the fate of *Gondolier*. Although it was probably not realised at the time, her arrival at Inverness on the evening of Saturday 2 September 1939 marked the end of the through passenger service along the length of the Caledonian Canal. The ship herself was taken away in February 1940 to be sunk as a blockship at Scapa Flow, where her hull still lies. There were some thoughts of reviving the service after 1945, since, as seen in the account which follows, *Gondolier* had remained consistently popular until rumours of war intervened. From Chris Fraser's account[3], it

1.36 Successors to *Gondolier*, two Maudslay buses with Park Royal bodywork await departure for Inverness from Fort William c1950. That nearer the camera is no.86 of 1948, while no.81 is beyond. (The Omnibus Society)

2   The North British Railway. C Hamilton Ellis. Ian Allan, London, 1955
3   *Christy Boy*. C Fraser. Fraser and Son, Glasgow, 1994

seems that MacBrayne's staff surveyed the piers concerned and that there were thoughts of using *Lochinvar* on the Canal, after she was no longer required at Oban. However, she was sold for excursion work on the Thames, and nothing came of this idea. After 1945, tourists who wished to complete the Royal Route had to do so by road. It was a great pity that a modern motorship, perhaps along the lines of the now-preserved *Balmoral*, could not have been built about 1950 for this service and once again, though not for the last time, Scotland lost a first-rate tourist facility for the lack of a fairly paltry sum of money and a willingness to take a long-term view. Modern vessels, operated by another firm, cruise on Loch Ness and these are well patronised, but they do not offer the facilities provided on board *Gondolier* and they do not afford the chance to sail the Canal from one end to the other as part of a longer Scottish trip.

Fortunately in her last summer, *Gondolier* had on board as pantry boy in first class a young lad named Charles Aitchison, with a photographic memory and a camera, and he later set down his detailed recollections of the ship and her passengers and crew. These are now reproduced with his kind permission, to give a taste of life on board as:-

First-Class Pantry Boy on Gondolier

"At Banavie we see RMS *Gondolier* – red funnel, white superstructure and shimmering brass." Thus did MacBraynes in the 1930s advertise their paddle steamer that was to take passengers through three locks and the Caledonian Canal between Banavie and Inverness.

Alas, I was the one that had to do most of the "shimmering". As first-class pantry boy I had to polish all the portholes aft of the paddles, while the third-class pantry boy was limited to those from the paddles to the bow – a less daunting task.

Strictly speaking, as she was a paddle steamer, she should have been referred to as PS *Gondolier*, but, as she carried the odd bag of mail, her owners chose the grandeur of "Royal Mail Steamer". Her service was all part of a two-day luxury trip from Glasgow to Inverness and vice-versa, the "Wonder Waterway" tour. *Gondolier* took passengers from Inverness to Banavie, where they boarded a train for the short journey to Fort William. This was to avoid lengthy negotiation of the eight locks (called "Neptune's Staircase") that formed the sixty-two foot drop from the Canal to Loch Linnhe. They then boarded *Lochfyne* and sailed to Oban, arriving at 6.45p.m. to spend the night there. On the following day they went by bus to Ardrishaig, where *Saint Columba* picked them up and took them to Glasgow. *Gondolier* sailed south from Inverness on Monday, Wednesday and Friday and north from Banavie on Tuesday, Thursday and Saturday

Obviously the trip could have been done in one day at a great deal less expense, so we had passengers who were pretty affluent and the catering reflected this.

But let us go back a bit. I had left school in 1939 and was looking for some interesting activity before taking up the serious business of training to be a civil engineer. My father's relations had a place in Fort Augustus called "Richmond House Hotel". Calling it an hotel was stretching things a bit. It had three public rooms, six bedrooms and a room for a maid. While on holiday there as a young lad, I had often seen *Gondolier* passing through the locks. She fairly towered above her surroundings and was clearly the highlight of the day, both for the locals and tourists. I was most impressed and this gave me a somewhat romantic view of the steamer.

As she ran only for the months of June, July, August and the first half of September, this seemed to be the answer to my search for a summer diversion. My father's cousin was her Purser, so it was a simple matter asking him to put my name forward for a job. I was offered pantry boy or chocolate boy. Chocolate boy did not seem to me to be a real job, so I chose pantry boy. Well, instead of being a diversion, it turned out to be the hardest work I have ever done.

At Inverness I rose at 6.30a.m. and my first task was to make up the beds of the Purser, Checker (Assistant Purser) and my own. We had no cabins and slept in first-class lounge after the passengers had departed. This meant that all my worldly goods were in a suitcase under the cushions in this lounge and I had to look out what I needed for each day, as I could hardly ask a first-class voyager to rise while I delved into this locker. The milk had then to be taken on board and stored. The ladder leading down to the saloon was scrubbed and the brass boiler for making tea had to be polished. Next I tackled the job of making 16 dishes of butterballs and by the time I had finished this, the ship had cast off and the passengers were appearing for breakfast. This consisted of a choice of cereal or porridge, followed by fried fish, then bacon and eggs. It was certainly a good start to the day. (The cost of breakfast was 3/- or 2/- in first class and 2/6d or 2/- in third.) The Officers then arrived for breakfast and by the time we had finished with them and cleaned up, we had our own meal at 10a.m. I had been up since 6.30 and all I had had was a cup of tea and a biscuit. Our meal was scarcely over when the passengers that had had their breakfasts were descending on us for their morning coffee.

My main work was to take whatever was necessary from the galley to the pantry and to wash up all the dishes, glasses and cutlery. The sink was filled with cold water and heated by a steam pipe that entered at the bottom of the sink. A bar of soap was placed in an old tin that was riddled with holes and this was held over the pipe until the water was very hot and soapy. It was so hot that my hands (we were not permitted to use cloths) could be in the water for only two seconds at a time. Glasses were first, cutlery next and dishes last. The drying was done with what was termed a pantry cloth and would be four feet long and two feet wide. We usually lifted and dried about five plates at a time.

The saloon steward, Andy Hexton, took in hand my training. He showed me how to make up the butterballs and how to dry dishes and cutlery at speed. MacBrayne's cups looked as if they had been specially designed for Andy's methods, for they could be picked up by the right hand and held firmly in the cloth, while the left hand inserted the other part of the cloth into the interior, the thumbs meeting in the centre of the handle. A short sharp twist in the opposite direction resulted in the cup being completely dry – and this meant even the handle. Andy had been a steward on trains and knew his stuff. He regularly carried five plates of soup from the pantry to the dining saloon. They were all balanced on his left arm while his right hand was free to do any steadying that was required. If he were pushed, he could manage seven plates at a time! We stocked Lea and Perrins Worcester sauce and one day Andy said to me, "Put a drop or two of it in your soup, lad, and you'll think that every day is your birthday". However, when taking his advice, the 2nd steward told me to watch while he put some of this sauce on a piece of cloth and dragged it across the copper boiler. It produced a very bright, shimmering swathe across the dull surface of the boiler. "That's what Lea and Perrins does to your stomach," said he. They were both having fun at my inexperience, for I did not then appreciate that there were acids in my stomach much stronger than any that the firm of Lea and Perrins could concoct.

I did not object to hard work, or even long hours, but I had a feeling that conditions were unhealthy. Most of the day I was working in the pantry, where there was no ventilation. The porthole in the pantry could not be opened while sailing, as it was aft of the paddles and, if opened, the water would have come pouring in. The heat was often so intense that I was compelled to discard all clothing save for trousers and white jacket.

For breakfast and high tea the stewards wore a conventional dark blue jacket, but with maroon silk lapels, on which were embroidered the famous MacBraynes' crest. However, for lunch they had a fancy white tunic, fastened diagonally down the front with silver buttons. It also had two silver buttons on each shoulder, ornamented with twisted blue silk cord between each button. It was most impressive.

On any day of the week, every ship in the MacBrayne's fleet had exactly the same menu. This was to ensure that any traveller going from one of their vessels to another would not have to face the same menu again. So if it was tapioca pudding on Wednesday, then it had to be apple tart on Thursday!

Lunch was a five-course affair and cost 3/6d, though a cheaper version was available at 2/6d (both figures in first class). For the former amount, a working man would have had to work three hours. Soup was followed by fresh salmon and salad, then there was a choice of joint or entrée.

After this came the dessert (quite a choice of puddings, jellies and fruit) and finally biscuits and a variety of cheese with coffee. This landed me with about 300 dishes, and there were two sittings, 12 noon and 1p.m. Add to this that the third-class saloon rang a bell for their lunch at 12.30p.m. and quite a few of them finished by mistake with us. As they were all potential tippers, the stewards did not turn them away. The stewards came to the hatch in front of the pantry and asked for whatever was required, and the pantry man served them. I distinctly recall that the sex of the diner was always mentioned. For instance, the steward might say, "One gent's roast beef and two lady's roast beefs" – the ladies always getting a much smaller portion. I was so conditioned by this idea that the man always came off the better that years later when I was about to be married and we were choosing furniture, I found out that in many ways the lady was now to come off better!

Third class passengers dined in the fore cabin and their lunch cost only 2/6d (12.5p), as they were not given the salmon and salad, or the cheese and coffee. Actually, this lunch was available to any of the tourists in first class if they were to choose it. I recollect that when the Chief Steward was carving up the joint in the pantry he would ask the steward if the recipient were a "half crooner" – meaning had the diner paid only 2/6d (half a crown) for the meal. If this were the case, he did not give as good a cut as the others got.

Back to *Gondolier*. After the second sitting, the officers came for lunch. By the time it was served and we had finished clearing up after them, it was after 2.45p.m. before we had ours. There was no meal hour or anything like that, the longer I took the more dishes were piling up for my return. By this time the passengers that had taken first lunch were coming at us for their afternoon tea, which consisted of toast, scones and cakes. The food served to the catering staff was excellent, although they did not have the salmon and salad, nor the cheese and biscuits and coffee! I do not suppose that it was MacBraynes' intention to see that we were all so well fed ; rather, I fancy, it would have been uneconomic to have provided two different lots of grub.

All the steam pipes leading to the pantry were not lagged and, when scrubbing the deck, I often had the misfortune to let my arm go too near one, and the result was a severe burn. These were dressed by the Checker, who was a second year medical student.

"It's a good job that we have someone like you here to do this sort of thing," I remarked.
"Why?" asked he.
"Well," I replied, "you must have had plenty of practice, seeing you are a medic."
"Oh no, " he countered, "all I've done so far is to cut up dead bodies. I learned to bandage in the Boy Scouts."

We arrived at Banavie about 3.40p.m. and the passengers left. The vessel was only four or five yards short of the width of the canal, so the galley boy and the two pantry boys had to turn out on deck to help the bosun and four deckhands cant the ship so that she was facing northwards for the return voyage. As soon as this was accomplished I had to go to the Post Office to collect any mail. I then joined the other deck boy and the galley boy on the quay, where they were peeling two large sacks of potatoes for the next day. While we were doing this, the deckhands were coaling the ship. It was quite a primitive method of pushing barrows loaded from a truck (in the railway siding on the pier) and wheeling them on to the ship. After this, she was washed down with fresh water and was always remarkably clean.

On the way north, I did not have to rise till 7a.m., as we did not sail until 11.30a.m, having to wait until *Lochfyne* delivered our passengers. It was before this that all the outside polishing had to be done. We were given Brasso to do this work and reminded how lucky we were as, up until recently, the job had to be done using oil and something called "bath brick". This time we had no voyagers for breakfast, but we had them for high tea when the ship was near Foyers on Loch Ness. If a flag were hoisted on the pier, we went alongside to pick up a few more passengers, otherwise we kept sailing for Inverness.

Once when heading up Loch Ness the skipper sighted an odd object and all on board were agog with the possibility of seeing the monster. Excitement was intense until we drew near and discovered that it was one of the spheres used by drift-net fishermen to buoy their nets. On the subject of the monster, my father's uncle Tom (father of the Purser) and my cousin Ian both claimed to have seen it. As Tom was returning from a funeral at the time, he was generally disbelieved. Many folk from the south fancy that the highlanders allege to have seen it in order to enjoy the publicity. I found the reverse much more likely to be true. Certainly there are people who may well have seen the monster but are disinclined to go public, for fear of being ridiculed.

We usually arrived at Inverness at 6.30p.m. I stocked up on biscuits, butter and other stores from MacBraynes' warehouse and, after I had laid out three beds in the saloon, I could go off for the evening. In the middle of the season, on Tuesday evening, we ran a cruise from Inverness to Urquhart Castle and back. By the time we were tied up and the trippers (including drunks) were off, it was near to midnight. No overtime was paid for this due to some legal quirk, which no one quite understood. After six weeks, *Lochfyne* had engine trouble and the new *Lochiel* took her place. Unfortunately she was about half a knot slower so that we now got away from Banavie half an hour later and did not reach Inverness till 7p.m.

The total crew was 24. The Master, Mate, Bosun and four deckhands made up the deck squad, while the Chief Engineer (there was only one!), a stoker, Colin MacKenzie and a donkeyman, also a MacKenzie, made up the engine room staff. In the catering department we had Chief Steward (yet another MacKenzie), 2nd steward, fore-cabin steward (to look after the third-class passengers), deck steward, saloon steward, cook, galley boy, pantry man, and two pantry boys. To complete this picture there were the Purser, Checker, stewardess and chocolate boy. The Mate, Hugh MacDonald, came from the village of Abriachan on the banks of Loch Ness. Duncan Cameron was Bosun. The four deckhands were Jamie (from Skye and very much the youngest), Hugh who came from Inverness, a fisherman from Buckie and Dan from Raasay, generally known as Raasay Dan. As many passengers would have had heavy luggage with them, the fourth deckhand, Hughie also served as baggage man and for this was paid an extra 2/6d per week. During the summer, the Cook was sacked – it is thought that he had been selling food to the deckhands – and he was quickly replaced by a man named Sneddon. The fore-cabin steward, one MacPherson, resigned at the same time, being replaced by Kenny MacRae from Skye. The Chief Steward was from Ross-shire, but was living in Inverness. This was one bed less that I had to look after when we were in Inverness, but I had to do his when we were in Banavie. He was diabetic and had to inject daily, the pantryman weighing out his food for him at mealtimes. When at Banavie, he, the two engine room ratings and another man gambled at cards. He was a very bad loser and, when he had lost, was in a foul temper all the next day. Although some of the crew, including those from Skye, were Gaelic speakers, the working language of the ship was English.

Our deck steward, Alec Beaton, was very religious and, as well as church attendance on Sunday, he went to a prayer meeting every Thursday evening. One Thursday we put a knot at the foot of his pyjama trousers and played tug o' war with them to make the knot really firm. As we all slept in the lounge, we got into our beds and waited for the fun to begin. Alec came in about 11pm and, as was his custom, sat for ten minutes reading his testament by means of a torch while we all pretended to be sound asleep. Then came the moment we had eagerly been awaiting. Alec tried in vain to get his legs into the trousers and, since we had no lights in the saloon then, it took him some time before he appreciated what had happened. When at last it dawned on him, he shouted "Out, out, boys" and proceeded to use the pyjama trousers to lash out at all of the younger members in turn. As there was the knot to be considered, Alec got some satisfaction in hearing our yells but, all in all, it was well worth it. Alec had a very red nose but in my innocence, and bearing in mind his religious proclivities, I drew no conclusions from this.

The ship's officers seemed to me to be a bunch of fads. The Purser insisted on having all his solids before being served any beverages; the Mate did not want gravy; the Skipper's tea had to be stewed for half an hour before he came to the table, otherwise he said it was too weak (maiden's water, I recall, was his favourite term); and the Chief Engineer had to have his fried egg turned while being fried. One morning as he was impatiently tapping his utensils on the table waiting his breakfast, it arrived with the egg "sunny side up" as the saying then had it. No one quite knew what to do and it was too late to take it back to the galley. Recognising that this was a *Gondolier* version of the Gordian Knot, I at once turned the egg upside-down on his plate and sent it out to him. He ate it with relish and did not notice the difference

To give some idea of the wages, the Purser was paid £5 per week and his keep, a fairly good wage in those days and about 40% more than a tradesman. The cook received £3 and the stewards (who relied a lot on tips) got only £1/17/8d. (£1.88). The pantry man got £1 and each of the pantry boys was paid 14/6d (72.5p). The chocolate boy was given 10/ -(50p), but his job was a sinecure. He looked after a small shop selling sweets, books and postcards. Twice a voyage he took a tray of his wares round the ship and on top of this he got tips. To be fair to him, he was so bored that he often helped me with the drying of the dishes. The deckhands were paid £2/15/- but had to find their own grub. Of my 14/6d, I sent home a ten shilling note every week and lived on the remaining 4/6d. I sent my clothes home to be laundered but had to keep myself in haircuts, shoe leather and bus fares from Banavie to Fort William.

We were paid on the Saturday afternoon and the cash for this was brought on board by my father's uncle Jack (from the hotel in Fort Augustus). I had swallowed the tale that he was strictly teetotal, but soon discovered that he had this veneer only when his sister Maggie was present. I could not believe my eyes when, on being asked if he would like a "refreshment", he downed a generous glass of whisky. On the subject of whisky, a bottle then cost 12/6d (62.5p), but when poured out with glasses, it brought in £1/2/6d (£1.12.5). It was a common practice for a steward to buy a bottle, secrete it somewhere in the dining saloon and, if a passenger should ask for a glass when the chief steward was absent, he poured from this bottle and pocketed the cash. Thus each bottle sold in this way could mean a profit of 10/- (50p) for the steward or, to put it another way, 80% profit. Of course, MacBraynes, who were buying their liquor at wholesale prices, were making much more than 80%!

One day when I had been told to throw overboard some biscuits that were broken and therefore unsuitable for first-class diners, I chanced to see one of the deckhands coiling a rope.

"Could you use these?" I asked him, thinking that it would be a shame to waste them on seagulls.

He grabbed the paper bag and made off at speed. The second time I did this, Andy Hexton was close by.

"What the devil do you think you're doing?" he demanded.

I explained that I thought the sailors would appreciate them.

"Just let the Chief Steward catch you at that game and you'll get the sack."

At that age, I was a trifle ingenuous and did not think anything through. To the pure all things are pure and I did not realise that the Chief Steward would think that the deckhands were paying me for the favours – and indeed that I might not be above breaking a few extra biscuits if the supply fell short of the demand!

The head lockkeeper at Muirtown Wharf (our berth in Inverness) had five daughters and I began dating the middle one, Cathie, who was fifteen. We were doing fine until the youngest sister began to attach herself to us everywhere we went. I do not know whether this was individual initiative or parental scheming but it became very irksome. Since she was on a bicycle, I put it to her that if she persisted in stalking us, I would let the air out of her tyres. She refused to stop and I carried out the deflation. She continued to dog us and ride the bike, claiming that if the wheels were damaged, her parents would send me the bill. I had an uneasy week until I realised that, damaged or not, the parents were not going to make an issue of it.

The highlight of my day on the trip south was a visit and a cup of tea at my relations' hotel at Fort Augustus. We arrived at the bottom of the five locks at 11.20am and did not leave the top lock until 11.55. The sluices were at that time opened by hand, as were the lock gates. Their opening was done by capstans, into which were inserted stout poles that were pushed by the lockkeepers and some of the deckhands. The Skipper, always keen to knock a minute or two off the time of the passage, used his charm to persuade tourists, on the banks of the canal, that manning the capstans was the best possible way to spend half an hour. The locks are now fully electrified and it takes twice the time to go through them. This is termed progress!

I became friendly with the Checker, David Watt, and one warm evening at the Banavie end, we swam together about half a mile up the canal.

"Do you fancy a swim across Loch Linnhe?" he enquired.

This took me aback – especially as I had just learned to swim a few months earlier. He explained that every year there was a race across the loch near Fort William. I did not relish the notion but he said, " Oh come on, I'm sure you can do it and you'll be company for me". He added that, although there was a gold medal and silver cup for the winner, the next five, regardless of time taken, would get silver medals.

So, on a very cold evening in August, I lined up with the Checker and two local lads. Other four entrants had wisely called off. I had no idea what was involved and did not even have any grease with me. Someone gave me a little Vaseline and I made the most of it. I was little more than half way across when I heard a muffled cheer from the other bank. This turned out to be the Checker winning the race. I plodded on for a while, accompanied by a boat containing two men and a boy. They kept me abreast of events and some time later let me know that the other competitors had given up. I was about only 60 yards from the shore when I felt really bad. My limbs had seized up and I was making little progress. I thought that I might be doing myself permanent injury and gave the distress signal to the boat.

I had a horrible feeling that, since I was so close to the shore and that I would get a silver medal for finishing regardless of my time, that they would try to persuade me to continue. Not so. They immediately hauled me into the boat and, while the boy rowed, the two men began using me as a punch bag. I could feel nothing. They carried me up to MacBraynes' shed on the beach and gave me first a brandy (which tasted like water), then a coffee, all the time pummelling away at me. They would put me near the fire then, just as I was beginning to feel warmer, they decided that I had had enough of the fire, took me away from it and resumed the pummelling. After about a quarter of an hour feeling began to return to my body and I was none the worse of the experience. Later I realised that I would never have been awarded a medal, as one of the conditions was that the swimmer would leave the water and walk up to MacBraynes' shed. That I could not have done. The episode was reported in the Highland edition of the *Daily Record* newspaper, much to the astonishment of my father who knew how little I could swim.

As I already stated, we were a luxury trip and had a fair share of celebrities. One day I remember seeing this distinguished-looking gentleman and heard the Chief Engineer say that he thought that it was Montague Norman - at that time Governor of the Bank of England. Pantry boys do not argue with engineers, but I thought that he was wrong and plucked up courage to ask the gentleman in question.

"Are you Sir Thomas Beecham?" I enquired.
"I am," was the reply.

Now, Beecham was one of the greatest orchestral conductors that this country had ever produced and, although I had never before asked anyone for an autograph, I decided to make an exception. I had to wait until the voyagers were disembarking before I could approach him. It was a Tuesday

– the day of the cruise down Loch Ness – and scores of passengers were crowding on to the ship as others were leaving.

"May I have your autograph?" asked I diffidently.

"Certainly," the great man said and signed away quite unconcerned while scores of people were jostling him to get on board for the evening cruise.

"Anything else?" he enquired.

"Please could I have one for my pal, the Checker?"

"By all means."

He was accompanied by a youngish blonde, Bettty Humby, a concert pianist, who was about to become his third wife.

One passenger that never paid a fare was a little terrier that came on board nearly every week at Fort Augustus, jumping on to the paddle-box, and getting off at Laggan. The dog returned by the same method a few days later. A pigeon with a broken wing landed on deck one day. The Checker made a splint for it and looked after it until the wing had healed. After that, the bird used to fly astern of us.

The steering on the ship was direct. That means that there was no engine to help move the rudder as one finds on larger vessels. So it was quite hard work turning the wheel and, in the tortuous sections of the canal, both the Mate and the Bosun were required for this. I learned to steer going up Loch Ness on one of the quieter days and can still remember that the course was north-east by a quarter east. In these days most compasses showed points rather than degrees.

I also asked one of the deckhands to show me how to make various knots and how to splice a rope, as I was more interested in seamanship than in catering. After showing me how to make a bowline, he demonstrated the way to make a back splice, an eye splice and a short splice, by taking a piece of rope and handed me a similar piece, with instructions to follow what he was doing. I learned all the stuff he taught me, but did not realise at the time that he was left-handed. Years after, when I was a deep-sea sailor, every time I was splicing, some one was sure to ask me if I were left-handed.

As war loomed, the number of passengers fell away and I had mercifully less work to do. Andy Haxton quit the ship earlier because of a dispute with the second steward and the deck steward. These two stewards had two tables apiece, each with eight seats, at the front of the dining saloon. As the ship tapered towards the stern, Andy had four smaller tables, each provided with six seats. When we were fully loaded with passengers, there was no trouble. Now that their numbers had fallen drastically the dining saloon would be scarcely a quarter full and Andy, being at the stern, came off badly. To make matters worse, the other two stewards would slyly put a hand on one of their chairs as the first passengers arrived. This gesture, however slight, was taken as an invitation to sit at that table and Andy would be left with four or five diners. I had a great deal of sympathy for Andy, for stewards depended a lot on gratuities and he was really the victim of sharp practice.

On the day war was declared, it was a Sunday and I remember Chamberlain's voice on the radio giving us the fateful news. Also it was later announced that all pigeons had to be reported to the government. This was quite amusing as ours was still following the ship. Although we still had two weeks of our season to run, it was not worth while carrying on and we were discharged. I had to pay my fare back to Glasgow (as I had done on the way up) because MacBraynes were exceptionally tight-fisted. They even made the other pantry boy and me go to a doctor in Fort Augustus and get him to examine us and give MacBrayne certificates to state that we were equal to all the hard work they were requiring of us. For this the doctor let us off with 2/- (10p) each.

I came home that day on a train loaded with soldiers. One of them was busy telling his friends that the war would not last long as the Poles were putting up a good show. Whether this was to calm their fears, or whether he really believed it I shall never know. Many of the troops were from Highland regiments and wearing kilts. Over the kilts were khaki garments of waterproof material; I was seeing for the first time trench aprons. On this train was the former fly-weight world boxing champion Benny Lynch of Glasgow. He had fallen on hard times mainly due to his love of drink, and had been reduced to fighting in booths. I recall his continually calling on the steward for more beer. When eventually the beer ran out, he immediately demanded lager.

I arrived at Central to find Glasgow a city of darkness. There was a "black out" and all windows had to be provided with some means of stopping light getting out. This was rigidly enforced by the A.R.P. (Air Raid Precautions) whose wardens were extremely zealous. Even the tramcar that took me home from the station had only two lamps, in place of the customary twelve or so, and even these were covered in dark blue paint. Next day half of the blue paint had been scraped away by irate conductors who had later found their bags to be nearly half full of assorted coins from all over the world.

(Readers who wish to learn more of Charles's career will be able to do so in his autobiography "*Making Waves*", to be published by Silver Link Publishing.)

Appendix 1. Timetable for Caledonian Canal service, southbound. 1936

Inverness	dep	8.30am
Foyers	"	10.25
Fort Augustus	"	12 noon
Cullochy	"	12.50pm
Laggan	"	1.45
Gairlochy	"	3.00
Banavie	arr	3.50

Appendix 2. The Evening Cruise

This was run on Tuesdays in July and August. The steamer left Inverness at 7.15pm and arrived back at 11pm. The adult fare was 2/6d (12.5p)

Appendix 3 – Fares in 1939

The single fare from Banavie to Inverness was 19/- (95p) in first class and 12/9d (64p) in third. However, many passengers would have taken through tickets from Oban (30/- (£1.50) and 18/9d (94p) single) or travelled on a circular tour, such as that known as LMS tour No.102/LNER Tour No.13. From London this allowed a rail journey to Glasgow and back from Inverness, steamer to Ardrishaig, motor to Oban, steamer to Fort William, rail to Banavie and the Canal sail to Inverness. For this fares were £9/4/2d (£9.21) in first class and £6/3/2d (£6.16) in third. These tickets allowed break of journey at any point en route and were valid for the summer season, up to a maximum of six months, although the rail journeys had to be completed within three months. Fares for the complete tour from Glasgow were ££2/2/8d (£2.13) first class throughout and £1/8/9d (£1.44) third class throughout. Return fares allowing a rail journey between Inverness and Glasgow or vice-versa were also available. As the tickets did not include hotel accommodation or meals the cost of a night in Oban and a night in Inverness, should be added. In 1936, dinner, bed and breakfast (with bath) at the Waverley Hotel cost 8/6d (42.5p) or 9/6d (47.5p).

There were by this date two through bus services linking Inverness with Fort William, as well as several connecting services, and the through buses did the journey in two and three-quarter hours. It has not been possible to find the Fort-William-Inverness bus fare, but a single from Inverness to Fort Augustus was only 3/6d (17.5p) and a return 6/3d (32.5p).

As mentioned above, £5 was a good weekly wage in 1939.

Unless otherwise credited, illustrations in this section are courtesy of Charles Aitchison

S.S. GONDOLIER LEAVING BANAIRE.

1.37 *Gondolier* and a North British railway 4-4-0 locomotive at Banavie. This is one of a class designed by Matthew Holmes and built from 1894 onwards to work on the West Highland Railway. This is an early post card, posted at Banavie in August 1902. (By courtesy of the Mitchell Library, Glasgow City Council)

1.38 With bandaged arms, Charles poses at the wheel. He did later learn to steer the ship and still remembers that the course up Loch Ness was north-east by east, a quarter east.

1.39 The Pantryman, the Chocolate Boy and Charles pose on *Gondolier's* bridge during her Sunday lay-over in Inverness.

1.40 Charles and David Watt, the Checker, on the steps of the paddle box.

1.41 *Gondolier* at Banavie about 1930. Apart from the addition of a deck house aft of the bridge, she is in the condition in which Charles Aitchison knew her. (By courtesy of the Mitchell Library, Glasgow City Council)

1.42 *Gondolier* in the locks at Fort Augustus, again about 1930. (By courtesy of the Mitchell Library, Glasgow City Council)

1.44 Passengers embarking on *Gondolier* at Inverness in the 1930s. (By courtesy of the University of St Andrews Library, RNWS-418-67)

1.43 An unidentified deckhand in the 1930s. Perhaps Hughie mentioned in the text? (By courtesy of the Mitchell Library, Glasgow City Council)

Bibliography

The King of Saxony's Journey through England and Scotland in the year 1844. Dr G G Carus, translated by S C Davison. Chapman, Hall, London 1846.

Black's Guide Book Advertiser, summer 1865.

Colour on the Clyde. A Cameron Somerville. The Buteman, Rothesay, 1959.

More Leaves of a journal of a life in the Scottish Highlands. Queen Victoria. Leipzig, 1885

Material on *Gondolier* in the Langmuir Collection, the Mitchell Library, Glasgow

Loch Lomond Passenger Steamers. Alan Brown. Allan T Condie Publications, 2000.

We steamed up the canal as far as Port Augustus.

S.S. GAIRLOCHY AT BANAVIE.

SOUVENIR OF THE CALEDONIAN CANAL.

A very early novelty card, with a pull-out section containing small views. The strip of minute photographs includes several of the steamers and gives good coverage of the cruise. (Author's Collection)

THE KYLES OF BUTE

C182

2 Columba

ONE OF THE BEST FORMS OF PUBLICITY which MacBraynes ever devised was this ship. She was ordered from G and J Thomson of Clydebank on 29 August 1877, this being confirmed by the builders by letter on the following day. Her contract price was £28,500, but the builder's letter contained a hint that, if the firm were satisfied with her after entry into service, they could feel free to pay a little more. Hutcheson and MacBrayne chose not to take the hint. She was to be on the general lines of *Iona*, but built of steel, to rather larger dimensions and with the improvement that her saloons would extend to the full width of the hull. Payment was to be in nine instalments, the last three of which were to be made after she had entered service, assuming that the builders kept to the delivery date of May 1878. A rather curious clause was inserted by Huthchesons allowing them the facility of deferring payment of the last two instalments (over £8,000 in total), provided that they paid bank charges. It is not known if this was actually done, but it would suggest that the Company did not have large reserves and wished to cover themselves in the event of cash flow problems arising. Construction was to be supervised by their agent Mr Muir. In the event, delivery was delayed and the ship ran trials on Saturday 29 June 1878, afterwards making a cruise to the Kyles with a party of distinguished guests on board, including representatives of the Caledonian Railway and the Board of Trade. David MacBrayne presided over an excellent luncheon, with the accompanying toasts. She did not actually meet her contract speed of 21.25 statute miles per hour, her best run on the measured mile being just under this, but this does not seem to have been a problem.

The only steamer to be described in any detail in the MacBrayne guide was, not surprisingly, *Columba* and here the writer gave him (or her)self the liberty of some slight exaggeration, since her length is given as 316ft (96.3m). This must have been the length over her fiddle bow, since her length between perpendiculars was 301ft (91.5m). With a ratio of almost eleven lengths to her breadth, she should, by all the laws of mathematics, have been a bad sea boat, but in fact she rode smoothly in the water and coped well with the few storms she encountered on her summer voyages. However, after her first season, additional stiffening had to be put in to the hull, as she had proved to be somewhat tender and her first captain was always careful not to swing her by her sponsons at a pier, relying instead on using the mooring ropes, worked by a steam capstan forward and steam warping sheaves aft. Steam steering gear, first tried on *Iona* in 1873, was also fitted, and the steering wheel was initially placed in the traditional position on the promenade deck, though there was also a simple plank bridge.

The press enthused about her appointments when she entered service and hailed her as "Far and away the most perfect ideal of a steamboat" and a "palace steamer". Of itself, her great length impressed and the uncluttered sweep of her promenade deck conveyed an air of great spaciousness, not met with on any other steamer at that time. Unfortunately this had been purchased at the price of an almost complete lack of any kind of ventilation below decks and conditions in the engine room were clearly horrendous, since cowl ventilators soon appeared admidships. In 1900 additional ventilators to the stokehold were installed. The dining saloon was also rather stuffy at first and this was improved firstly by provision of two ventilators against the rear of the main saloon, then, in 1884, by four others admidships on the promenade deck. The funnels were originally too short and showered smoke and smuts down on to the promenade deck until their height was increased in 1884. The bridge was greatly enlarged about 1900 and the steering wheel transferred to it. Not long after the steamer came into service, cycling became a popular pastime and the first tricycle in Skye was recorded in 1880. The Bicyclists' Touring Club, founded in 1878, had 10,000 members by 1883 and 56,000 by 1900. While touring cyclists certainly swelled MacBrayne's' passenger numbers, their machines became a nuisance on board ship and in 1891 a small platform for these was added aft of the bridge on *Columba* and *Iona*. The Club complained long and bitterly about the flat rate charge of 1/6d levied on bicycles and finally this was reduced to a sliding scale in 1899. From that year, bicycle charges were as follows :- 6d (2.5p) up to 10 miles, 1/- (5p) up to 25miles, 1/6d (7.5p) up to 50 miles, 2/- (10p) to 75 miles, 2/6 (12.5p) up to 100 miles.

In 1901 a new cloakroom was added in a deckhouse aft the second funnel and passengers could leave bags and other articles there for 2d per item. Two years later this was enlarged to give a smoke room, over which was created an upper deck, available to passengers for the first time on a Clyde steamer. Even with all these additions, there was still plenty of deck space. It was not only her great size or the expanse of her decks that impressed contemporaries – they also praised the compact nature of the facilities and the means by which a great deal had been made to fit into a relatively small space. Much of this was attributed to David MacBrayne himself and the close personal interest he had taken in the construction of the ship.

The upper saloon for cabin passengers was 60 ft (18.28m) long, as was that of *Iona*, but on the new vessel, this was 27ft (8.22m) wide, instead of 20ft (6m) and this must have made a considerable difference to the comfort of her passengers. It was luxuriously appointed, being upholstered, originally, in saffron, then in crimson velvet, with red curtains at the windows. The ceiling was stencilled slate blue on a background of ribbed gold and the woodwork was of Austrian ash. The pillars which supported the roof were surmounted by crowns. A novelty was that the seats, variously referred to as "lounges" or "tempting divans", were arranged at right angles to the windows, which were much wider than those in *Iona*. There were eight of these "lounges" per side, with seating back to back, and they would have accommodated about 160 passengers in total. Unlike those of *Lord of the Isles,* the windows at the end gave a good view out over the stern of the ship, although this was slightly marred in early years by the presence of her only lifeboat, which was mounted on davits over the stern. However, after 1900 she had two boats mounted on the sponsons and the view aft was now unimpeded. After 1912 two more were located on the upper deck. The after end of the saloon was originally fitted up as a drawing room or "boudoir", for use by lady passengers, and was fitted with revolving chairs and separated from the main saloon by lace curtains., It is not clear how long this arrangement lasted. In the "boudoir", the main saloon and the dining saloon, footstools were provided for use by ladies. Mirrors on the inner bulkhead enhanced the already light and spacious atmosphere. Silver paraffin lamps were fitted, but little used, as she seldom sailed after dark. (An experiment with gas light on *Iona* in 1880 seems to have been unsuccessful.) There were reading tables and writing desks, as Victorian travellers expected to be able to write letters while on the move. Racks on this desk contained stationery, the notepaper being headed in red lettering and the envelopes carrying a reproduction of the MacBrayne flag. A Bible, its cover embossed with the ship's name, also lay on the desk, for use at marriages or burials at sea, but it has not been recorded if this was ever used. It had been a gift to the ship from one of the directors of G & J Thomson when she was built.

On the floor was a "warm-tinted" carpet. There was a tea room at the entrance to the saloon, but this was not mentioned as an original feature and was probably a later addition. There were also some small tables and chairs in the centre of the saloon and these too were intended for the use of ladies. In 1883 it was mentioned that a grand piano, similar to those on American river steamers, was to be placed in the saloon, but as there are no further references to such an instrument, it was presumably decided that passengers would not appreciate anything which smacked of Transatlantic influence. It would seem in fact that, unlike the majority of Clyde steamers, *Columba* did not have any music on board until late in her career. In the 1920s and 1930s, one Mr MacNollie, was granted the privilege of playing a dulcimer on board MacBrayne steamers and, according to the author's grandfather, this included *Columba*.

Entry to this saloon was carefully monitored by stewards and, at a late date in the ship's career, the travel writer Maurice Lindsay, who considered that the saloon gave an impression of well-established opulence and time-saturated sea-going, fell foul of one of these gentlemen. The Lindsays were going to Innellan on holiday and Maurice had been given the responsibility of looking after the cat, a venerable beast, in its basket. At first all went well and the cat remained obligingly silent. When he entered the saloon, a steward loftily enquired about the contents of the basket and with a flash of inspiration, Maurice replied "Provisions". The steward grunted and let the family past, to settle themselves in one of the seating bays. Maurice's account continues "At five past seven a long thin stream of clear liquid suddenly raced down the linoleum floor (it would seem that the carpet had gone by this date). Its place of origin was unmistakably the basket at my feet. In a moment the steward was at my side. "Your provisions seem to be leaking, sir" he observed acidly. "You'd better take them on deck". The cat spent the rest of the voyage as a deck passenger with Maurice, who was in fact delighted to be able to escape from the saloon.[1]

Sporting dogs were carried in considerable numbers in the run-up to the "Glorious Twelfth" but these were likewise barred from the saloon. There was a separate tariff for sporting dogs, at a lower rate than the 2/- charged for lesser breeds for a Glasgow-Ardrishaig single.

Below, in the dining saloon, which could seat 130 diners at one time, meals were served at any time, in contrast to normal practice on the Clyde, where fixed sittings continued as long as meal service did. Instead of the usual long tables, there were individual round tables, affording diners a degree of privacy. It was estimated in the 1880s that about 500 cabin passengers per day would take meals in this saloon. The chairs were of maple and covered in dark yellow velvet and the general decor was in polished bird's eye maple, imported from Hungary, set off by teak pillars with gold flutings. The ceiling was covered by "a new kind of canvas fabric", with a groundwork of blue and gold. Heavy, richly-chased silverware emphasised the atmosphere of luxury. One of the drawbacks of a dining saloon located on the lower deck was that food was sometimes cold by the time it arrived at table. To minimise this risk, the counter of the steward's pantry was fitted with steam heating and dishes could be kept warm until a waiter arrived to carry them to a table. In the middle of the saloon stood a large table, on which were piled cuts of salmon and cold meats, and condiments in silver pots. Until 1914 on-board catering was contracted out to the Chief Steward for a flat fee and, according to a reliable rumour, this was in the region of £1,000 per annum. Even so, those who occupied the position seem to have done well out of it. For much of the period up to the first world war, the post of Chief Steward was held by James R Turner, who lived in Rothesay. His brother Colin was also involved in catering on MacBraynes' steamers and presided over the meal on her trial trip. Passengers travelling up from England by the night sleeper could order breakfast before leaving Euston and the Steward was then advised by telegram of the total who would require breakfast at Glasgow on the following morning. A set of painted glass panels illustrating old Scottish sayings ("A low bush is better than nae bield"), painted by the Glasgow artist W Keir, was placed around the saloon and a stained glass window by the same artist, depicting the landing of Saint Columba in Scotland in 563, adorned the comapnionway leading to it. These panels were apparently "strictly conventional in the modern sense", which meant that they were vaguely Pre-Raphaelite. A tea room was added after 1900.

A menu for 16 May 1891 offers the following courses for dinner:-

Soup, Salmon and cucumber, Roast or corned beef, Roast lamb and mint sauce, Roast mutton and caper sauce, green peas, vegetables, Sweets, Cheese and salad, Tea or Coffee.

A copy of the ship's wine list has also survived, dating probably from about 1895, and it gives a very good insight into the kind of passenger who was expected to dine on board. It offered no fewer than six vintages of champagne, all priced at 10/- (50p) for a bottle and 5/- (25p) for a half bottle. There was also sparkling moselle at he same prices, while sparkling hock was rather cheaper, at 8/-

---

1   "Clyde Waters". Maurice Lindsay, Robert Hale Ltd, London, 1958. Reproduced by kind permission of the publishers.

2.1 *Columba* sweeping into Rothesay Bay on a summer morning about 1890. Her funnels have been lengthened from their original stumpy height, but the expanse of her promenade deck aft is still totally uncluttered. (Author's collection)

2.2 A view of the cabin section of the promenade deck, at about the same period. Obviously this was taken on a day when the ship was not very busy. (National Maritime Museum, Greenwich, London, neg.no.P20532)

2.3 Another view, with rather more passengers. (By courtesy of the Mitchell Library, Glasgow City Council)

2.4 At Rothesay pier on the return voyage, between 1885 and 1900. The photograph was taken in the 1890s. The statue has since been moved to the further end of the Esplanade and the area is now the site of the restored Winter Garden theatre and restaurant. (National Maritime Museum, Greenwich, London, Francis Frith Collection, neg. no. GO2864)

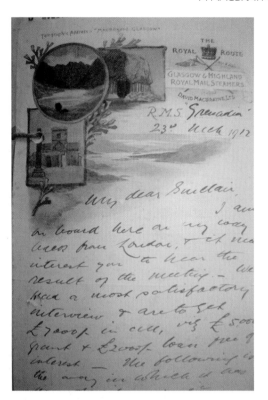

2.5 An example of MacBraynes' headed notepaper, on a letter written on board *Grenadier* in March 1912. by Mr Henry D B MacTaggart, who became provost of Campbeltown in that same year, but died within a few weeks of assuming office. He was on his way back from a meeting in London, at which application for financial assistance for the upkeep of roads had been made. This topic was becoming of increasing concern to local authorities with the growth of motor traffic. It had clearly been a successful meeting, since Kintyre was given a grant of £1,000 and an interest-free loan of £600. The total amount paid to Argyll County Council was £7,000. Another surviving epistle, written on board ship in 1906, has Fingal's Cave as a letterhead. (Argyll and Bute Archives)

2.6 From 1902 official MacBrayne post cards were available on board all "swift steamers" and these featured a drawing of *Columba*. On some, senders had to write the message on the front, as the back contained a quotation from Wordsworth "A land of rainbows spanning glens whose walls, Rock-built, are hung with many-coloured mists...." This example is a full view, without the quotation. (Author's Collection)

(40p) and 4/- (20p). For those whose wallets could not meet such prices, French white wine, of undisclosed type and vintage, was offered for 5/- (25p) or 6/- (30p) per bottle. Claret and red burgundy were sold by the quarter pint, at 3/- (15p), 5/- (25p) and 7/- (35p) and 6/- (30p) and 8/- (40p) respectively. Bass beer cost 6d (2.5p) per bottle and whisky was available at 4d (2p) or 6d (2.5p) per glass. Dinner for four, with a bottle of champagne, at a total cost of 22/- (£1.10), would be well beyond the range of even a skilled workman.

The shampooing and hairdressing establishment was originally managed by an experienced assistant of Messrs Sturrock of Glasgow and later by a gentleman named Felix, who had also become known as producer of a special kind of hair oil, still available many years after he had retired from *Columba*. When he retired this facility was withdrawn but re-opened on an unofficial basis after 1920 by a Greenock man who travelled on board to cut the hair of the crew and would also oblige any passengers who asked him. Until there was a hairdresser in Ardrishaig, the professional men of the town would sail to Tarbert on board *Columba* for the sole purpose of having their locks trimmed, returning on *Iona* or *Inveraray Castle*. In the bathroom, which was under the control of the Chief Steward, passengers could have "the luxury" of a salt water bath to revive themselves after an overnight journey from England. Each class of passenger could shop at the book- and fruit- stalls provided for them, those of the first class being located at the foot of the companionways leading down to the saloon. Latterly the fruit and confection stalls were run by Malcolm Campbell, the well-known Glasgow greengrocer and fruiterer. A young lad with a tray of chocolate, sweets and newspapers also toured the cabin accommodation at regular intervals. The on-board post office had a paragraph to itself in the MacBrayne guide and the writer enthused over the 100,000 letters which passed through it per month, many of these being apparently local letters between the places served en route. Postal orders could be issued and cashed and a post restante service was offered, letters to be addressed to "RMS *Columba*", Greenock., N.B. That form of the address left no doubt

2.7 The saloon of *Columba*. Umbrella stands were fixed to the end of each seating bay. (By courtesy of the Mitchell Library, Glasgow City Council)

2.8 A comparison with the saloon of *Iona*, in a view taken about 1900, shows the improvement of the new layout. (By courtesy of the Mitchell Library, Glasgow City Council)

2.9 The dining saloon of *Columba*. (By courtesy of the Mitchell Library, Glasgow Coty Council))

about the identity of the kind of passenger who might take advantage of this facility. A cloakroom was added during a refit in 1881 and articles could be deposited for 2d per item. The post office service ceased on 14 April 1917, due to war time difficulties, and was not resumed in 1919.

Her summer passenger complement on a Steam V certificate was 2116 and her crew numbered 74. Even if she were fully loaded, which was seldom the case, this gave a ratio of one crew member to 28.6 passengers. This was far in excess of that on other Clyde steamers, and even the Caledonian Steam Packet Co's flagship *Duchess of Hamilton* carried a crew of only 42, for 1780 passengers (1:42). These figures give an idea of the standard of on-board service offered to travellers.

To carry all these passengers between Glasgow and Ardrishaig required steam from four boilers, fuelled by 16 furnaces, into which between 18 and 20 tons of coal per day were shovelled by the sweating firemen. Although even the steerage accommodation had been described as "light and airy", conditions in the stokehold were more like those of the nether regions often mentioned by local ministers in their sermons. It was no wonder that the firemen went on strike, successfully, during the post-war industrial unrest in 1919. The engine room was not much better and until electric light was fitted in 1929, conditions were so dark as to be positively dangerous.

Columba was certainly a fast ship, though as built she was, at 18 knots, slower than *Iona*, but unusually, her speed increased later in life, as a result of reboilering. But other Clyde steamers were equally fast and it was her ability to accelerate quickly and maintain very tight point-to-point schedules, particularly in earlier years, which established her reputation as a racer. In the 1890s she covered the Gourock-Dunoon stretch in only 15 minutes and the Tighnabruaich-Tarbert section in the even hour. Later ships required 20 minutes for the former and 65 minutes for the latter.

The passengers on board were certainly a mixed bunch. In 1875 the author of "The royal Route – a ten day tour" mentioned "Laudy-daudy" (sic) swells and Yankees as prominent among the passengers (on board

Iona). He also listed "Fat manufacturers, smug tradesmen, worthy parsons, dignified dandies, MPs, popular barristers, London journalists, reading parties and smart young surgeons". Like any other Clyde steamer of her time, *Columba* carried many local people, who used her almost as later generations would use buses – young girls from Kintyre going into service in the West End of Glasgow, commercial travellers such as Mr Baldwin in J J Bell's "Christina" or Neil Munro's Jimmy Swan (though neither of these seem to have sailed on her), other business men, school inspectors, travelling people ("tinkers") with their wares, bright youngsters from Tarbert or Ardrishaig who had won a scholarship to Dunoon Grammar School and who would not see home or parents again until the end of term, housewives from the Kyles going shopping in Rothesay, emigrants on the first stage of their voyage to a new world, French onion sellers, young men going to work on a building project near Colintraive.....In summer there were also middle-class Glasgow families, such as the Lindsays mentioned above, en route to "a month at the coast", although most of these preferred to use the railway steamers to the Kyles and neither Tarbert nor Ardrishaig was a holiday destination for many of them. Around Glasgow Fair (second fortnight in July) and noted for their "wee tin trunks", there would be large numbers of expatriate Highlanders going back home while their masters and mistresses were on holiday. Until about 1900 many of returning Ileachs would have used *Columba*, as far as Tarbert, where they changed on to *Pioneer*. To cater for this group, return tickets were offered at single fares during the Fair. The normal return fare from Glasgow to Tarbert (in 1905) was 6/- (30p) cabin and 3/6d (17.5p) steerage, but the single fares were only 4/6 (22.5p) or 2/6d (12.5p) and to a servant girl earning perhaps £24 per year, this represented a useful saving. In the 1930s, Maurice Lindsay noticed "Sad-faced crofters, shepherds and fishermen" who "filled her wooden, uncomfortable steerage quarters with low-voiced Gaelic and the tang of thick black tobacco. Tweeded lairds, some who hoped to be mistaken for tweeded lairds and wealthier English tourists strolled about her decks, binoculars dangling against their flapping overcoats". He did not record any foreign visitors.[2]

All these could of course be found on *Grenadier* or other steamer in the off-season. The passengers whose patronage distinguished *Columba* above all other Clyde vessels were the well-to-do English and, to a lesser extent, foreign tourists on the first stage of their journey north. Some would be on one of the circular tours detailed in "Summer Tours in Scotland", while others, complete with guns and gun dogs would be en route to a shooting lodge. The men would have brought their game register, to record the date of shootings, number of guns out and quantity and variety of prey killed. Added to the mountains of luggage which they and almost all other passengers brought, there were piles of gun cases, golf clubs and fishing rods. There could be problems when there were too many dogs and fights broke out. Purser Ftizgerald remembered the French as being full of the romance of Scotland, courteous and polite, while the Germans carried maps and wanted to know the why and wherefore of everything. On one occasion members of the Vanderbilt family from the USA travelled on the ship and in the dining saloon, where they had their own table, were waited on by their own butler and attendants.[3]

The baggage man – in the 1920s a commanding figure named Lachie – and baggage clerks dealt with all this. One of his assistants was Neil MacArthur, who hailed from Kilmartin and had begun his career with Hutchesons as a postillion on one of the four horses which drew *Sunbeam* on the Crinan Canal, when she relieved *Linnet*. As Mr MacArthur was 70 in 1936, this would suggest that the practice of using the barges as reliefs continued until at least the 1880s. For this work he wore a red jacket. He returned to MacBraynes after a short spell of going deep-sea and joined *Columba* in 1894. He became very fond of her and praised her as a good ship, easily worked and doing her job well, with never a murmur or complaint. He did not retire when *Columba* did, but carried on aboard *Saint Columba*.

In the earlier part of the season, the English passengers would have been preceded by a wave of

2 *Clyde Waters*, op.cit.
3 Isles of Youth broadcast, 1936.

servants, en route to open up the shooting lodges and make everything ready for the owners and their house guests. As the timetable stated firmly that servants travelling in cabin class paid the full cabin fare, many of these travelled in steerage and were, to Scottish eyes, quite strange. While some were imposing personages in their own right, others were noted as "Shilpit (pinched), shaven valets and pert, trim lady's maids". They sometimes had difficulty when stating a destination, particularly if the name of the place was Gaelic – place names such as Onich could be a problem and "Acharacle" was almost impossible! The paper "Mercantile Age" in 1884 commented on this problem and added that "The cockneys could be so inquisitive too". However, it is unlikely that many cockneys travelled on board, other than as servants.

On many occasions the ship, like other Clyde steamers, was chartered to carry special parties, but whereas the others might carry a works or office outing, *Columba* was often hired by professional institutions, or to act as club steamer during the Clyde yachting "fortnights". Those who found themselves on board might well have been familiar with the ship from their holiday travels. It would seem that MacBraynes were able to command a high fee for the privilege of chartering *Columba*. Her greatest triumph came on 31 August 1912 when, already 34 years old, she was chartered by the organisers of the centenary celebrations of the steamer *Comet*, to convey the Secretary for Scotland, T MacKinnon Wood, and his guests down river from Glasgow to a review of naval and merchant shipping at the Tail of the Bank.

In the post war years, there were changes in the passengers carried and the hiker with his or her rucksack had to an extent replaced the tourist with the Inverness cloak and deerstalker. The gun dogs and "sporting" equipment had gone and been replaced by additional sets of golf clubs.

Columba ended her career, without any particular ceremony, when her last few passengers disembarked at Greenock on Saturday 18 September 1935. If any MacBrayne steamer inherited her mantle, it was not her successor *Saint Columba* on the Clyde, fine ship though she was, but *King George V*, which became something of an international institution on the Staffa and Iona cruise after 1936 and until her sad demise in 1974. By the 1960s only local passengers remained for *Lochfyne* to carry between Gourock and Ardrishaig and if there were 200 on board, she was busy. When she had to go elsewhere in winter, to cover for another ship, she was replaced by a bus. The glory had definitely departed.

Few people can now remember *Columba*, but this description in George Blake's excellent socio-economic study "The Firth of Clyde" (1952) was probably made from personal recollection and gives an idea of the ship in her heyday. The scene is Tighnabruaich on the afternoon of the first Saturday in July 1908.

"She sat low in the water and had the curved bow of a racing yacht. Her two funnels were red with black tops like the *Mercury*'s, but they had a sharper rake and the hull was black. Her paddles, within small black boxes, elaborately gilded, turned with the swift grace of a ballerina's toes, purposefully but without fuss. Into the pier she carried with her an air of consequence, and the young boys observed with particularity the human air of consequence worn by the bearded captain and the purser on the extension of the bridge over the paddle-box; such an authoritative pride as you might find in the officers of a crack Atlantic liner. The varnish of her paddle deckhouses gleamed freshly in the afternoon sun."

2.10 Ardrishaig pier staff manhandle a large gangway onto the foredeck, to deal with the mountain of luggage which can just be glimpsed under the extension of the promenade deck forward of the saloon. (By courtesy of the Mitchell Library, Glasgow City Council)

2.11 Accompanied by their own pipers, members of the Rob Roy Four-in-hand Brake Club pose in the height of Edwardian finery. This was clearly a charter sailing. Special terms, including food if required, could be arranged for large parties. (By courtesy of the Mitchell Library, Glasgow City Council)

2.12 The ship near the end of her career. (Author's collection)

Captains

Despite her long life, *Columba* was commanded by only five men, one of these being only for one year. Their names and dates of service were as follows:-

John MacGaw	1878-1885
Angus Campbell	1886-1903
Lachlan MacTavish	1904-1913 and 1916 to 1923 (some sources give 1925)
(?) Alistair MacKechnie	1914
Charles Cameron	1924-1935

(She did not sail in 1915)

Captain MacGaw had commanded *Iona* from half way through her first season (1864) and transferred to *Columba* when she entered service.

    Captain Campbell was born in Tarbert (Argyll) and served Hutcheson and MacBrayne for 44 years, during 30 of which he held the position of captain. He was stated to be a "singularly able and efficient officer" with a frank and engaging manner. His first command was *Glencoe* on the Oban-Gairloch service (qv chapter 6), on which he remained for about ten years. He then served as Master of *Iona* and later *Columba*. In the autumn of 1903 he became ill and died on Christmas Eve. A fund was set up by local people to commemorate him and this raised over £600, of which £20 was used to erect a cairn at Tarbert, unveiled on 24 September 1904. The balance was placed in trust to help his widow and daughters. Captain MacTavish served with the Company for over 50 years, 35 of these as captain. He served on *Gael*, *Glendale*, *Lovedale*, *Cavalier* and *Claymore*, before being promoted to *Columba* in 1904. He finally retired at the age of 74 and died in November 1927. Little is known about Captain MacKechnie, but an Alistair MacKechnie was briefly captain of *Claymore* before 1914 and may then have gone on to *Columba*. He suffered at that time from ill health and gave up seafaring to work ashore, which seems to have suited him better, as he went on to become a local provost.

2.13 The impossible scene. MacBraynes were so proud of the attractions of both Fingal's cave and *Columba* that they combined the two in this view, purporting to show the ship at Staffa, on the back cover of the 1905 timetable. As mentioned elsewhere, *Columba* did not once leave the confines of the Clyde. (Author's Collection)

2.14 Passengers disembarking at Tarbert in August 1912. Captain MacTavish supervises the operation. (National Maritime Museum, neg.no.N30203)

2.15 Captain Campbell. (By courtesy of the Mitchell Library, Glasgow City Council)

2.16 Chief Engineer R MacPhail (left) and steward Duncan Young on board at an unknown date. (By courtesy of the Mitchell library. Glasgow City Council)

2.17 A view of *Saint Columba* at Glasgow before 1939. (By courtesy of the Library of the University of St Andrews, RNWS-14-18))

2.18 The upper deck of *Saint Columba*, looking forward to the bridge, in April 1948. (By courtesy of the Mitchell Library, Glasgow City Council)

Even more strangely, only two pursers were ever in charge of the ticket office. The first was Alexander Paterson from 1878 to 1910. He had also begun his career on *Iona*, as a youth in the 1860s, when he was assistant to John Murray and was promoted to *Columba* when she came out. As he was still then a fairly young man, he must have shown signs of exceptional promise. He was succeeded by James FitzGerald – often known as "Fitz" – from 1911 until the ship was withdrawn, after which he transferred to *Saint Columba*. Mr Paterson was remembered as being "deservedly popular and obliging". Mr Fitzgerald began his career as his assistant in 1894 and retired just before the outbreak of the second world war. He then volunteered to return to service and worked in the audit department until 1945. The purser was assisted by six to eight checkers, usually university students, and luggage clerks.

2.19 *Saint Columba* in berth 3 at Rothesay pier on 18 August 1954. Captain Robert MacLean, Commodore of the fleet, surveys operations from the bridge..A fine selection of traditional wooden gangways lie on the pier. Beyond that which leads to the ship's upper deck can be seen the destination board, the last item of which read, romantically, "Oban and the North". (Author)

Competition

A foretaste of competition came in 1865, when the Wemyss Bay Railway Company briefly entered the Ardrishaig trade with its new steamer *Kyles*. However, she was based at the Loch Fyne port and gave a service up to the railhead in the morning and down in the evening. Chaotic management drew much criticism and the Ardrishaig link ended in mid-July, without challenging *Iona*'s position.

Serious competition came in the following year, when the North British Railway, having just taken over the Edinburgh and Glasgow Railway, decided not merely to start a steamer service on the Clyde but to do so on the premier route to Ardrishaig, in a direct challenge to Hutchesons. Unlike the latter, the railway company did not plan to run in the winter months, but was interested only in creaming off some of the profitable summer traffic. A subsidiary North British Steam Packet Company was formed and it ordered two handsome saloon steamers, *Meg Mirrilees* and *Dandie Dinmont*. Advertisements referred to the first of these as *Meg Mirrilees* and she opened the new service on 1 May. A train left Glasgow Queen Street at 7.30am, running via Maryhill, and the connecting steamer left Helensburgh at 8.55. Arrival at Ardrishaig was timetabled for 12.05pm and connecting coaches left for Oban at 12.30pm. That which went via Kilmelford arrived at 6.30pm, while that which took passengers via Loch Awe did not reach the town until 8pm. In the return direction, coaches left Oban at 7.45am and 6.15am respectively and arrived on Loch Fyne at 1.45pm. The ship left at 2 o'clock and passengers were in Glasgow at 7.45pm. Connecting services from and to Edinburgh were widely advertised, as was the possibility of hiring through carriages from places as far off as Berwick-upon-Tweed. The single Glasgow-Oban fare, cabin and first class rail, was 12/6d (62.5p), plus 1/- (5p) driver's fee for the coach. However, the railway steamers did offer the possibility of a day trip to Ardrishaig with almost two hours ashore.

In the event, there was once again no need for the Hutchesons to worry overmuch. Although the new steamers were smooth-running and quite fast, both were plagued by mechanical troubles during the first two months of the new service and in June the NBSPC had to resort to chartering *Petrel*, a much smaller and hardly luxurious vessel to keep it going at all. The long coach drive no doubt militated against the success of the service to Oban ; roads were poor and outside passengers must have suffered a prolonged soaking when it rained. Possibly David Hutcheson had seen, or heard of, what was coming, since it was in the same year that he placed in service *Linnet* on the Crinan Canal and, with *Mountaineer* on the connexion from Crinan to Oban, they between them provided a much more civilised method of making the Ardrishaig-Oban journey. But the NBR's finances were by the autumn of 1866 hopelessly over-stretched, the Chairman, Richard Hodgson, was obliged to resign and retrenchment set in. The steamers were advertised for sale in April 1867. Although only *Meg Merrilees* was actually sold, that was the end of this particular challenge to the Royal Route.

The next new entrant to the field was *Lord of the Isles*, of the Glasgow and Inveraray Steamboat Company, which went into service in 1877, at fares basically similar to those charged by Hutcheson. A superb ship, she certainly gave *Iona* and then *Columba* a good run for their money, but she did not call at Tarbert or Ardrishaig and the only passengers she actually took from Hutcheson were those whose destination was Inveraray itself, since previously they had had to change at Ardrishaig into the old and slow *Inveraray Castle*. Passengers for Oban were also tempted to the new service, especially after the opening of the Callander and Oban rail line in 1880, since a coach connexion was provided between Inveraray and Dalmally station, a three hour drive. Oban was reached at 6.30pm. But the Inveraray Company was also interested in developing other circular tours which did not directly compete with the Ardrishaig service and the growth of tourist traffic in the west of Scotland meant that there was ample business for both operators. The daily tussles between *Columba* and *Lord of the Isles* from Rothesay through the Kyles of Bute were spectacular and in themselves good publicity for both companies, but they were not really driven by commercial necessity.

From 1902 both MacBraynes and the Inveraray company had to face much stiffer competition from the new steamers of the Turbine Steamer Syndicate Ltd (later simply Turbine Steamers Ltd), which in that year began to serve Tarbert and Ardrishaig and in 1908 extended their sailings to Inveraray. MacBrayne's response was to increase the frequency of sailings to Ardrishaig and in the end it was the second *Lord of the Isles* which succumbed, in 1912, to become part-owned by MacBraynes.

1HOS. KELLY, C.A., Secretary, 34 West George Street, Glasgow.

2.20 The address given below this picture of a jolly coachman indicates that this was no MacBrayne publication, but in fact one from the competitor, the Lochgoil and Inveraray Steamboat Company, which continued to operate road services after its ships had been sold to MacBraynes, in association with Turbine Steamers Ltd, in 1912. It conveys an excellent impression of coach travel — at least, on a fine day,.

The guide book of which this is the cover actually dates from the mid-1920s, by which time motor buses were used on the Inveraray-Dunoon service and fashions had changed considerably from those worn here, but clearly the operator thought that the coachman was still a good advertisement for its tours. (Author's Collection)

A Glasgow Goodbye to the Old Brigade

1864-1878-1935

We heard it rumoured here and there, but now it's quite the truth
That we must lose two honoured friends, first met in early youth;
Their names were ever household words, well known the country over,
Their pictures graced each station wall, from John o' Groats to Dover.

We'll never see their like again, yet that fame must ever last,
While we would ponder over scenes and pleasures of the past;
For they were part of Scotland's life, when Glasgow Fair came round
As boys we met those treasured friends, when to the Highlands bound.

We'd board *Columba* at the Bridge, then start our trip at seven,
This prospect viewed for months ahead, the Royal route was heaven,
Iona left from Tarbert then, when round near Toward they'd meet,
Each with great funnels crimson red, the pride of all the fleet.

The grand Saloon like Castle Hall, each side yon massive table[4],
We gathered round the festive board and ate as we were able;
Breakfast – Herring, Ham and Toast; Lunch – Salmon, Chicken, Pie and Roast,
For we went "Doon the Watter" then, but now it's "To the Coast".

The broth that Neil MacInnes made, how can we e'er forget,
With barley, peas and leeks "intilt", we taste the flavour yet;
But what's "intilt" the Queen did ask, what could oor Neilly say,
There's water, beef and saut "intilt", with carrot, turnip tae.[5]

The Royal Route must still remain, though motors are the rage,
Ardrishaig Pier to Oban Town makes quite a charming stage;
Kilmartin, Ford, Loch Melfort, touching Sea and Hill and Dale,
Yet Crinan had a charm itself, when all the way we'd sail.

Columba packed from stem to stern, leaving Glasgow at the Fair,
If you had room for your twa feet, then you had quite your share;
We stood like well-packed Sardines, till touching Rothesay Pier,
While *Clansman, Clydesdale* came behind and helped the folks to clear.

You'll come and see the engines now, doon in the "Furrit End",
Be sure you've got some Siller, for it's there the cash you spend;
Meet Johnnie Begg, and Walker, Crabbie, Grant, Bell, Black and White,
In fact you're quite a lucky chap, if you get hame the night.

In youth we'd wander round the North, reach home up Clyde with you,
Majestic, Rugged, Grand, Sublime, Lochaber's scenes to view;
Inverness, down Neptune's Staircase, Corpach, Corran, Oban Town,
Then *Chevalier* to Crinan Pier, dainty *Linnet* dropping down.

---

4   Memory is clearly playing tricks with the poet here. *Columba* had individual tables in the dining saloon.
5   This story refers to a conversation between Queen Victoria and a countrywoman at Balmoral. The woman had offered soup, which the Queen so much enjoyed that she asked what was in it. Queen Victoria did not sail on *Columba* at any time.

Let's view that picture once again, Peace, Happiness and Wealth,
The Barber's Shop, the Dogs, the Guns, when August neared the Twelfth;
Great folks then bound for Islay's shore, Small Isles and Jura too,
Brave Old *Glencoe* for Gigha's Sound, would see them safely through.

Iona take this bright farewell, *Columba*, staunch and true,
We've spent long years of pure delight, our memories fond of you;
Those souvenirs of bright design, from your timbers and your brass,
Perpetuate these treasured scenes, while generations last.

You've gone the road we all must go, you "Famous Bonnie Twa",
No more you'll paddle through the Kyles, nor see the Broomielaw.
But visions sweet must linger, o'er the Route you made so dear,
The Burnt Isles, then Colintraive, round Rothesay Bay and Pier.

1936. J.W

It has been impossible to trace the author of these verses.

Columba had the distinction of appearing on two cigarette cards. The first (top) was no.39 in the series *"Celebrated Ships"*, published by the tobacco manufacturer Wills. It refers to her as "This well-known" old steamer and, since it also mentions the post office, dates from the years before 1914. The second was issued by Mitchell of Glasgow in the mid-1920s and is no.6 in the series *"River and Coastal Steamers"*. It shows the ship in her 20th century condition. (Author's Collection)

3   Captain James Hodgson

ONE OF THE BEST-KNOWN COMMANDERS whose career spanned both many years of sailing under the MacBrayne flag and also a period under Caledonian MacBrayne was Captain Jimmy Hodgson.

James Gordon Crighton Hodgson was born in Glasgow on 17 October 1921. His mother was from Isle Martin, one of the Summer Isles off Ullapool and his father from Govan. The family lived in Govan and as a boy, like so many in Glasgow, he found the comings and goings on the River Clyde a constant source of interest. Among the ships which he particularly liked was MacBrayne's *Claymore*, then in the final years of her career. It was not surprising that he decided to go to sea on leaving school in 1937 and his first ship was the Donaldson line *Letitia*, later well known to emigrants to Australia as *Captain Cook*. When war was declared in 1939, he was one day out from south Wales on a ship bound for the USA and sailing alone. Despite the lack of protection, she reached her destination safely.

In 1942 the war really caught up with Jimmy Hodgson. On 8 October he was serving on board the Ellerman liner *City of Athens* when she was torpedoed off the Cape of Good Hope. The crew were rescued by the destroyer HMS *Active*, which went on to sink the offending U-boat before going on to land the men at Simonstown. As a "distressed British seaman" Jimmy then took passage on another Ellerman ship, *City of Corinth*, which made for Recife in Brasil. From there she headed for Trinidad, but incredibly she was also torpedoed, on 17 November, and this time it was a US patrol cutter which came to the rescue. Thereafter he served in six different ships, latterly, from June 1945, as Second Mate, and fortunately the young seaman had no more adventures. The end of the war found him safe in what was then Bombay and he was glad to know that the fighting was at an end. In the immediate post-war period he spent some years on board SS *Carslogie*, trading out of ports in the north east of England. At all times, his conduct was rated as "very good".

He had begun to think that he would like to try his hand in the Scottish coasting trade and thus it was on 29 June 1948 that he joined the MacBrayne fleet, as Second Mate aboard the cargo steamer *Lochgorm*. This was a very temporary post, as he moved on after six weeks to the Clyde Shipping Company's SS *Copeland*. He stayed with her until returning to MacBraynes and *Lochgorm* on 25 May 1949 and he was to remain with the Company until retirement 34 years later. MacBraynes seemed at that time to believe in moving their officers around and he served on a variety of cargo vessels, including the steamers *Clydesdale* and *Hebrides*, the latter having been acquired with the fleet of MacCallum, Orme and Co. in 1948. Apart from a spell on *Lochness*, all his experience at this time was on board cargo ships, mainly on *Lochbroom* and *Loch Carron*, and his first spell as Mate came in August 1950, again on *Lochgorm*. However, it was to be some years before he secured a permanent post in that rank, this coming on *Lochmor* in the summer of 1956. On 2 October 1956 he went on to *Loch Seaforth* in the same capacity under Captain MacKinnon and remained with her until 4 March 1959. He was then back on *Lochmor* for two years until transferred back to the cargo service until 1963. Finally he came back to *Lochmor* from New Year's Day 1963 until April 1964. All these turns of duty had given him a very wide experience of west highland waters and also of the workings of the MacBrayne services, both goods and passenger.

He later commented that it should not be thought that the cargo service was in any way an easy number compared to the passenger ships. Whereas on the latter it was often possible to spend at least every second night at home, crews on cargo vessels might go for weeks without a chance to

3.1 Before he obtained promotion – the young sailor.

3.2 In his deep sea days, Jimmy Hodgson is spruced up by one of the crew.

3.3 On board *Loch Carron* – the Captain, whose identity is not known, is on the left and Jimmy Hodgson on the right.

3.4 An shot of Captain Hodgson, taken when he was relieving on *Loch Seaforth* in the 1960s.

3.5 *Loch Carron* in Oban bay. The Hutcheson monument on Kerrara is prominent behind. (Laird Parker, courtesy of Frank Walton)

3.6 A very early colour view of *Lochmor* arriving at Kyle

see their families. Jimmy had married during this period, having met his wife Ina Macleod when one of the cargo ships called at Tarbert (Harris) and in due course a son, Donald, was born to the couple, who had taken up residence in Mrs Hodgson's family home in Tarbert. At that time he was serving on *Loch Ard* on the Glasgow-Islay service and, after seeing a month-old baby, he did not have a chance to go back to Harris to see his growing son for another nine months.

On 1 April 1964 he signed on at Aberdeen as Mate on board the new car ferry *Hebrides* and, under Captain Donald Gunn, duly brought her round to the west coast from her builder's yard. On 15 April she opened the service between Uig on Skye and Tarbert in Harris and Uig and Lochmaddy. His later opinion of the workmanship of Hall, Russell and Company was high and when he retired, he commented that "They don't build them like that any more". One year later, after a brief spell as relief skipper on *Loch Seaforth*, he became her captain and remained on her until his retirement in 1983, at the age of 62, latterly, when rosters became more intensive, sharing duties with Captain Archie MacQueen of Staffin, Skye. He described his time on *Hebrides* as a "tremendous experience". Given that she was MacBrayne's first car ferry, that was probably an understatement on a par with his comment about the Minch, that "it can be fairly treacherous at times".

Adapting to change

On traditional MacBrayne steamers such as *Lochmor*, cars were loaded by the ship's derrick. A sling arrangement of ropes was laid out on the pier and the car was carefully driven on to this, the driver having to ensure that his four wheels each aligned with the sling. The slack was then taken up and cushions or hessian sacks filled with straw were placed between the ropes and the sides of the car, to prevent damage or scratching while it was being hoisted aboard. It was then carefully deposited on to the forward deck and lashed down to prevent movement when at sea. If it was rough out in the Minch, it would be drenched. The whole business of loading took about five minutes, but as only six cars at most would be involved, there was time enough to deal with them all. Car space had of course to be pre-booked and a certificate of the vehicle's weight had to be produced at the time of loading.

Unlike occasions in the past when a ship had been replaced by a newer vessel, the advent of the car ferry meant, for officers and crew, a complete change in the method of working a ship, especially in the matter of calling points. When, for example, *Lochiel* had replaced *Pioneer* on the Islay service, the on-board facilities were greatly improved, but the basic timetable remained unchanged. In the past, as Captain Hodgson himself remarked, it did not matter if *Lochmor* spent extra time at Lochmaddy when the amount of cargo to be shipped required this. The lost time could easily be made up elsewhere and an hour here or there was nothing in a schedule spread over two days. Now ships often had to be in and out of port within 45 minutes and timetables were so tightly drawn that a delay at a pier inevitably had a knock-on effect on services to other piers for the remainder of that day. When a company official deplored to Captain Hodgson the lack of "characters" in the modern MacBrayne fleet, the latter retorted sharply that crew members had no time to be "characters" as they had to keep to the timetable. The basic schedule (in summer 1972) provided two return trips from Uig to Tarbert daily Monday to Friday. Lochmaddy had a single trip on Monday, Wednesday and Friday and a return trip on Tuesday, Thursday and Saturday, when Tarbert was served by one single and two return journeys.

Hebrides and her sisters could carry up to 50 cars, which were loaded and unloaded by a side ramp connected to a lift. This ramp had a capacity of five average-size cars. Loading it required up to two minutes, partly depending on the skill of the driver, and it then took another full minute to raise or lower it – it thus required at least three minutes to deal with five cars. Deck hands learned the necessary new skills fairly quickly but passengers, especially summer visitors, took longer to do so. If a full load of cars was on board, the chances were that the ship would leave port late and at busy times there were also occasions when cars would appear on the road above Uig village, horns blaring and lights flashing, just as *Hebrides* was casting off. There must often have been a battle between the Captain's innate courtesy and his determination to keep his ship on something resembling her timetable. Courtesy usually won the day and it was not unknown for her to put back to the pier for latecomers. As the day wore on, this delay would become cumulative. Another problem mentioned by Captain Hodgson was that, in the time alongside, there could be quite a marked rise or fall of the tide, by up to fifteen feet, and by the time the last cars were being loaded, the ramp would have assumed a fairly steep angle relative to the pier and cars could be "grounded" when negotiating it.

Another difficulty for the Uig ferry crew was that many drivers now came by road through Kyle of Lochalsh and in summer, with the small turntable ferries then in operation on that crossing, long queues developed at Kyle. Ferry staff there would sometimes ask motorists for Tarbert or Lochmaddy to identify themselves and they would then pass on these numbers to the MacBrayne agent who would telephone them on to Captain Hodgson, with instructions to await these cars at Uig.

Perhaps these occasions were part of the reason that, under his command, *Hebrides* seems to have been known as a happy ship. In November 1979 the Aberdeen newspaper *The Press and Journal* reported that the ship had been given a "Service with a Smile" award in a BBC programme. This followed a letter from a Miss MacDonald, who made a minimum of 12 crossings on board every year. She particularly commended the help given by crew members to her mother, who, because of arthritis, had problems in walking. Sometimes a cabin was placed at the lady's disposal for the crossing from Lochmaddy to Uig. At other times she was allowed to remain in the family car on the car deck, rather than face the somewhat steep companionway. On one occasion her family left her there to go to the cafeteria, promising to bring back something for her. What they had forgotten was that this was the 6.30am sailing and the cafeteria did not open until later. Seeing the lady sitting alone, a crew member (thought to be an engineer) went over and asked if she would like a cup of tea "and do you take milk and sugar?" A few minutes later he was back with the tea, and biscuits, and Mrs MacDonald was able to enjoy a cuppa in comfort while the others waited hungrily above for the opening hour.

It was quite common for MacBrayne skippers to take members of their family on some sailings and when he was serving on board *Lochmor* Jimmy Hodgson brought young Donald along for a trip. At one port, he was given the task of ringing the ship's bell, a practice which warned anyone on board who was not travelling that it was time to think about going ashore. To Donald's horror, the rope and clapper came away in his hand and no warning could be given. The crew members who saw his predicament were kind enough to conceal their laughter. Visits to the bridge by members of the travelling public were often arranged and it was not uncommon to find several people being shown around, viewing the ship from the bridge wings or chatting amicably to members of the crew. Captain Hodgson seemed to be forever having his photograph taken with passengers enjoying their trip over the Minch, made more memorable by a visit to the bridge and by the personal touch for which the whole crew eventually gained a reputation. It says a great deal for his ability to manage change that he carried on this kind of personal touch from the more leisurely times into the era of the car ferry, with its exacting schedules. He was noted for his "conscientiousness, concern and capabilities" and his unfailing courtesy.

Another novelty which came with the car ferries were the cruise passengers who would stay on board overnight, using the 50 berths provided. There had of course always been those who made a trip for pleasure, sleeping on board during the voyage, but now there was provision both for motorists who could arrive the night before and sleep on board to avoid an early rise in the morning and for passengers on inclusive tours by MacBrayne coach and steamer, which were marketed intensively, with excellent results. There were 15 such tours offered in 1969 and *Hebrides* was involved in most of these. They were excellent value; in 1969 a four day tour to the Uists and Skye from Glasgow cost only £21/10/- (£21.50), with a reduction for those in May. All this meant that the cabin and restaurant stewards had to provide something approaching a hotel service, in

3.7 The bridge of *Hebrides* was a good deal more sophisticated than any of those on which Captain Hodgson had previously sailed. Here Captain MacQueen supervises the man at the wheel.

addition to their normal duties. Embarkation was allowed up to 11pm. In 1972 the charge for a single-berth cabin was £1.70 and for a berth in a two-berth cabin £1.40, and as cabins had en-suite facilities, this represented a bargain compared with shore prices.

Yet another new venture was the offer of MacBrayne's picnic packs, at a charge of 40p. These contained salad, a finger roll, biscuits and cheese and an apple, with paper plate and plastic cutlery. Drinks were available for a separate charge. These could be ordered in advance or purchased when travelling and they were made up freshly on board.

Apart from cars, *Hebrides* was sometimes called on to carry unusual cargoes and perhaps the most unusual was a bear. This animal, Hercules by name, was shipped out to North Uist in the late 1960s as some kind of publicity stunt. He did not take to life in the Isles and managed to escape from his mentors. In due course he was recaptured and returned to Uig and the mainland on board *Hebrides*. The voyage passed off witthout incident.

There were very few days when *Hebrides* did not sail and only one occasion on which, having managed the crossing to Skye, she did not succeed in coming alongside Uig pier. On that particular voyage, with the wind somewhere between Force 10 and Force 12, she was sadly carrying a coffin and, when she took refuge in Aros bay, that was transferred to a fishing boat. Unfortunately, someone watching from the comfort of firm ground in Waternish penned a letter to the *West Highland Free Press* criticising Captain Hodgson's handling of the situation and he later confessed that that did hurt. Yet, no matter the weather, the travelling public and the crew had every confidence in Captain Hodgson and only once (in 1981) was there any complaint against him, and that mainly because passengers thought that they should have been informed that the crossing would be very rough. He was more concerned about the direction of the wind than its strength, but did admit that he worried about crossing in a force ten or twelve gale. Sometimes, as he later admitted to Brian Wilson of the *West Highland Free Press*, he had to take a calculated risk.

With all these developments happening in a very short space of time, it can be seen that MacBrayne captains, officers and crews had to adapt very quickly to a step change in their traditional routines and the success of the first three car ferries shows how well they adapted to the new order. Within two years, *Hebrides* was carrying 1,400 vehicles per week in summer, an average of 39 per voyage. *Lochmor*, when really busy, might have carried 35 cars in the course of her two-day wanderings to the Outer Isles! Details of the number of vehicles carried on summer sailings between 1966 and 1974 are given below. The decrease in the number of commercial vehicles carried in the last three years was no doubt due to the opening of the direct ferry service to Stornoway

MV *Hebrides* (1964) Summer Sailings

	5/5/66–1/10/66	1/5/67–30/9/67	4/5/68–1/10/68	5/5/69–/10/69
Passengers	32,841	43,817	53,033	54,967
Cars	7,996	11,097	13,077	15,421
Commercial	511	487	785	1,298

	4/5/70-3/10/70	3/5/71-2/10/71	1/5/72-1/10/72	30/4/73-30/9/73
Passengers	60,672	72,169	73,517	63,513
Cars	15,996	17,719	18,736	16,062
Commercial	2,006	2,068	1,970	1,641

	29/4/74-28/9/74
Passengers	62,816
Cars	15,107
Commercial	1,148

The figures for the period from her entry to service on 15 April until 31 December 1964 were:-

Passengers 47,325, Cars 10,335, Commercial vehicles 754.

3.8 The coming of the car ferry also meant the coming of the traffic jam to Harris. Cars waiting for shipment stretch up the hill into the village. Loading arrangements are now rather tidier, as vehicles line up on reclaimed land to the left of this photograph, away from the centre of the village.

3.9 A close up of the lift.

3.10 *Hebrides* unloading cars and passengers at Tarbert

3.11 Hercules enjoying some on-board refreshment.

3.12 The wreck of HMS *Belton*.

The wreck of HMS *Belton*

In October 1971 a team of scientists was despatched by the British government to study the habits of the seal population in the waters around North Uist and the Sound of Harris. One of their number, a young lady, was assigned the task of observing their breeding habits from one of the uninhabited Monich Islands off the coast of North Uist. All went well until a fierce storm blew up and, as her tent was in danger of being blown away, she asked to be taken off. An inshore minesweeper, HMS *Belton*, arrived from Oban and duly brought her to the safety of Lochmaddy.

On Friday 22 October Captain Hodgson took *Hebrides* away from Uig twelve minutes late on the last run of the day, to Lochmaddy. The delay was due to Stornoway passengers and merchandise being diverted to an earlier service due to gales in the Minch. The crossing was made in a Force 3 to 4 wind and the ship arrived safely at 21.02. The captain noticed the naval ship moored in the bay about two and a quarter cable lengths off the pier. Having landed Uist pasengers and cars, he then sailed for Tarbert to land those bound for Stornoway, finally arriving back at Lochmaddy at 06.05. By now the gale had increased in strength and it was obvious to those on the ferry that *Belton* had dragged her anchor and gone ashore on Eilean Phail, three cables to the north east of Lochmaddy pier. Her commanding officer asked for help by radio telephone, but as it was still blowing hard and completely dark at that hour, Captain Hodgson had to reply that he would come to their assistance as soon as there was sufficient light to allow him to see what was happening. By 07.49 it was light enough to sail and he took *Hebrides* to anchor near the minesweeper. It was intended that the commander of *Belton* should pass a line to *Hebrides* by means of his "Gemini" craft, but this attempt had to be abandoned as this craft was soon in difficulties due to the gusts of wind. There were then two attempts to fire rockets with towing hawsers from *Hebrides* to the stricken ship but these also failed. About 09.30 the wind shifted slightly to S SW and Captain Hodgson gave orders for the anchor to be heaved in, preparatory to taking his ship to a position eastward of Ard a Bhail, where he could anchor relatively close to *Belton*. Her towing hawser was then hauled on board *Hebrides* and made fast, but when an attempt to pull on this was made, the line parted, as *Belton* was now hard and fast on the rocks. It was now clear that the ferry herself could be in a dangerous situation and it was decided to abandon the rescue attempt, the Commanding Officer assuring Captain Hodgson that all his crew were safely on Eilean Phail. In his report, the Captain commended all the crew who were involved in the rescue bid, instancing the engine room staff who responded speedily to frequently changing instructions over a period of three hours, the radio officer who had maintained constant contact with *Belton* and the officers and seamen who had handled the Wessex launching apparatus on deck. The efforts of all concerned were commended in a letter from Rear-Admiral Dunbar-Naismith, Flag Officer, Scotland and Northern Ireland, dated 25 October. Their efforts, he said, were most creditable and much appreciated.

Belton was raised and towed to Greenock, but the damage was such that it would have been uneconomic to repair her and she was scrapped. *Hebrides* and her crew were soon back on their normal station – attempting to rescue a grounded ship was all in a day's work!

Man overboard

It was a wet, fairly miserable night as *Hebrides* left Tarbert and most passengers had sought the comforts of the bar or restaurant as she moved down the East Loch. But suddenly a girl approached Captain Hodgson and informed him that there was a man in the water. It was not possible to turn the ship around at that point, but a boat was quickly lowered and searchlights played on the sea. After about half an hour, a man was indeed spotted in the water, hauled aboard the boat and taken back on to *Hebrides*, which immediately returned to the pier. The casualty, a young man named Stephen Lake, was rushed by ambulance to hospital in Stornoway, where, after being treated for shock, he was found to be little the worse of his experience.

Given that it is quite difficult to fall overboard from a modern ship, especially in a calm sea, it is hard to know what really happened to cause this accident. Eyewitness accounts said that he had been seen balancing on the ship's rail after a quarrel with his girlfriend. If he did then think of suicide, the half hour in the cold water soon changed his mind on that point and in the charming letter he afterwards wrote to Captain Hodgson, he said that he had never been so glad to see a boat as he was that night. The Captain's view was that it had been a 10,000 to 1 chance of finding him and he was lucky to be alive.

Captain Hodgson retired in 1983, when he had reached the age of 62. Sadly his wife died after a couple of years and this had a profound effect on him for some time. He then moved down to Glasgow to be near his mother, who lived to celebrate her 101st birthday. He returned to Harris regularly and, being near Gourock and Greenock he made frequent visits to these places, to keep in touch with ships and the sea. He died in Glasgow in 1997 and his ashes were brought home to Harris to be scattered in the Luskentyre cemetery, within sight and sound of the wild Atlantic billows which he had known so well.

He also has a memorial of an unusual kind. When the car ferries were new, radar was not as refined as it now is and so Captain Hodgson had two reflectors constructed and placed on either side of the entrance to East Loch Tarbert. On really murky nights, these were illuminated by the searchlights on the bridge wings of *Hebrides* and guided her safely to the pier. They became known locally as "Hodgson's lanterns" and are still in place to-day.

Off-duty, Captain Hodgson enjoyed painting in oils and, unsurprisingly, ships were his most frequent subject. One of his finest works was a painting of *Lochmor*, which he did for Captain Gunn, who had had a spell commanding that ship. He had also a musical talent and, self-taught-played both the piano and mouth organ. Old black and white films were another hobby. Any chance to go loch fishing he seized with alacrity and would go off with his rods and bait at the drop of a hat. He smoked cigarettes and cigars from an early age, and preferred to roll his own cigarettes, generally using Old Holborn or Golden Virginia tobacco – a short cigarette stub hanging from his bottom lip was almost a trade mark. A happy-go-lucky person with a very good and subtle sense of humour, he was a devoted father and fun to have around. It was always a pleasure for the family to have him home from sea and he was well loved by all of them. He was also highly regarded by the extended family and by the community which he served. He is truly missed in Harris.

The View From The Galley, as narrated by Donald Hodgson

In my teenage years, prior to leaving school at Christmas 1969, I worked in the *Heb*'s galley washing the enormous numbers of plates, dishes, pans and cutlery generated by the then huge numbers of passengers carried onboard. This was a semi-official Saturday job and was probably the most labour intensive work which any young lad would ever have to undertake.

The several hundred passengers carried on most sailings during the summer months meant that not long after the ship sailed at 6.30am the cafeteria opened and within minutes I would be filling up the massive sinks with hot water filtered through a large catering-size tin can filled with a string handle, pierced with holes and hung over the hot tap. The can itself would be filled with soap bars which would emit a lather and froth when the hot water passed over, through them and into the sink. This was the normal way of obtaining a lather and was common practice in all MacBrayne's ships before such luxuries as washing-up liquid appeared. It was rare in the summer months to have more than a few minutes to have a quick cup of tea before the constant stream of dishes and cutlery would pile up severely and it would be back to the sink once again.

When the ship tied up at her next port of call, there was generally only enough time to complete the washing up, commence drying the crockery and cutlery, and then slot them into their allocated receptacles before the cycle repeated itself all over again, as the cafeteria regularly remained open, or shut only for a very short period to re-stock before sailing again.

On completion of the working day, rarely before 10.45pm, I would be asked to go along to the Chief Steward's office, where he would give me a receipt to sign for his book-keeping, and pay me the enormous wage of a Ten Shilling note. Even in the late 1960s, it was extremely long hours and hard graft for such a minimal amount, and, allowing for inflation, I doubt whether anyone nowadays would entertain such a job for such a pittance, were industrial dishwashers not readily available.

3.13 The spotless bridge wing of *Hebrides*

3.14 A neatly attired lady passenger

3.15

3.16

3.15/16/17 Captain Hodgson and passengers. The first two photographs were taken on *Loch Seaforth*.

3.18

3.18/19 MacBrayne ships sailed at all hours and in all conditions. An evening shot of *Hebrides* at Tarbert and a view of the ship at Uig in wintry weather.

3.20 The Captain relaxing in his cabin with a cigarette and a crossword.

3.21/22 Cabins on the car ferries were comfortable and passengers enjoyed the luxury of their own facilities, something undreamt of on earlier vessels.

3.23 One of the last vehicles bought by MacBraynes was this Bedford VAS5, no.34, which arrived in 1969 and was sold to W Alexander in 1970. In its brief period with the Company, it is seen on one of the tours operated in conjunction with the car ferries. (R L Wilson, Online Transport Archive)

3.24 MacBraynes also operated service buses in North Uist and Benbecula and Bedford no.154 is seen on the latter.. It was bought in 1952 and remained in the Outer Hebrides when sold in 1967 to MacAulay of Lochboisdale. It had a long life, not being scrapped until 1977. (C Orchard, Online Transport Archive)

3.25 Acquisition of the business of Cameron of Harris in 1964 brought this 11-seater Ford, with Kenex body, into the MacBrayne fleet, in which it was numbered 32. It was the smallest bus ever owned by the Company and is seen in the garage at Tarbert. (Malcolm King)

3.26 The cook on a cargo ship, probably *Loch Carron*. He is preparing for the messy job of gutting more than a dozen herring.

3.27 Some of the crew of *Hebrides* heaving a line over the bow.

3.28 *Hebrides* leaving Tarbert.

NEW LOOK 1964

Next year when you visit the Highlands and Islands why not bring your car with you? Towards early Spring 1964, David MacBrayne Limited will introduce three modern, up to date drive on — drive off car ferries. These ships, the very latest in design and equipment for the handling of cars speedily and safely, will operate:—Between Oban, Craignure (Mull) and Lochaline (Morven), Between Mallaig and Armadale (Skye); and the third ferry will operate on a triangular service between Uig (Skye), Tarbert (Harris) and Lochmaddy (North Uist). The ships will be fitted with stabilisers, and provided with cabins. Observation lounges, restaurants/cafeteria and bar, will also be available. Here is a way to visit the Highlands and Islands with convenience and in comfort.

Illustration is an artist's impression of one of the new car ferries.

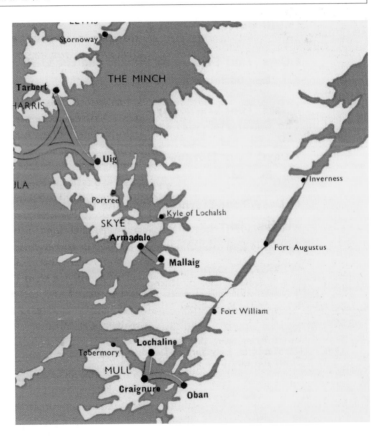

Publicity of early 1964 for the introduction of the car ferries and a map of routes. (Author's Collection)

(Unless otherwise credited, all illustrations in this chapter are by courtesy of Donald Hodgson)

THE
WESTERN ISLES

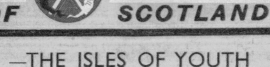

OF SCOTLAND

—THE ISLES OF YOUTH

by

The Royal Route

DAViD MACBRAYNE LIMITED

CLYDE HOUSE, 44 Robertson Street, GLASGOW, C.2
LONDON OFFICE: 227 REGENT STREET, W.I

Printed in Scotland

4 Stornoway

WHILE MACBRAYNES DOMINATED THE TRAFFIC in most of the smaller ports and in Oban, this was certainly not the case in Stornoway, where the Company's ships formed only a small part of the total tonnage using the port. Perhaps it was difficult for the managers to appreciate this, since relations with the Stornoway Port and Harbour Commissioners, a body set up in 1865, were usually strained and sometimes degenerated into outright hostility. The role of the local agent could be crucial in securing fair treatment for the Company's ships using the port. When it seemed to be at a disadvantage, the Company reacted strongly and, as will be seen, this led to one of the longest legal battles which ever involved MacBraynes.

The Hutcheson connexion with Stornoway antedated the formation of the Commission, since it began in 1853, with the construction of the first ship to bear the name *Chevalier*, for the Glasgow – Stornoway service. She had a very short career and was succeeded by the first *Clansman*. MacBraynes became more involved in sailings to Lewis when in 1880 they took over the working of the Ullapool and later Strome Ferry – Stornoway mail service from the Highland Railway. On the former service, they placed a succession of handsome ships – *Clydesdale, Clansman* (1870), *Claymore* (1881) and *Chieftain*. On 11 May 1904 Captain Duncan MacKechnie of *Claymore* died aged 74. He was a native of Mull and had been in the Hutcheson/MacBrayne fleet for about 40 years, of which he was a captain for 15. He had been ill but was expecting an early return to duty. Ships on the latter service, worked from Kyle of Lochalsh from 1897 and also Mallaig from 1901, became equally well known and included *Sheila, Lochness* and *Loch Seaforth*. These ships were perhaps of more concern to the Leòdhasachs, since from about 1880 the main passenger link with the mainland, as far as essential journeys were concerned, was that to the railhead. The guide book for 1881 described the inhabitants of Stornoway as "enterprising and intelligent".

One of the longest-serving MacBrayne agents at Stornoway was David Simpson, who held that office from 1903 to 1923, at a time of strained relations with the Port and Harbour Commissioners. He was succeeded very briefly by J Archibald, then by Alexander Livingstone, whose period at Stornoway was to be equally long. He was not a native of Lewis, having been born at Plockton in 1879, one of three sons of Murdo and Margaret Livingstone. His father was a shipowner and was drowned at sea. On leaving school about 1894, Alexander went to work for the Highland Railway at Kyle, but transferred to MacBraynes in 1902. His first appointment was as chief clerk in Stornoway and he remained in that post for eleven years. While in Stornoway he married Alexandra Macleod of Lochs. The couple had two sons and one daughter. Of his sons, Murdo went on to become the Company's agent at Kyle. Promotion took Alexander to Mallaig as agent, then on to Kyle in a similar capacity, before returning to Lewis in 1923, as agent in Stornoway. He remained in that post until ill health obliged him to retire in 1944, although he had by then reached what would now be considered retirement age in any case. However, he seems to have recovered to an extent, as he lived until New Year's Day, 1957 and was remembered as being "remarkably agile and brisk in manner". Appropriately *Loch Seaforth* carried his body back to the mainland on the night of Wednesday 2 January and he was interred in his native Plockton. He was a freemason and his hobbies were golfing, gardening and bowling.

In these days, when two daily sailings by *Isle of Lewis* and one by *Muirneag*, are scarcely sufficient to cater for all the traffic offering on the Stornoway service, it is difficult to remember just how few passengers and how little freight traffic there was one hundred years ago. In the early years of the

20th century, few people, other than "commercial gentlemen" and members of Ross and Cromarty County Council, travelled regularly to and from Lewis. A family might receive the occasional letter from a son who had emigrated to Canada, but few, other than professionals such as doctors and lawyers received any quantity of mail. As Mr Livingstone remembered, there was a time when one labourer could easily trundle all the island's mail in a handcart from the pier to the post office after the arrival of *Sheila*. Until 1903 the post office was located in Perceval Square, but that building was then condemned as overcrowded and insanitary and in 1906, as new premises were not ready, the staff had to move to temporary accommodation in the town hall until the present premises in Francis Street were opened in 1908. These were rather less handy for the pier and no doubt the move was not welcomed by those who had to push the cart, but motor vans later took over. All the goods destined for Point could be accommodated in a box cart and twice a week two carts, run by a Mr MacRae of Callanish, carried all the arriving merchandise for Bernera, West Uig and Callanish. Despite the glowing recommendation of the town in the MacBrayne guide – several hotels, four churches and a court house – Stornoway did not become a tourist destination until well into the 20th century. Even the details of Lewis Castle and its grounds, with ten miles of carriage drives and five miles of footpaths, the extensive hot houses filled with the most exquisite flowers (and tropical fruits) failed to draw the crowds. By 1957 the volume of incoming mail required the attendance of two motor lorries to carry all the bags swung ashore from *Loch Seaforth*.

James MacLeod became manager at Stornoway in 1955 and continued in post until well into Caledonian MacBrayne days. He was a local man, having begun work in the office as a junior in 1928. Between 1933 and 1939 he acted as relief purser on various services and was then on war service until returning to Stornoway in 1945. He became chief clerk in 1949.

Stornoway Harbour Commissioners v David MacBrayne Ltd.

In most of the west highland harbours which they served, MacBraynes were the principal provider of shipping services. Only in Stornoway were their steamers simply a few among many and the story of their relationship with the Harbour Commissioners is therefore an interesting one.

For most of the second half of the 19th century, relations between the Company and the Commission were reasonably smooth, despite a remark by the latter's auditors that the former was always in arrears with dues for their steamers and the rents owed for buildings which belonged to the Commission. It was the arrival in 1908 of the magnificent new steamer *Chieftain* on the Glasgow-Stornoway run which was to lead to outright warfare between the two. With her comfortable lounge, fine dining saloon, electric light and well-furnished cabins, she was a very great improvement on *Claymore* and it was obvious that MacBrayne was setting out to capture some of the more lucrative tourist traffic from the ships of Messrs Langlands, which had for some years provided what were described as "yachting cruises" and whose shipboard amenities ran to sprung mattresses in the berths, electric light and a piano, facilities not to be found on the MacBrayne ships.

By an order of 1882, the Harbour Commissioners were allowed to charge 3d per registered ton on vessels discharging cargo from home ports and the same on those loading. From 1895 a reduced rate of 4.5d was levied for ships which were both discharging and loading. At some point after 1884, Langlands obtained a concession by which the two calls made by their steamers when sailing to and from Aberdeen would be treated as one and they later received a further concession in that only 3d per ton would be charged in the summer months, when some of the space normally occupied by cattle was converted into temporary cabins for passengers. Somehow this concession, which had not been advertised in any way, came to the attention of MacBrayne's agent in Stornoway, David Simpson, who clearly thought that this represented unfair competition for his own company's new vessel. He had a quiet word with the Commission and an oral agreement was reached that the same concession would be made available to MacBraynes in respect of *Chieftain*. A further concession was granted in respect of her registered tonnage; this was actually 497t, but it was agreed to rate her as 306t. Nothing was put in writing between the two parties, but Simpson

4.1 *Clansman* of 1870 coming alongside the wharf at Stornoway. This view, by the local pharmacist and photographer Tolmie, later formed the subject of a post card and an example exists postmarked 1902. Mr Tolmie was obviously keen to ensure that Lewis would not be left behind in the latest craze. (Stornoway Port Authority)

4.2 A group of well-dressed passengers on board *Lovedale* at Strome Ferry, between 1893 and 1896. (Highland Photographic Archive)

4.3 *Lovedale* at Kyle between 1897 and 1900, shortly after the opening of the railway to the port. (Courtesy of the University of St Andrews Library)

4.4 MacBrayne staff at Stornoway pre-1914. On the left is Alexander Livingstone, Chief Clerk, and it is thought that the gentleman next to him is the Company's agent in Stornoway. (Courtesy M Livingstone)

did communicate with management in Glasgow and had been instructed in May 1908 to accept the arrangement. There was even a suggestion that a similar concession should be sought in Oban, but it would seem that nothing came of this. The ship then called on 32 occasions and MacBraynes saved £76/8/- (£76.40) on these visits.

When on 13 April 1909 the vessel's tonnage was re-rated as 603, MacBraynes did not bother to mention this to the Commission and by 1912 they had saved the sum of £803/17/6d (£803.87.5) on her visits to Stornoway. She went on to call on 198 occasions between that year and 27 November 1915. (This would suggest that she was in commission for much of the year, although her spacious accommodation would have been under-utilised in the off-season.)

Unfortunately in January 1912 the Commission's Collector of Dues, A R Campbell, who had authorised the agreement, was replaced by a new broom in the form of Angus MacLeod, who immediately pointed out that there was a discrepancy between the ship's registered tonnage and the figure which was used to calculate dues on her calls in Stornoway. The Commissioners decided to put an end to the concession and Mr MacLeod sent the company an invoice for £811/9/6d (£811.47.5). This was promptly returned, unpaid, by MacBraynes and a battle commenced which was to last almost as long as the world war which broke out soon afterwards. In December 1913 the Company ceased to pay any dues at all on any of its vessels visiting Stornoway. The Commission, at its meeting of 30 December, resolved to write to MacBraynes demanding a resumption of payment and were rather surprised to receive a reply from D Campbell Brown, Managing Director, saying "we think that you are under an entirely erroneous conception of the case." Mr D H MacBrayne was ill at this time. The Company then threw additional fuel onto the fire by asking that *Claymore*, which was charged at a compounded rate of £750 p.a., should receive similar consideration. A special sub-committee of the Commission was set up to deal with the issue and immediately rescinded the minutes of 1884, 1900 and 1902 recording the concessions made to Langlands, thus annoying that firm also. As their yachting cruises had of course been suspended on the outbreak of war, the matter was for them, for the time being, academic.

In April 1915 MacBraynes offered a meeting to discuss the dispute, but their letter was simply allowed to lie on the table. In July of that year, the Commission wrote to the Company demanding that they settle all outstanding sums at once and threatening legal action if they did not do so. As this produced no result at all, in November 1915 it was agreed to go ahead with an action. On 8 December MacBraynes again offered to meet, but this was declined. MacBraynes then brought up the point that the Commissioners were in breach of the Harbour, Docks and Piers Act of 1847, in that they had failed to display a board giving a list of dues which would be charged to ships using the port. Apparently there had been one, but it had been blown down at some date after May 1912 and not replaced.

On 12 February 1916 the Commissioners threatened to prevent any MacBrayne ships using the harbour. The latter, having gone to the Court of Session to obtain an in interim interdict against this, were in a stronger position and, as the legal advisers to the Commission cautioned that it would be impossible to enforce this ban, it was agreed on 6 March to withdraw it. It was also decided to exhibit rates to be charged and a new board was immediately erected. Counsel continued to recommend a meeting with the Company and finally the Commissioners accepted this. However, when they met in Glasgow on 7 April, they found the Company in "a very uncompromising attitude", now claiming that they wanted adjustment of accounts pre-1908. Arbitration was suggested as a way out of the impasse, but rejected by MacBraynes, since the Commission had on 23 May brought the question of dues to be paid on the mail steamer, *Sheila*, into the argument. The rate was £2/1/8d (£2.08) per visit and she made six calls per week. The only way forward seemed to be legal action and this was begun, but the solicitors advising the Commission clearly thought that they did not have a very good case and finally an agreement was reached out of court in April 1918, by which time the amount outstanding on harbour dues from December 1913 plus water rates was £1743/18/1d. (£1743.91). By this settlement, MacBraynes agreed to pay that amount plus interest of £184/16/- (£184.80) and a payment of £200 in lieu of the £811/9/6d (£811.48) claimed for *Chieftain*. For their part, the Commission agreed to extend to MacBraynes all concessions made to Langlands. The legal costs to the Harbour Commission were £206.

Thus ended a dispute which should never have reached that stage of legal action. The Commission had been uncompromising for too long and clearly in the wrong in the preferential treatment they had given to the ships of one firm. On the other hand, MacBraynes had not always shown any urgency in settling the affair, claiming at different times not to have received letters, or saying that their lawyer was "away for a few days". It says much for the pier staff and the ships' crews that the services continued to operate more or less smoothly while the legal arguments raged and despite war-time conditions. Very shortly afterwards, in June 1919, *Chieftain* was sold to the North of Scotland, Orkney and Shetland Shipping Company. Although post-war patterns of trade had not yet had time to become established, she was an expensive ship to run and it may have been that the question of paying increased dues tipped the balance against retaining her as a member of the fleet. With her departure, MacBraynes retired for a time from the upper end of the cruise market, although *Claymore* retained a loyal following until her withdrawal in 1931. She had accommodation for 62 berthed passengers, of whom twelve slept in open berths around the saloon. Passengers enjoyed dining at the communal table, presided over by the Captain, the social life organised by the Purser and the impromptu concerts, though young men had to beware of the matchmaking mama and daughter.[1]

Another problem which occurred from time to time over the years was the matter of the crowds "meeting the boat". It was long a custom in west highland places, where the arrival of the MacBrayne boat was the event of the day, to go down and watch the proceedings, to see who was coming home and who was off to Glasgow, or on the first stage of a journey to Canada. There might be Uncle Murdo, back home from Oregon for the first time in 42 years, there might be a newly-graduated student back from Glasgow with a First in Classics, a potential new minister over to preach, commercial travellers or one of the "daoine dubh"[2] with their wares, Effie MacX back from another shopping spree in Glasgow, some adventurous English tourists – the possibilities were endless. And apart from the folks, there were goods being unloaded – a piano for the doctor's daughter, a new bike for Calum Beag and, in later days, even an Austin Seven car. Some people came down to collect parcels which were being brought by the steamer, although mostly these were put into the Company's store and distributed later by local carriers. It all made good viewing and, later, good crack over a cup of tea or a dram. In small places it did not matter if the entire village turned out, as there were not enough people to cause a problem, but in Stornoway, there could be distinct congestion if even 10% of the town's population came down to King Edward pier to see *Lochness* come in. And in due course, just after seven, as the crowd grew, a cloud of smoke and the sight of two tall masts above Arnish point told that she was not far away and she soon was sweeping majestically up to the quay and the gangway was put aboard. Then the crowd became excited and there were joyful reunions – after a couple of days or a couple of decades – and in time they all went off to their warm homes and supper. And the MacBrayne boat had once again brought "a little more colour into the lives of certain poor, tired creatures".[3]

But the crowds could be a problem, even although there was not in those days the emphasis on Health and Safety that excites us now. MacBraynes had in the 1920s invested in a new mobile crane which greatly assisted unloading and loading, but there were times when it had to remain immobile due to the mass of people on the pier. On a Friday in August 1930, the local manager had to stop the unloading of the mail steamer and the Company wrote to the Commissioners about the problem The reply suggested that they should ask for the services of a constable for

1 *Across Hebridean Seas.* Iain F Anderson, Chatto and Windus, London, 1937
2   The "Daoine dubh" were people from the Indian sub-continent who travelled around remote areas selling household wares such as brushes, polishes and smaller utensils. They performed a valuable service and were made most welcome in rural communities.
3   George Morrison. *One Man's Lewis.*

half an hour prior to sailing time and also stationing two members of crew on the pier to assist passengers. The congestion still occurred and finally the Commissioners began to close off the pier at times of arrival and departure of *Lochness*, but this brought complaints from the press and public and long queues would from near the gates, stretching back almost to the site of the present terminal.

The legal case was certainly not the last occasion on which the Commission and MacBraynes would disagree, but none of the later arguments reached the stage of legal action. Later disputes concerned storage space, office space (1919), dues again (1925) or, in August and October 1930, the problems caused by congestion around the berth of the mail steamer. There was also an argument in the 1930s when the Commissioners asked shipping firms to collect dues on their behalf. But ultimately all these were solved with a certain amount of goodwill.

Sheila

This ship was built in 1904 and was named after a character in the novel "A Princess of Thule" by William Black. Apparently he in turn chose the name after meeting a pretty young Sheila at Garynahine in Lewis. She was warmly welcomed when she first arrived in Stornoway, under the command of Captain Cameron, who was to remain with her for most of her career. The ship had a very steady career, despite the exposed nature of much of her daily route and had few problems. Her lack of capacity was sometimes a drawback and it is not recorded what the herring girls thought of her steerage accommodation, when several hundred made the crossing at the height of the season. It also caused problems in the war years and ultimately contributed to the disaster of the *Iolaire*, since *Sheila* did not have room for all the service personnel and civilians who turned up at Kyle on Hogmanay, 1918 and the yacht was brought into service to take the naval contingent. A collision with a fishing smack in November 1923 was the most serious event in her own career, until she met her end.

That came early on New Year's Day 1927 (a Saturday), while she was inbound from Stornoway, in what was described as a gale and "thick weather", with a relief master in command. She ran aground on a remote part of the coast of Ross-shire, south of the entrance to Loch Torridon. The stranding in itself was a fairly minor affair and a passenger, writing to his parents in Stornoway, reported that the vessel glided gently up on to the shore. He was asleep and did not know that anything untoward had happened until a steward woke him. The six passengers and some of the crew were put into a lifeboat and rowed clear of the ship until daylight broke, by which time the tide had ebbed. They then came back on board and had breakfast, but with the angle at which she was lying, "it was hardly necessary to chew your food : it just slipped over with the angle of the boat". The wireless operator was very busy and eventually picked up Malin Head and a US ship off Barra Head, but in the meantime some of the crew had gone ashore and ultimately reached the nearest post office, 15 miles away, from which they sent off telegrams reporting the accident. Meanwhile the passengers waited on board until about 2pm when it was arranged that they should go ashore and they were then cared for by the villagers of Caoig, most being accommodated in the farm house of Mr M MacRae. With Captain Robertson in command (qv), *Plover* arrived about 4.30pm and they were rowed out to her, to sail off to Kyle. *Claymore* then called in at Kyle and brought the mails and passengers back to Stornoway, making a return trip to the mainland on Monday 3 January. It looked as though it would be possible to salvage *Sheila*, but before this could be arranged, bad weather set in and she went to pieces where she lay. No convincing reason for the stranding was ever given and it has been said that it may have occurred because of New Year.[4]

The loss of *Sheila* was discussed by the Stornoway Town Council after its next meeting and most members used the occasion to air their views on her, saying what a dreadful ship she had been. They now wanted something bigger and better and a boat which would do the crossing to Kyle in four and a half hours, to allow passengers to catch the early morning train to Inverness,

---

4   Not all accounts of the stranding tell the same story and some suggest that the passengers were not picked up by *Plover* until the Sunday afternoon.

a facility which county councillors would welcome. Councillor Hugh Matheson suggested joint action with the District Committee and Parish Council. Councillor Tolmie mentioned tourism. Only Councillor Mrs J Fraser had anything good to say for *Sheila*. She had made stormy crossings, including one on which a boat was washed off its davits, but had never been afraid. (It would seem that Mrs Fraser was a lady not easily scared.) "You may get a bigger boat" she said, "but I doubt if you will get a better one." A small committee was set up to draft a memorial to the Secretary of State, the President of the Board of Trade, the Chancellor of the Exchequer and the Post Master General, and to send a copy of this to Mr MacKenzie Livingstone MP. There is no record that any of these took any notice whatsoever of the Council's concerns.

Travelling by *Sheila* was only part of the journey for many people and, coming north, that journey might have started in a cab in Edinburgh, in the dark of a December morning, somewhere before 4am. There was then a long wait at Perth, in winter time still in the dark. From there on, progress was slow. There was more waiting at Inverness then on to the green train (of the Highland Railway, pre-1923) "which wanders by slow and easy stages to Kyle". The ride was hard and there was always jolting. It seemed that anything would do for the people of the isles. What passengers wanted was a good solid meal with eggs, toast and strong tea, but at that time, there were no on-board refreshments, since dining carriages did not come to the Kyle line until the 1920s, when the LMS transferred some elderly but very fine ex-Midland Railway vehicles to work in Scotland. Some people would be nibbling at sandwiches, some would be eating oranges or chocolate or bananas or unsatisfying things like that and by the time that they boarded *Sheila*, they felt like nothing on earth. The cabins were comfortable, but the expense could be justified only for night journeys when ."To be thus cradled in my own Hebridean waters was a delicious experience". Those who did not have a cabin, had to make do with red plush seats in the white-painted saloon, with a red cushion at one's head. In fact it was not clear if the covering was actually plush – it was a "strangely smelling, soft material, as red as the MacBrayne funnel itself". On *Sheila*, the saloon was right aft, the end of it over the propeller, which kept up a constant chugging, with a kick of the shaft to "finish off the beat". Ceaseless rattling of some silverware, teapots or other such utensils, suspended in racks overhead, added to the cacophony. Passengers could of course escape this by going out on the raised after deck (assuming that they could negotiate the companionway), but it could be horribly cold there, an intense and stupefying cold, a cold which found its way through all the defensive layers of clothing a man might have. They were usually glad to go back below again. Those who were not beginning to feel the effects of the Minch welcomed the merry ringing of tea bell and the food – tea, white bread and marmalade or perhaps a piece of fish or cold meat – served by the sure-footed stewards. When passengers had dined, the tables then cleared and with slow and steady pace in came the Captain and perhaps an officer or two. Later followed a nondescript company, grime-bestrewed people that suggested the engine room. Those who were not feeling so good, to whom the thought or sight of food was "loathsome", had to lie in torture in the midst of all this and it seemed quite a long time before what was to them a hideous repast came to an end. Sometimes the latter poor souls would eat something, which they did not much enjoy, not to stave off hunger, but to stave off the awfulness of sea-sickness on an empty stomach.[5]

But in the end, quieter waters always came, with Cabeg Head and the Lochs coast and, with a sweep round the lighthouse at Arnish and much ringing of the engine-room telegraph, *Sheila* and her passengers were home in their own good town. [6]

---

5   Despite stabilisers, the problem has not entirely gone away. After a recent, bumpy crossing on board *Isle of Lewis*, when waiting to disembark at Stornoway, a kindly lady asked a rather pale little boy if he was all right. The lad smiled bravely but said nothing and it was left to his father to explain that "he's had the dry boak a' the way over".

6   This account of travelling on board *Sheila* was written by John N Maciver, "Jack" otherwise known as "Scratch". He wrote regularly in the *Gazette* over a period of 30 years and was a gifted musician. He trained as a teacher but soon gave it up and came home to Stornoway where he spent the rest of his life recording the scenes and goings on round the harbour. He died suddenly in 1948 aged 62.

4.5 *Sheila* at Kyle. (By courtesy of the Mitchell Library, Glasgow City Council)

4.6 and 4.7 Victorian passengers on the after deck of *Claymore*. (By courtesy of the Mitchell Library, Glasgow City Council)

4.8 Captain Cameron on board *Sheila* c1923. (© Duncan Macpherson Collection, Dualchas Heritage Service, The Highland Council))

4.9 Some of the Macpherson family of Kyle on board *Sheila* in the early 1920s. The ladies are Mrs Margaret Macherson and her sister Chrissie, the children are Mary and Neil. (© Duncan Macpherson collection, Dualchas Heritage Service, The Highland Council)

Lochness

This ship was built subsequent to the setting-up of the new Company in 1928 and appeared in service remarkably quickly thereafter, as though the new owners wanted to prove their good faith to the travelling public. Probably this was largely due to work done on the specification under the old Company, although the new vessel was rather larger than that proposed by MacBraynes. She was ordered from Harland and Wolff of Govan in January 1929, her keel was laid in March, she was launched on 6 June and entered service on 1 August. Under command of Captain Norman MacArthur, she took up her roster at Mallaig and gave a good account of herself on her maiden voyage, as she arrived early at Stornoway, despite a strong north-easterly wind. The Engineer was Mr MacColl, while Mr MacRae was Chief Steward. Captain MacArthur, who had joined MacBraynes in 1903 and become a captain in 1911, remained with the ship for many years and gained a reputation as being equally affable to the fishworker crossing in steerage and the more affluent visitor travelling first class.[7] Like Captain Robertson, he counted Sir Harry Lauder among his friends. He was clearly proud of his ship and in 1936 commented that over the past ten years, the people of Stornoway had not once missed a mail or newspaper.[8]

Passengers in first class had a lounge, "prettily" decorated in yellow, with imitation windows at which hung dainty curtains. It was furnished with comfortable settees and there was also a "neat" writing desk. The electric lights were shaded by silk lampshades. The smoke room was finished to resemble an old country inn, a scheme much favoured by Coast Lines in its cross-channel vessels. Apparently it was "realistic", at least until the ship began to pitch and roll. The finely-furnished, indeed "dainty" dining saloon on the main deck was decorated in green and had small tables for four, with matching individual chairs. No longer did those suffering the effects of the Minch have to lie and watch while others ate and this must of itself have made the passage easier for many. The nine cabins and five staterooms were large and airy, with good headroom. The greatest improvement, however, was in the third class accommodation, which was laid out both fore and aft. It consisted of a dining saloon, a smoke room and separate lounges for ladies and gentlemen. At times of peak traffic, as when the herring girls were travelling, part of the cargo space aft could be floored and fitted with seats, to give increased under-cover accommodation. In both classes there was ample deck space, including some under cover. The deck space was divided longitudinally, thus giving passengers in each class the run of the ship from stem to stern. She was hailed by the local press as a "miniature liner". Initial publicity had shown her with the traditional black hull, but she entered service with the grey hull favoured by Coast Lines at that time. It was disliked by the public, proved impractical for ships on the kind of duty that *Lochness* had, and was soon abandoned.

A great advantage of *Lochness* was that, with her increased speed, a departure from Stornoway at 11pm now allowed passengers to reach Kyle at 4.15am. and thus be in ample time to catch the early train (5.10) and be in Inverness by 10.30, and Dingwall rather earlier. This facility was much appreciated by county councillors and council staff, who had to attend regular meetings in Dingwall. Those who wanted to reach Glasgow earlier and have more time to sleep on board could continue to Mallaig and be in Glasgow by 1.56pm. The stop at Kyle, with associated cargo handling, did tend to lessen the chances of a good night's sleep for the latter.

The new vessel certainly represented a step change in Scottish coastal shipping and it was perhaps rather unfair of George Morrison to say (referring to the subsidy paid to MacBraynes) "S'e glè bheag a ràinig air an truaghagh" (Very little of it reached the poor soul).[9] Unfortunately she thus made most of the rest of the fleet seem even more obsolete.

She had been in service for less than two weeks when she ran down a small boat in Stornoway

---

7   The opinion was that of Mr D MacPherson of the Kyle Pharmacy, who often travelled on the ship and came to know the Captain well.

8   Isles of Youth broadcast, May 1936

9   George Morrison (1906-88), better known as 'The Breve', was one of the most influential Lewismen of his generation, although his professional life was spent outwith the island. He was an extremely funny man, and was best known for being the writer of the Brevities published in the Stornoway Gazette, which ran from the late 30s to the early 80s. His writing was often satirical, sometimes playful, sometimes serious, but never malicious. He spared no one, least of all MacBraynes.

4.10 Captain MacArthur on the pier at Kyle, with *Lochness* behind. Behind is the carthorse which was used for shunting operations (see Ch 8) © Duncan Macpherson Collection, Dualchas Heritage Service, The Highland Council)

harbour. Then on New Year's Day 1930, she ran aground on Goat Island when leaving, having had to take action to avoid two trawlers which were lying in her normal path. No doubt the date had something to do with this. MacBraynes tried to pin responsibility on the Harbour Commissioners, but the latter had no intention of giving in to "unreasonable and unnecessary demands". They added that they were always willing to give every possible facility for the quick despatch of the mail steamer. Thereafter *Lochness* settled down to give a decade of good service to Lewis but as early as December 1936 the gilt had definitely worn off and the renewal of the mail contract in the next year was seized on by the Leòdhasachs as an opportunity to press for a new and larger ship. Although the renewal of the contract went through without too many problems, it was to be a decade before the promised new ship would enter service. Matters were made worse when, in September 1940, *Lochness* had to have a brief spell off for overhaul and *Clydesdale* was put on the run. Naval men, inured to seafaring, described conditions as "tough" and passengers in third class found them "appalling but degrading". There was nothing that the Company could do – the fleet was at full stretch and *Lochness* was in commission for about 16 hours per day, six days per week, leaving very little time for minor repairs. Matters became even worse in August 1945 when an infestation of cockroaches was discovered on board. MacBraynes explained that this was due to the number of passengers who had been travelling in foreign parts, but no one was convinced by this argument. Two months later she had a brief period off for overhaul and was replaced by *Hebrides* (on charter). Passengers were glad to see her when she came back and seem to have stopped complaining.

Only three accounts of crossing in *Lochness* have appeared in print. In 1930 a lady writer, Ethel Pickworth, had been looking forward to the voyage with a kind of dreadful anticipation but in fact sailed in a flat calm, her only complaint being that a thick sea mist prevented her seeing anything at all. However, she seems to have liked the ship.[10] In *"Isles of Sunset"*, published about 1930, Walter Mansell found her to be a handsome vessel, a vast improvement on her predecessor, with the appearance and comfort of a pocket liner. Later, when she was no longer new, George Morrison, in *"One Man's Lewis"*, was much less complimentary, suggesting that, as MPs were used to sleeping on benches, they could perhaps sleep in the steerage of *Lochness*. He also commented on the huddles of poor folk in the steerage, who could either "freeze beneath the stars or rot beneath the decks".

---

10   Ethel Pickworth *"By Sea to the Isles"*, published by the author, Llandudno, 1953

4.11 *Lochness* at Kyle c1930. Cloth caps and cloche hats seem to be de rigeur in steerage. Over the starboard rail can be seen the ferry slipway, with a few cars awaiting shipment across to Kyleakin. The railway hotel is still in its original form, rebuilding not having started (© Duncan Macpherson Collection, Dualchas Heritage Service, The Highland Council)

4.12 Construction of the oil tank to hold fuel for *Lochness* at Kyle in 1929. (Duncan Macpherson Collection, Dualchas Heritage Service, The Highland Council)

THE MAILBOAT "LOCH NESS" AT STORNOWAY.

4.13 *Lochness* at Stornoway in the early 1930s. (Author's collection)

MARITIME BUILDINGS, STORNOWAY,
(BUILT ON SITE OF THE OLD STRONGHOLD OF THE MACLEODS OF LEWIS).

A.5116

4.14 The new harbour building of the mid-1930s, which housed the terminal for passengers. (Author's Collection)

4.15 By the 1920s, *Claymore*'s visits to Stornoway were less frequent, but she did continue to offer trips to remote places in the north-west mainland, such as Lochinchard, where she is seen about 1925. Motor transport has arrived even in this remote area. (Stornoway Port Authority)

Applecross

To passengers wanting a fast passage to or from Stornoway, one of the drawbacks of the service was the time spent diverting to serve the remote village of Milton in Applecross. Not many people travelled to Applecross, but the service was a lifeline to the area. A passenger on *Lochness* in the 1930s commented that the total business handled on one call was the setting down of one lady passenger, a few boxes of goods and some mail bags and in the 1950s George Morrison, perhaps thinking back to Saint Maelrubha, who arrived in these parts in a coracle in the sixth century, mentioned the "moth-eaten coracle" which served as the ferry boat and recorded that all that was unloaded was three trunks, two boxes of margarine and a dear English lady. This call was made about an hour after leaving or before arriving at Kyle and thus, inbound, took place about 3am. It probably added about half an hour to the overall journey time and could also have been the cause of *Sheila*'s stranding in 1927, as, when altering course to make the call, the officer on the watch may have become confused about various lights in the vicinity. It certainly was not an easy task to take a ship the size of *Loch Seaforth* into an anchorage of this nature, let alone meet the ferry, in the dark of a December morning and latterly, in winter, the call on the inbound run was by prior arrangement only. In 1956 it was given up altogether, the area then being served from a new pier at Toscaig, about four miles south of Applecross, by the small motor vessel *Loch Toscaig*. With Captain Gordon in command, she left for Kyle at the more civilised hour of 8.30am and returned at 2.45 in the afternoon. As she lay idle between these times, Mr MacFarlane, the Company's agent at Kyle, conceived the idea of using her on short cruises to beauty spots such as Loch Duich and these proved to be popular, the pleasure of the trip being enhanced by the tea and biscuits served by the crew. This piece of local enterprise lasted until the vessel went to Oban in 1964 and *Lochnell* was placed on the service. With the construction of a new road to serve the area, the ferry service was withdrawn in 1971.

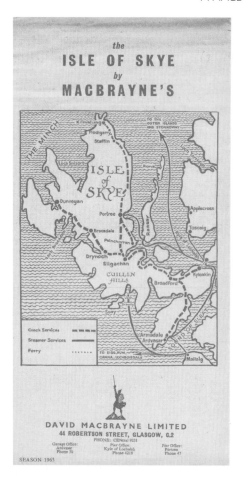

4.16 A MacBrayne timetable leaflet for Skye in 1963 shows the normal route of the Stornoway steamer and the ferry to Toscaig. (Author's Collection)

4.17 The "moth eaten coracle", as seen from *Loch Seaforth* in June 1950. Three passengers, a large hamper and assorted boxes of goods are being taken ashore. (By courtesy of the Mitchell Library, Glasgow City Council)

4.18 *Loch Toscaig*, seen at Oban in May 1964, when working the Lismore service. *Claymore* lies at the railway pier. (Author)

4.19 On board *Loch Toscaig*. Duncan Macpherson is on the left and the other passenger may be Mr Dalby Porter, who regularly visited the area c1950. (Duncan Macpherson collection, Dualchas Heritage Service, The Highland Council)

Loch Seaforth

The replacement for *Lochness* was ordered from Dennys of Dumbarton in late 1945, but steel shortages and other post-war problems delayed construction and she was not launched until 19 May 1947, finally arriving in Stornoway on 6 December.

Initial impressions, as recorded in the *Stornoway Gazette*, were very favourable. Particularly striking was what the paper called the "outlook tower" – the observation lounge for first class passengers on the upper deck. This was furnished with armchairs and settees upholstered in red or green, and was certainly a comfortable apartment, if somewhat chintzy in style. Unfortunately the windows were set rather too high to allow seated passengers to admire the view and not everyone seemed to appreciate the furnishings. In January 1950 it was reported that five chairs and three cushions had been slashed. Perhaps the time of year had had something to do with this. There was also a lounge for those in third class, aft on the promenade deck and a great advance on the facilities on *Lochness*. A most welcome innovation was a small hospital cabin on the same deck and patients travelling to the mainland could now have more privacy than that given by a curtained-off alcove in the saloon. The dining saloons were also considered handsome, but the smoke room for first class was a rather gloomy little apartment aft of the engines and that in steerage was even less appealing. However, the reporter questioned the need for the extensive deck space, which was of little use on the inward journey, and in the matter of seating capacity and berths as a proportion of her total capacity, the ship was not any advance on her predecessor. The idea of a seat under cover for everyone would not be implemented until the arrival of *Isle of Lewis* in 1995. *Loch Seaforth* was originally licensed to carry 500 passengers. She also introduced the luxury of single-berth cabins in first class and in both classes the provision of two-berth cubicles, rather like couchettes on European railways. In 1959 the charge for the former was £1 and for the latter, in either class, 5/- (25p). The report also mentioned that there was plenty of space for the carriage of cars, although by the time that the vessel had been in service for ten years, this no longer sufficed and additional car space had to be created by plating over the forward hatch on the cargo space. Although the press did not mention the accommodation for the crew, this was also a great advance on that on earlier ships and, depending on status, crew members had either single- or twin-berth cabins. .

In the 1950s Peter Flett, who hailed from Stornoway, was Purser and on one occasion, on a crossing to the mainland, was called upon by no less a person than the Company's Chairman, to check the tickets of two passengers in the first class lounge, who looked as though they did not properly belong there. Having looked at their tickets and found this to be the case, Peter duly took them to the third class quarters and reported back to the Chairman that he had dealt with "Two first-class drunks".

Although the advent of *Loch Seaforth* did not require any physical alterations to the port facilities at Stornoway (or at Kyle), the arrival of the fine new ship was the occasion for a renewal of hostilities between MacBraynes and the Harbour Commissioners over the matter of dues, which, at £750 per annum, had not been changed since just before the loss of *Sheila*. The new rates proposed, it was calculated by the Company, would work out at £5,508/16/- (£5,508.80), and they promptly returned the first invoice they received, for December 1947. The matter was ultimately referred to Arthur Woodburn[11], now Secretary of State for Scotland, and on his suggestion, a compromise of a 45% reduction in the new rate was agreed in June 1948.

For much of her time on the Stornoway run, *Loch Seaforth* was commanded by Captain John Smith, who was on the bridge from 1953 until she left the area in 1972, apart from a few years after 1964 when, against his will, he was transferred to the new car ferry *Clansman*. Many would have seen this as promotion, but Captain Smith did not like the car ferries and was glad to be able to return to the more traditional ship after 1966. John Smith was born in South Dell in Lewis in 1908, one of a family of three boys and one girl. Both his grandfathers, John Smith and Angus Graham, were skippers of sailing ships. He went to sea, after education at Cross and Lionel schools

---

11   Arthur Woodburn, Secretary of State for Scotland in Attlee's government, from 7 October 1947 to 28 February 1950. He was MP for East Stirling and Clackmannanshire.

4.20/21 The first and third class dining saloons on *Loch Seaforth*. Although the latter is definitely smaller, there is little difference in the furniture and fittings and there is a marked change from the accommodation on *Sheila*, on the route only twenty years earlier. (Glasgow University Archives)

4.22 Captain John Smith in the wheelhouse of *Loch Seaforth*.
(Courtesy of Mrs D MacDonald)

4.23 Captain Smith bringing *Clansman* in to Mallaig in stormy conditions in February 1965. The car ferry was then relieving *Loch Seaforth* on the Stornoway run. (Alasdair Munro)

and served with a number of shipping companies. Of his wages, half was sent back to his parents and half went to pay college fees, to allow him to continue to study for his master's certificate at what was then the Royal Technical College in Glasgow. In May1939 he joined MacBraynes, as Second Officer on *Lochearn* on the Inner Isles run from Oban. During the war, in 1942, he moved to the Stornoway service as Mate on *Lochness* and transferred to the new ship in December 1947 in the same capacity. His first command was also of that ship, on a short term basis and, after spells relieving on various ships, he became Master of *Loch Seaforth* in December 1953. As she was generally considered to be part of the "Skye navy" – the bosun and carpenter, for example, were both from that island – it was rumoured in Stornoway in 1953 that he was cultivating a Skye accent before he took up his new command. He was of course a native Gaelic speaker and much of the on-board business was carried out in the language. He finished his career with brief spells of service on *Iona* and *Clansman* on the Stornoway car ferry roster and retired from the latter ship in 1973. One of his brothers followed in his footsteps as Mate on *Loch Seaforth* but sadly was killed in an accident on board.

In 1937 John married a lady from Lewis who had been a cook in Glasgow, and there were four children, all girls, of this marriage. Sadly his wife died at an early age and he re-married in 1968, but his second wife also pre-deceased him. Ultimately he was grandfather to 13 children, two of whom have made the sea their career. Away from the sea, John's hobbies were fishing and gardening and he greatly enjoyed foreign travel, in particular a visit to the Holy Land. In recognition of his services to Lewis, he was in 1973 presented with the Cuach Comunn Leòdhais agus na Hearaidh Glaschu, a cup awarded each year to a person who has brought honour to himself or the island. He died in 1985, at the age of 77.

Captain Smith was a superb seaman and it was said that he never missed a crossing on account of bad weather. He was especially skilful at berthing a ship in the worst of conditions and it was said that you could then hold an egg between the quay wall and the ship and he would not break it. He himself would probably have passed on the credit to the ship herself, being both a modest man and also immensely proud of her and of her sea-going capabilities. During all the time that he commanded her, not a single sailing was missed due to bad weather even although on some nights, he admitted, she "found every hole in the Minch". On others "she just danced across". His worst crossing was on 31 January 1953, in the storm in which the Stranraer car ferry *Princess Victoria* sank. Due to the intensive timetable worked by the Stornoway mail steamer, Captain Smith had a special leave allowance of one week off in every six. When he was away, the ship was entrusted to relief captains, of whom some, such as Captains Alasdair Matheson and Jimmy Hodgson, were also held in high regard.

In her later years, *Loch Seaforth* had a number of accidents, which ultimately led the popular press to report that the ship was "jinxed". The first of these was a stranding at Kyle on 2 March 1966, when she failed to complete a 180 degree turn and ran aground on the mainland shore. She was well and truly stuck on the rocks and it was some days before she could be pulled clear. *Loch Ard* came up to maintain the cargo link and passengers were diverted, for the first time, via Uig and Tarbert. Then, not long before her transfer away from Stornoway, she ran aground on the small island of Longay, south of Raasay, on a stormy night in October 1971. On the bridge was a relief captain who had taken the inside course between Skye and Raasay, to lessen the discomfort to passengers. No one was injured and the damage was slight, but local politicians in Lewis worked themselves into a fine state of indignation about the continued use of an "unsafe" ship.

Even with the alterations mentioned above, it was not long before the demand for car spaces was once again outstripping the vessel's capacity and in February 1960 the *Stornoway Gazette* was complaining about the long waiting lists for car passages and the need to book months in advance in summer. There seems to have followed a suspicion in Lewis that the successful introduction of the Uig-Tarbert car ferry, and in particular the growth of commercial vehicle traffic by that route, might threaten the continued operation of the direct service to Stornoway. Perhaps this was not unfounded, since some of the civil servants charged with formulating plans for the car ferries had shown little grasp of the geographical realities of the Hebrides and it had even been rumoured that they had suggested that two ferries could adequately serve the three routes opened in 1964. There had also been plans by a new Stornoway-based company, Ullapool-Stornoway Ferries Ltd, to introduce a car ferry service, but these came to naught when, firstly, the ship which was to be used, a vessel from internal Danish services, failed to secure a certificate from the Board of Trade, and then when the founder of the company, Charles Alexander, died suddenly in May 1965.

For a further three years nothing happened to bring the introduction of a car ferry service any nearer. In the meantime, passenger numbers on *Loch Seaforth* declined, but, perhaps surprisingly, there was an increase in the tonnage of goods traffic. However, in November 1968, MacBraynes drew up plans to transfer the existing mail service to a different mainland port, Ullapool, Gairloch and Aultbea all being considered. There was little to choose between these three in terms of distance and length of open water passage, but Ullapool scored in having a pier which could easily be adapted for a car ferry and also had fairly good approach roads. An informal meeting was held in Stornoway in November 1968, at which Mr Leith outlined the Company's ideas, stressing that the timetable could later be adapted for a car ferry. Unfortunately these proposals were immediately leaked to the public and an outcry arose in Lewis, where people wanted a car ferry and were no doubt afraid that agreement with the new plans would postpone this for some time. Mr Leith said that the immediate introduction of a car ferry would be "premature", though he gave no reason for this. The crossing time would be three hours and departure times from Stornoway would have been 7.30am and 3.30pm in summer, 10am in winter and from Ullapool, 11.30am and 7.30pm in summer and 6.30pm in winter. A coach connexion with Inverness would allow Glasgow arrival times of 8.45pm and 6.05 next day, and, as at that time, the night trains between Inverness and Glasgow still conveyed a sleeping carriage, passengers could have a comfortable journey. Fares would be higher than via Mallaig[12] and goods services would have had to be diverted. The lorry service to Glasgow could run on three days per week. Some commentators feared that these arrangements would have an adverse effect on the economics of the Kyle line, which had been threatened with closure. The proposals were rejected in January in a joint meeting between Stornoway Harbour Commissioners, representatives of the Burgh Council and Lewis District Committee and Mr Leith then intimated that the reorganisation would not go ahead. In 1970 *Loch Seaforth* broke down and was off service for some days, while passenger traffic was diverted via Uig-Tarbert. The Commissioners were very unhappy about this and were concerned that the arrangement might be made permanent. They no doubt feared loss of revenue. A complaint was made to the local MP, who passed it on to the Secretary of State, but this received short shrift, as Mr Ross replied that he thought that intervention by his office would not be justified.

In January 1971 Gordon Campbell [13], now Secretary of State for Scotland, finally announced that he had approved the introduction of a ferry service between Stornoway and Ullapool and that a 75% grant would be made available for the construction of linkspans at the two ports. This decision aroused a good deal of local opposition in Lewis, but this time the objectors did not manage to alter the plans. *Loch Seaforth* soldiered on until March 1972, when she was rather disastrously replaced by the nearly-new car ferry *Iona*, still running to Kyle and loading vehicles by hoist. Her behaviour on this exposed service, despite Captain Smith's excellent seamanship, generated a great volume of complaints, some of which even went to the Prime Minister, Edward Heath, but he seems to have paid as little attention to these as Lloyd George did in 1919. She made the last crossing from Kyle on 25 March 1973. Problems with the linkspan delayed the start of the new service until May 1973, when it was inaugurated by *Iona*, she being very soon afterwards replaced by *Clansman*. The connexion with Kyle, which had just outlasted David MacBrayne Ltd, had finally been severed.

---

12   At that date, the Stornoway-Glasgow fares were:- via Mallaig 87/9 (£4.39), via Kyle 101/3, via Mallaig, Armadale and Tarbert 95/6 (£4.77)
13   Gordon Campbell, Secretary of State for Scotland in Edward Heath's government, from 19 June 1970 to 5 March 1974 and MP for Moray and Nairn.

4.24 Cars for shipment by *Loch Seaforth* queuing at Kyle in the 1960s. A Hillman Imp, a Volkswagen Beetle and a Triumph Herald are fourth, third and second in the queue, waiting while a crate of goods is hoisted aboard. Not only was the ship's car space restricted, but loading and unloading took a considerable time and led to queues such as this. (By courtesy of the Mitchell Library, Glasgow City Council)

4.25 Some lady tourists take a stroll on the pier at Stornoway, while barrels and bales of wool await shipment on the left and, on the right, *Loch Seaforth* rests before her next departure. The ship's distinctive figurehead can be seen on her bow. (T B MacAulay Collection, by courtesy of Mrs K MacIver)

4.26 MacBraynes did not operate stage carriage services on Lewis, but with the coming of inclusive tours by car ferry and coach, their buses began to be seen on the island. In this view, no.67, a Bedford VAS with Duple coachwork, awaits passengers outside the Royal Hotel in Stornoway. It was based in Glasgow. (Chris Orchard, Online Transport Archive)

4.27 Plenty of MacBraynes' goods vehicles were in attendance at the new car ferry terminal in Stornoway in 1972, when this photo was taken from the deck of *Clansman*. Much of the traffic was now carried in containers and demand was such that MacBraynes sometimes had to hire additional capacity from local hauliers. (Bill Lucas)

4.28 Captain Smith taking *Iona* out of Kyle for the last time, March 1973. (Alasdair Munro and Mrs D MacDonald)

MACBRAYNE'S STEAMERS

EXCURSIONS
from Kyle of Lochalsh

DAILY (except Sundays) to
Mallaig (by Steamer)
(Via Sound of Sleat) .

Steamers dep. Kyle	arr. Mallaig	Steamers dep. Mallaig	arr. Kyle
5.10 a.m.	7.5 a.m.	12.30 p.m.	2.15 p.m.
M.O. 8.30 a.m.	10.30 a.m.	S.O. 1.30 p.m.	3.30 p.m.
10.0 a.m.	11.40 a.m.	Th.O. 5.30 p.m.	7.30 p.m.

M.O. Mondays only.   S.O. Saturdays only.
Th.O. Thursdays only 2nd June to 22nd September only.
* Passengers may travel by any service in either direction.

DAY RETURN FARE, Saloon 15/.

DAILY (except Saturdays and Sundays) to
Stornoway (by Steamer)

Steamer depart Kyle 2.30 p.m. :   arrive Stornoway 7.0 p.m.
Steamer depart Stornoway 12.30 a.m. :   To Mallaig and arrives
back to Kyle at 10.0 a.m.

SPECIAL TWO DAY FARE, Saloon 50/-
(Berths extra)

THURSDAYS (2nd June to 22nd September) to
Loch Scavaig (Loch Coruisk ISLE of SKYE)
By Steamer
Allowing time ashore

Steamer depart Kyle	... ...	10.0 a.m.
Steamer due back	... ...	7.30 p.m.

FARE, Saloon 22/-
Passengers are advised to wear low heeled footwear

MONDAYS, THURSDAYS and SATURDAYS only
Circular Tour to
Mallaig and Armadale (Tour No. 22)
By Steamer and Motor Coach

Steamers depart Kyle 8.30† a.m. 10.0 a.m.:   arrive Mallaig 10.30† a.m., 11.40 a.m.
Steamer depart Mallaig 12.30 p.m.:   arrive Armadale 12.55 p.m.
Coach depart Armadale 1.0 p.m., 2.0* p.m.: arrive Kyleakin 2.25 p.m., 3.10* p.m.
Ferry from Kyleakin to Kyle of Lochalsh

† Mondays only.   * May to September only.
FARE, Saloon 15/8

MONDAYS, THURSDAYS and SATURDAYS only
Circular Tour to
Armadale and Sound of Sleat (Tour No. 23)
By Motor Coach and Steamer

Ferry from Kyle of Lochalsh to Kyleakin.
Coach depart Kyleakin 9.45 a.m.:   arrive Armadale 11.10 a.m.
Steamer depart Armadale 12.55 p.m.:   arrive Kyle 2.15 p.m.

FARE, Saloon 13/2   P.T.O.

An undated handbill giving details of excursions from Kyle of Lochalsh. An overnight trip to Stornoway was available at a special fare of 50/- (£2.50) but allowed little time to see anything of Lewis. (Author's Collection)

Table
14 MALLAIG . KYLE OF LOCHALSH . STORNOWAY
(Stornoway Mail Service)
DAILY (EXCEPT SUNDAYS)

Conveys Motor Vehicles

			A	B					NS
Mallaig ..	Steamer	dep.	1215	1215	Stornoway	Steamer	dep.		2330*
Armadale ..	"	"	—	1245	Kyle of Lochalsh	"	"		0400†
Kyle of Lochalsh ..	"	arr.	1400	1430	Kyle of Lochalsh	"	dep.		0500†
Kyle of Lochalsh ..	"	dep.	1500	1530	Mallaig	"	arr.		0655†
Stornoway ..	"	arr.	1915	1945					

NS—Not Saturdays.   A—1st to 17th October 1970 only.   B—19th October 1970 to 30th April 1971.   †—Following morning
*—On Sunday evenings passengers will embark at normal time but vessel will sail at 0015 on Monday morning from Stornoway, arriving Kyle of Lochalsh at 0430—
remainder of timetable as above.
All car and passenger tickets must be paid in advance in both directions.   For car space and sleeping berths apply to Head Office.
AT STORNOWAY.
Sleeping berths must be claimed on board ship by sailing time.   Passengers may embark on the vessel from 2130 onwards.
All cars and motor cycles to be on the pier by 2000.
All cars and motor cycles for the 0015 Monday morning sailing to be on the pier by 2000 on Saturday evening.

FREIGHT RATES

MOTOR CARS, CARAVANS, Etc.

	From Mallaig or Kyle	Mallaig to Kyle of
Not exceeding:—		
7 cwts.	£3 15 0	Lochalsh
10 cwts.	5 13 0	80/- p. ton
15 cwts.	7 11 0	Minimum
20 cwts.	11 8 0	Charge: 40/-
Over 20 cwts.	11 8 0 p. ton	

These rates are for the single journey only, but a concession of 50 per cent. is allowed on the return booking provided cars are brought back by the same route within three months of the outward date of shipment.

PASSENGER FARES

			Single	Return
Mallaig to Kyle of Lochalsh	..	..	11/10	20/-
Stornoway	..	..	40/-	74/-
Kyle of Lochalsh to Stornoway	..	..	30/-	51/-

SLEEPING BERTHS

Single Berth Stateroom	..	..	..	£1 10 0
Two Berth Stateroom	..	..	..	1 5 0 per berth
Four Berth Stateroom	..	..	..	0 15 0 per berth
Single Berth Cubicle	..	..	..	0 12 6
Two Berth Cubicle ..	..	..	..	0 10 0 per berth

The timetable for the Stornoway service, winter 1970-71. (Author's Collection)

Bibliography

Minute books and letter books of Stornoway Pier and Harbour Commission 1905-1918, 1925-39, and papers relating to proposed car ferry services.

Court of Session papers on action of Stornoway Harbour Commissioners v David MacBrayne Ltd, 1917-1918

It must be Stornoway. The story of the Stornoway Pier and Harbour Commission 1865 to 2004. Catherine Mackay. Argyll Press, Glendaruel, 2008.

Stornoway Gazette, 7, 14 and 21 January 1927 (Loss of *Sheila*), 14 June and 9 August 1929 (*Lochness*), May 1933 (Travelling on *Sheila*), 1947 (*Loch Seaforth*) and material by George Morrison)

Information on *Loch Seaforth* supplied by Alasdair Munro, Inverness

Ethel Pickworth. *By Sea to the Isles.* Published by the author, Llandudno, 1953.

Duncan Macpherson. *Where I Belong.* G and W Fraser, Aberdeen, 1964.

Landing Staffa.

Gilfillan

5 The Lordly Ship

"*A ND HERE ON KING GEORGE V, is every combination and device to turn us to a holiday humour. The ship's lordly appearance, her spacious decks, her restful lounges, the resources of every service above and below, make her an ideal ship for a day so full of sights and wonders. Better get a deck chair and you and I will sit down.*"

So began the account of the Staffa and Iona sailing in the 1939 guide. After her post-war refit and much more prosaically, the General Manager would rate her in 1946 as "Sound for the job". If any later MacBrayne ship inherited the mantle of *Columba*, a ship which would be known the world over, it was *KGV*, as she was often called, rather than her direct successor, *Saint Columba* on the Clyde. The guide did not exaggerate. She was a lordly ship, with a tremendous and very loyal following, and there were many sore hearts when she was finally withdrawn in 1974. It is said that her sailings were profitable to the end. Attempts at preservation followed, but she met her end as a burnt wreck on a South Wales beach. She deserved better, but perhaps preservation would not have been appropriate. A ship which delighted to turn Rhu na Gael to face the Atlantic – with an announcement from Captain John Gray that "in their own interest passengers are advised to clear the foredeck" – might have resented a static role as a restaurant on an inland river.

She was for a time replaced by the car ferry *Columba*, but even her sailings came to an end in 1988 and Caledonian MacBrayne seemed content to allow the Staffa and Iona cruise to lapse. Only in some years can it now be enjoyed, courtesy of *Waverley* and her operators. Tourism in Scotland is the poorer.

This account gives an idea of what went on behind the scenes, to provide this cruise. The first part is based on information supplied by Rev. Archie Lamont and the description of the running the catering service is by John Gallacher of Oban.

The Lamont family came from Bunessan in Mull, where Archie's great-grandfather had lived and out of which he had carried on a trade with Greenock, using a fishing smack. With this he served all the small ports in the Ross of Mull. His grandfather had worked as a crew member on *Cygnet*, before transferring to the ships of the Northern Lighthouses Board. With them most of his time was spent on *Hesperus*, which was based in Oban. While the rest of Scotland was celebrating VE day in 1945, Archie was incarcerated in an exam hall in Edinburgh, taking the university bursary examination and he went on to study divinity there. In 1946 he was looking for a vacation job and a family friend suggested that he should approach David MacBrayne Ltd to ask about work as a purser on board one of their ships. Without any interview, he was duly appointed to that post on *Lochfyne*, which in that season was running excursions out of Oban. On three days of the week she went to Iona, on one of these starting from Fort William, and on the other three she carried out cruises, such as to the Six Lochs. Evening cruises were also run on some days. As these involved spending a fourteen-hour day on board *Lochfyne*, the purser very often had a sore head by the time they finally returned to Oban, due to the constant vibration. As this was the first post-war summer, demand was brisk and the weather was generally fine. After one and a half day's training, the new purser was on his own and indeed very shortly afterwards found himself training an even more raw recruit, who was to take up duties on *Robina*, sailing on short cruises out of Oban. Passengers in 1946 were mainly tourists from England, with a smattering of Scots, but scarcely any foreigners.

Compared to other services, the duties on the Iona run or on the cruises were not onerous, although the purser was expected to be available to passengers during the entire trip. Ships on this cruise were operated as first class only and that must have simplified the clerical work. The day started about 8.30am with a visit to the Oban office with the previous day's takings, these having spent the night in the on-board safe. Almost all tickets were bought on board and, unlike present-day practice, these were collected only when passengers disembarked. Many left the trip to the ticket office until the last minute and it was not unknown for passengers to be redirected from the gangway to the ticket office to buy their tickets before leaving. Most passengers would require tickets either for the round trip to Iona or the cruise and there was not the multiplicity of bookings that was found on other services. Meal tickets were not then issued, diners simply paying the cashier as they left the saloon. Little cargo was handled and what there was consisted mainly of parcels. However, on one occasion *Lochfyne* was charged with the delivery of a boat to a man on Lismore. The boat concerned was large and not new. As *Lochfyne* had been designed as a passenger-only vessel, she lacked a derrick and much careful manoeuvring was required from the crew to get it into place on the vessel's foredeck. Unfortunately one man took hold of a section of the boat's gunwhale and was then horrified when this came away in his hand. It had clearly rotted through, but this did not prevent the consignee from suing MacBraynes for damages.

The purser was not only expected to usher passengers ashore at Iona and later to count them back on board, but also went with them to give a brief conducted tour of the abbey and nunnery. It seems that there was a tradition that the purser on the Iona tour should be a student of divinity, presumably to be able to give a more detailed account of the island's history than other students would have done. No landing was made at Staffa in the immediate post-war years, as the landing stage had been damaged by a stray mine during the war and could not be repaired for some years. (This call was in due course resumed, until a rock fall on 13 September 1967, which occurred when passengers were landing on the island, put paid to it for good.) It was also important that everyone was back on board at the correct time, to allow the ship to keep to her schedule. *Lochfyne*, being a diesel-electric ship, had no problem with this, but it was a different story when *King George V* resumed her normal place on this service in 1947. Difficulties arose, since she was a coal-burner and the quality of fuel available in these years was poor. When she ran late, as she very often did, time ashore at Iona had to be curtailed and this was virtually the only source of complaint that the purser had to deal with, as passengers felt that they had been cheated.

Of course there were also questions, of varying degrees, and perhaps the prize went to one lady who came to the ticket window to ask if Columba had discovered America before or after he came to Iona. There was also, in 1946, the matter of the stray mine among the Torran Rocks, just off the south end of Mull. Two rather twittery elderly ladies came to ask if it was true that there was a mine there, not, they assured the purser, that they were afraid of it, but simply because they wanted to see it. The errant mine had in fact already been reported to the Admiralty by the Captain and, after a reminder from him some days later, dealt with by the mine disposal team from the Clyde. Some weeks later, when *Lochfyne* returned to Oban one night, a large bomb disposal expert bore down on the purser as he saw the last passengers off and asked to be directed to the ship's captain. What passed between them is not recorded, but it may have been that the expert was somewhat annoyed that the captain had sent that reminder.

Lochfyne was a happy ship, with a distinct family atmosphere. In 1946 she was commanded by Captain Angus MacKinnon, an affable man from Gometra, who was very often accompanied on board by his son, a tall, well-built boy known as "the wee fella". Captain MacKinnon went on to become commodore of the fleet. From mid-August Dougie MacCallum was Mate and adored the ship, to the extent that he was visibly upset when transferred to *Robina* as Captain. Even though this meant promotion, he would not be reconciled to the idea of leaving, even if only for a few weeks, his beloved *Lochfyne*, to which he very soon returned. This story ultimately had a happy ending, since he later progressed to be her captain, remaining with her for many years. While he was absent, Ian MacIver from Ardnamurchan via Greenock acted as Mate and Bob

MacVicar was pilot. As the ship was in commission all the year round, most of the crew remained with her, in some cases for many years. Most of them came from somewhere in the western isles, particularly Barra and the Uists, and were Gaelic speakers, although the business of the ship was always conducted in English. The officers were also generally from the Isles or from Loch Fyne. On *King George V* Captain MacKechnie from Skye was in command and the Chief Officer was Neil Campbell from Tiree, who later became Captain Campbell. In 1948, Captain MacKinnon was back on the run, with John MacCallum – also from Tiree – as Chief Officer. Captain MacKinnon remained in command of the steamer until the end of the 1954 season and later referred to this period as a very happy time.

One of the purser's other duties was to pay out the weekly wage packets to members of the crew, including the firemen. The Chief Officer and Chief Engineer submitted to head office in Glasgow weekly time sheets as appropriate to their departments. In head office a list of payments due to each man was made up and the Oban office was authorised to issue cash in bulk to the purser, who then had to disburse this on pay day to each man, according to the list supplied by head office. The bulk cash was brought on board by a clerk from the Oban office and delivered to the purser. As this transaction usually happened at a time well after the office had closed, a hectic hour or two then followed for the purser, what with the clerk desperately rushing to get home and firemen already lined up at the door desperate to get their pay and equally desperate to get ashore to spend it. The seamen, in contrast, were calm – they were later at the window, as they had deck duties to perform well after the ship had docked. The seamen, typically, conserved their pay for their families and, particularly in the case of men from the Outer Isles, for the winter maintenance of their domestic properties at home.

Both firemen and seamen catered for themselves on board and Archie was frequently amazed at the ability of the seamen to feed themselves adequately and, particularly, economically, in order to take home as much as they could at the end of the season. The purser did not deal with the officers or the stewards and stewardess (Amy MacPherson).

King George V was then still a coal-burning steamer and the firemen were rather a mixed bunch, mostly being recruited in Greenock or Port Glasgow, between which there was great rivalry in many fields. As she came into commission later than the railway steamers on the Clyde, the latter had already creamed off the pick of the available labour and MacBraynes had to take what was left, this including some characters, and most of whom were great fun. The bars of Oban took a substantial share of the weekly pay packets and fists were a common way of settling the disputes which later arose. One night, in the small hours, the Oban constabulary were called to the ship, to find a free-for-all in the firemen's cabin, the walls of which were running blood. Once order had been restored, someone thought to ask the reason for the fight. The question at issue had apparently been whether men from Greenock made better safe-breakers than those from Port Glasgow. At a later date, some of the older firemen signed an agreement giving the purser the right to send a proportion of their pay direct to their wives by registered post, thus making sure that their families would not be left totally penniless. One of the men fancied himself as an amateur boxer and when shore time permitted, he would go off to some fairground and, for the sum of £2 – almost equivalent to a week's wages – allow himself to be punched almost senseless by someone with rather more talent in his fists. This same man also fancied himself as something of a dandy and when dressed to go ashore sported what was then known as a stag pullover – a pullover decorated with a circle of stag heads round the middle. Another fireman was Lachlan McLoghlin Ponsonby, generally known as Lachie. He distinguished himself one day by failing to report for duty and the police were called to *KGV* before she sailed. They were unable to cast any light on the mystery of the missing fireman and were considering trawling the sea around the North Pier after the ship had vacated her berth. She had just cast off when through the arch in the pier buildings ran Lachie, shoeless and without a jacket, clearly hoping that the ship would wait for him. This Captain MacKinnon refused to do. The other firemen had to cover for him and Lachie forfeited a day's pay, clearly a salutary lesson, since he took care thereafter to be back on board in time for departure. But Lachie also had a very honest streak in his make-up. One night after the last passengers had disembarked, he knocked at the purser's ticket window, looking very puzzled indeed, his pay slip in one hand and his pay in the other. On admission to the office, he said "You've paid me too much, one pound too much" and proceeded to hand over a pound note. It would have been a temptation to many to keep the money and hope this would not be noticed.

In 1947 the engine room was under the command of Mr W MacGregor, who was then coming up to retirement. He worried. He worried about the engines, perhaps because the steamer had been somewhat temperamental in her younger days. Not without reason, he worried about the supply and quality of coal available. And he worried about the firemen. When someone was tactless enough to suggest that a bunch like that were not worth worrying about, he simply pointed out that without the firemen, there would be no cruise to Iona. He was replaced by Mr MacKillop, who took equally great care of the engines, but did not worry so much, perhaps because the ship was converted to oil firing in the winter of 1950/51 and the problem of the firemen was solved.

The weather in 1946 was generally good and that of 1947 was brilliant, but there was one bad day when there had been some doubt if the ship would sail, especially as only 40 passengers turned up on the North Pier in the morning. However, it was decided to set off, going via Tobermory, and on the passage up the Sound of Mull, *KGV* passed some deep sea trawlers which were running for shelter in Oban bay. Iona was safely reached, despite a heavy swell in the Sound and the passengers had time ashore. On the return trip, huge waves were encountered off the south end of Mull, but nonetheless most of the passengers, who clearly enjoyed a rough passage, went down to the dining saloon for tea. For fear of the windows on the weather side being smashed, the Chief Officer got the passengers who had chosen seats at tables on that side to move over to join those on the lee side. From the shelter of the promenade deck, those looking out could see one enormous wave approach the ship. They braced themselves against any convenient wall and in a few seconds found themselves horizontal, looking up at the sky through the windows of deck shelter. From below there came a most horrendous crash, suggesting that one or more of the large windows in the dining saloon had been smashed. This had not happened, but the elegant saloon was a shambles, with passengers, chairs, food, broken crockery and tablecloths thrown all over the floor. In a few seconds the ship was back on an even keel, and, remarkably, meal service was resumed quickly afterwards. Miraculously there were no injuries. Possibly because of this happening, the ship did not always sail on the numerous bad days which marked the summer of 1948.

John Gallacher was brought up in South Uist and on leaving school looked around for work. He heard that there was a vacancy for a pantry boy with MacBraynes and thus in 1958 made his first acquaintance with *King George V*; he was subsequently promoted to be galley boy on *Claymore*. Thereafter he had a spell of deep-sea work, with Elders Fyffes to the West Indies and to West Africa. He returned to MacBraynes and served on board *Lochearn* and again *Claymore* However, it was to be on *King George V* that he spent most time and this account of the running of the dining saloon is based on John's memories of life aboard.

"Enjoy the excellent cuisine on MacBrayne's vessels" ran a slogan which appeared over the years in many issues of the timetable. Given the length of many voyages and the appetites sharpened by the sea air, most passengers were happy to avail themselves of the cuisine and generally they were not disappointed. A full meal service was maintained throughout the second world war and even in the immediate post-war years, when rationing was still in force, the Company managed to maintain a very high standard in its catering and to serve what were for those times generous portions. In the case of the Oban-based excursion ships, this success may well have been due to their close co-operation with suppliers in the town. Vegetables came from Breckenridge's shop, fish from Binnie the fishmonger, meat from Jackson the butcher and teabread and cakes from the baker, Kirkwood. These suppliers knew what was likely to be required, but definite orders were placed on the previous evening and food was delivered on board in the morning. Generally the system worked perfectly but there was one panic when the order which had been left in the letterbox at Jackson's was found to be illegible when opened, rain having flooded the box in the night! However, by some quick thinking on the part of Jackson's staff, the necessary items were made up and delivered to the ship before sailing time. On long distance services, where passenger numbers were relatively low and timetables easy, there was no problem catering for everyone who wished to take a meal, in a fairly leisurely fashion, but it was quite otherwise on the day excursion from Fort William and Oban to Staffa and Iona. Most passengers wanted to take lunch and of course most also wanted their full time ashore in Iona. To meet this demand, the catering staff developed a kind of production line in the service of the mid-day meal and *King George V* built up a very good reputation for the on-board catering.

The catering establishment formed a large percentage of the total crew numbers. In the 1960s, under the command of Chief Stewards, David Hayburn and, later, David Samson (formerly of *Lochinvar*), there were six stewards, two stewardesses (who served in the cafeteria on the lower deck) and a barman. In the galley there were the cook, second cook, a pantry man, a galley boy and three pantry boys. The galley was originally located admidships but about 1950 it was relocated in an enlarged form in the stern of the ship, this being marked by a large, upright galley chimney, which slightly spoiled her elegant lines. The dining saloon was situated aft on the main deck and accommodated 220 at tables for ten each. Meals were brought to the diners by silver service, many of the pieces having clearly been in MacBrayne ships almost as long as the Company had existed. The silver was cleaned by stewards once per week, being washed in soda then polished. The stewards wore white shirts and black trousers, with black ties and black shoes. Large windows, some of which could be opened, allowed diners to view the passing scenery as they ate. However, there was no time to linger, since everything had been planned down to the minute, to allow the service of four sittings of lunch in the time available. The first sitting began at 11.30, when the Captain and officers also had lunch, and half an hour was allowed for it. This was followed by 15 minutes to lay up the tables afresh and so on until on a busy day four and a half sittings would have been served. Before meal service started, stewards would already have laid out plates of salad on the long tables in the middle of the saloon and it was an easy matter to add to these slices of cold meat as required. Lunch invariably began with soup and stewards had developed the skill of carrying six full plates at one time, balancing four in their arms and securing the other two in their hands by hooking their fingers around them. In the galley two large containers would be simmering with the main courses, possibly stew and mince. Sweets were usually cold, but often served with custard, and these would also have been prepared in advance. When diners opted for a salad, the stewards could be seen balancing seven plates of these at once. High tea was served on the return journey, but was less hectic, since many passengers would be taking an evening meal in their Oban hotel or boarding house. But there were few more delightful dining experiences than enjoying a salmon salad while *KGV* steamed along the cliffs of the Ross of Mull on a sunny evening, through the open windows the sound of the gulls mingling with that of the ship's wash.

John later transferred back to *Claymore*, as night steward. This involved a twelve-hour stint, from 8pm to 8am, but was less hectic than lunch on the Iona run and sometimes there was a chance to enjoy a dance at Tobermory, music being provided by Bobby MacLeod and his band in the Mishnish Hotel. While on *Claymore*, John met several distinguished passengers including Gordon Jackson and his wife and also R A Butler. A frequent passenger was Mr A Oliphant of the Coll Hotel.

The war service of *King George V*

When Archie Lamont served on *King George V* at Oban in 1947 and '48, she was not long returned from war service. Most of this was spent in home waters, acting as a tender from Gourock and Greenock to ships at the Tail o' the Bank, in the course of which duties she carried many distinguished passengers. But in 1940 she was on very active service and played a distinguished part in the Dunkirk evacuation. This is the timetable for that period in her history.

On 17 May 1940 she left Dover at 14.30 and arrived in Dunkirk at 19.50. Early on the morning of the next day she sailed along the coast to Oostende, reaching the Belgian port at 09.50 and leaving again at 12.40 for Folkestone. There were clearly problems in finding a berth in the harbour when she arrived as she did not dock until 20.45. Most of her passengers would have been refugees, since the great evacuation had not yet started. She then had a day off and on both 20 and 21 May carried out ferry duties to and from Boulogne, leaving Dover in the morning at 07.30 and returning from Boulogne at mid-day. On the second day, she was caught in a bomber raid off the French coast and came near to being lost, but managed to escape before becoming a casualty. She did not see further service until the Dunkirk evacuation began.

Her next crossing was from Dover to Dunkirk on 29 May, leaving at 03.20 and arriving at Dunkirk at 09.20, again probably having to wait off-shore for some time before going alongside. She left with troops at 11.00 and crossed to Margate, arriving there at 18.30. Having disembarked her troops, she then went up to Sheerness and left there again on the next day at 13.15 for Dunkirk, reached at 19.15. She left again for Margate at 22.30 and was alongside there at 07.30 on the next morning. Again she must have had to wait for a berth, since she would normally have made the passage in about four hours at most. In the afternoon she went back up-river to Sheerness and left again for Dunkirk at 20.00. She was in Dunkirk at 09.40 on 1 June and after a very quick turn-round, left for Margate at 10.30, arriving in Kent at 17.00. Again she went on to Sheerness, perhaps to refuel, but this time came back down to Margate and left at 19.00. After a fast crossing she was in Dunkirk at 22.40 and left at 23.00, to return to Margate, arriving at 04.30. She left again that evening, 3 June, but did not reach Dunkirk, returning at 07.30 on 4 June. She then proceeded to Southampton and ultimately back to the Clyde. She had been under shell fire several times, but fortunately sustained no significant damage.

The rest of her war service was spent as a tender on the Clyde, during which she carried many distinguished passengers, including Winston Churchill, en route to a meeting with President Roosevelt.

Lochgarry also took part in the Dunkirk operation.

On her six cross-channel trips *KGV* had carried abut 18,000 men and for their part in the rescue, Captain R MacLean and Chief Engineer W MacGregor received the DSO, while Bo'sun D J MacKinnon was awarded the DSM. Apart from their bravery under fire and superb seamanship, the logistics of embarking over 2,000 soldiers in 20 minutes, as on her last trip, under the conditions of Dunkirk, must have called for a high degree of organisation and discipline. Perhaps the Iona run had been good practice. Captain MacLean, was able to return to France in 1957 to a ceremony to honour Dunkirk veterans, along with Alan Galbraith, Quartermaster and A MacDonald, a crew member.

5.1 *King George V*, in Caledonian MacBrayne colours, crosses Oban bay to the North Pier to collect cruise passengers on 1 June 1973. (Author)

5.2 Off Lismore, *King George V* meets *Claymore*, inbound from Barra, June 1969. (Author).

5.3 *King George V* backing out of Tobermory. (By kind permission of the Mull Musuem)

5.4 *Lochfyne* at Staffa in 1931. In practice, she would have anchored rather further out from the cave than appears to be the case here. This is one of a series of cards from paintings by Tom Gilfillan, who also devised the logo of a highlander which adorned the Company's road vehicles. (Author's Collection)

5.5 *King George V* waiting off Iona in June 1973. (Author)

5.6 Small but vital members of the fleet were the red boats which ferried passengers ashore at places at which there was no pier. To cope with the crowds arriving on the cruise steamer, it was necessary to station four at Iona at the height of the season and one is seen here at the jetty in June 1969 Unlike most of these boats, *Loch Shiel* boasted some shelter, since she had formerly been employed on the services on the loch of that name. (Author)

5.7 A deck view on *King George V* off the Ross of Mull in June 1973. (Author)

5.8 A perfect Oban evening in May 1964. *Lochfyne* was still used on the Iona cruise for a few weeks before *KGV* came out and is seen here at the Railway Pier along with *Claymore*. (Author)

5.9 The dining saloon of *King George V*. (By courtesy of the Mitchell Library, Glasgow City Council)

T.S. King George V.

5.10 Not many writers of postcards say much about their ship, but on this card, dated 20 August 1936, a little girl, Sheila, says that she was nearly sick on a trip to Iona and that the ship is rolling terribly, although "Dad says it is not". The card itself is interesting, since it shows the vessel in the colours of Turbine Steamers Ltd. Presumably MacBraynes had not yet had time to have cards prepared of her in their own colours and were using up stocks which they acquired with her in October 1935. (Author's Collection)

5.11 John Gallacher perched nonchalantly on the stern rail of *Claymore*, 1958

5.12 Other crew members – Hughie MacAllister (Mull), Duncan Campbell (Vatersay) Angus Morrison (Harris)

5.13 Crew members on *Claymore* in the late 1950s. They are, left to right, Shamus Bhan MacKinnon, Duncan Campbell, Jonathan Galbraith and John Gallacher

5.14 The stewardesses, Jean and Mabel

A brochure published by Caledonian MacBrayne for the last season of *King George V*, 1974. This was a time of rapid inflation and no prices are quoted either for the cruises or meals. (D Henderson Collection)

Illustrations 5.12 to 5.15 are reproduced by kind permission of John Gallacher

Bibliography
Turbine Steamer King George *sails again – in pictures*. David Kerr. Published by the author, Glasgow, 2000.

S. S. *Gairlochy from S. S. Gondolier. Loch Oich.*   *Caledonian Canal.*

ch^d Macintyre, Fort William

6   MacBrayne Publicity – The Tours and the Tourists

D ESPITE THE VOYAGES OF MARTIN MARTIN in the 17th century and the travels of Dr Johnson and James Boswell in the late 18th, not many people ventured to the Hebrides until after 1820, unless they had to travel on business or, in the case of those leaving the area, had little or no choice but to travel in search of a better life. The coming of what was at first called the steamboat did not greatly alter the situation, though it no doubt made life far easier for businessmen and opened up the area to commercial travellers. It may, however, also have contributed to outward migration; it has been noted that there was a considerable movement from Campbeltown to Glasgow in and just after 1826, the year in which the Campbeltown and Glasgow Joint Stock Company was formed to run a service of steamers between the two places. Tourism was also beginning. Keats visited Staffa in 1819, Sir Walter Scott made a West Highland tour in 1821. Berlioz' Waverley overture, first performed in 1828, and translations of Scott's novels, brought the western highlands to the attention of mainland Europe. In the summer of the next year, the German composer Felix Mendelssohn Bartholdy, with a friend Karl Klingemann, visited Staffa, having travelled from Fort William to Oban on *Maid Of Morven*, then on the Glasgow-Inverness service. From Oban they went on to Tobermory on *Benlomond* (sic), aboard which they had to spend a night, due to problems in landing. They went on to Staffa on the next day, probably on *Highlander*, and, despite seasickness, the composer was sufficiently impressed to make the island know in his Hebridean overture. On 1 June 2009, during a concert held on board *Waverley* on a cruise to Tobermory and Tiree, this overture and other music were played to commemorate both the visit and the bi-centenary of the composer's birth. By 1833 advertisements appeared in the Glasgow press for trips to Iona and Staffa, by the steamers *Saint Mun* and *Maid of Islay*, while *Fingal* cruised on Loch Ness.

At that time, publicity was confined to advertisements in the *Glasgow Herald* and local papers in the highlands. These simply listed sailing dates and times and were in no way designed to attract casual or pleasure traffic. But the tourist business prospered and the Company, from 1851 David Hutcheson and Co, received a welcome financial boost in the early 1860s, when it was able to dispose of no fewer than four of its steamers, at a very advantageous prices, to the agents of the Confederate States, to run the blockade imposed by the northern states during the Civil War in the USA. With this windfall, the Hutcheson brothers were able to commission their first saloon steamers, *Fairy* in 1861 and two years later *Iona*, actually the second of that name. Although the latter was very soon sold off to serve as a blockade runner, she was replaced in 1864 by an even better ship, which inherited her splendid deck saloons, the after one being 60ft long by 20ft wide, allowing a reporter to claim that she offered all the comforts of a perfectly furnished private mansion. In 1866 the Crinan Canal barges were replaced by a little saloon steamer, *Linnet*. In the same year, two other new saloon steamers were commissioned, *Chevalier* for the excursion route from Oban to Staffa and Iona and *Gondolier*, for the Caledonian Canal service from Banavie to Inverness. Now Hutchesons could offer passengers superior accommodation on all stages of the journey from Glasgow to Inverness and the cream of Victorian society was not slow to take advantage of this. A one-day sailing from Oban to Gairloch was introduced soon afterwards. In 1875 a service was begun on Loch Awe, as an alternative route to and from Oban, and, in the next year, the screw steamer *Lochawe* was built for this. In the same year, Hutchesons also began to serve

Islay, an island which was then, in contrast to most of the others in the Hebrides, fairly prosperous. This prosperity was due in no small measure to its numerous distilleries, but despite these, it did not then see many tourists.

An account of 1875 lists the passengers on *Iona* as including "Fat manufacturers, smug tradesmen, worthy parsons, dignified dandies, MPs, popular barristers, London journalists, reading parties, smart young surgeons, and their ladies".[1] This was clearly quite a well-to-do company and to attract more of the kind of passenger whom he wished to see on his tourist steamers, David MacBrayne, who had taken over in 1878 and traded under his own name from the next year, began to publish, from 1880, the guide book "Summer Tours in Scotland". At first this was a small paper-back volume, illustrated only with sketches, but in 1883 it blossomed out into a handsome book, bound, at first, in green, then later red leather with gold print on the covers and gilt edges to the pages. It was priced at 1/- (5p), or about £5 in present-day values. A golden *Columba* graced the front cover. A cheaper version, in paper-back and without the gilding, could be bought for 6d. Given that £2 would have been considered a good weekly wage at that time, it was evident that the book was not aimed at the Glasgow working-class day tripper and his family, nor at the residents of the Gaeltacht, who would use MacBrayne's services on their way to and from Glasgow or Inverness, or when en route to a port to take ship for Canada or the USA. The market was clearly those who had the money and time for extended touring and who would loyally follow where Her Majesty had led. Travellers were expected to be curious about the history, the natural features and the contemporary "improvement" of the area.

The book was well illustrated, the original sketches soon being supplemented by coloured engravings, then, from about 1883 with handsome photographs. In that year these were rendered in a curious blue finish, but in 1884 sepia was used and soon black and white was chosen as standard. Many of the illustrations were full-page views of places mentioned in the text and quite a few showed the steamers which a traveller would use in the course of a tour. It made a fine holiday souvenir, to be kept to bring back memories, long after the tour was over.

From 1881 to 1926, the form of the guide did not vary much from year to year, though from 1910 the steamer timetable was issued separately, allowing more space for descriptions of points of interest. In the 1880s and 1890s it contained twelve chapters, divided into three sections. The first of these covered, in four or five sections, the Royal Route from Glasgow to Inverness, via the Crinan Canal, via Loch Awe and via the Mull of Kintyre. In early editions this covered also the extension of some sailings round Cape Wrath to Thurso, but this enterprise proved to be too ambitious and was dropped in the next decade. The second chapter devoted four or five sections to excursions from Oban and Inverness. From Oban these consisted of the day tour to Staffa and Iona, sailings to Fort William and Inverness, with associated tours to Glencoe, and the day-long sail to Gairloch, with an extension to Loch Maree. By the 1890s local trips to Mull and Loch Sunart were also advertised. The third chapter dealt with longer trips to the Uists, Barra and Lewis and Harris from Portree or via the west coast of Skye. From Inverness the tours listed were to Gairloch, linking up there with that from Oban, and to Ullapool. The services from Glasgow to Islay, both via the Mull of Kintyre and by connexion at Tarbert were originally linked in with the Royal Route but later given a chapter to themselves. A full list of places at which the steamers called followed the travelogues. The last part of the guide contained timetables of all the services to be used, beginning once again with the journey from Glasgow to Oban and Inverness, by what MacBrayne always classified as "swift steamers". These certainly included some flyers, such as *Columba* and *Iona*, but also some, such as *Fusilier*, which could manage 13 knots with a favourable wind and whose swiftness was relative, perhaps best judged in comparison with what were called "deep sea steamers".

The Staffa and Iona tour was given in the form in which it continued for so many years, though with a slightly earlier departure from and arrival at Oban (8am and 5.30pm). Generally the Victorians seem not to have minded early rising when on holiday, although the magazine "Leisure hours" did comment (c1880) that "The 100 tourists (at Oban) look as if they had all risen too

---

1   A A'Beckett. *Our Holidays in the Highlands*, 1875

early and were trying to appear wide awake by unwinking eyelids". While all the main hotels were within easy reach of the steamers, guests who stayed at the Columba Hotel, of which the first part opened in 1887, had the best of it, since it was situated right on the North Pier. Ninety minutes were spent at Staffa, to allow all passengers the chance to visit the island. Boatmen came over from Gometra prior to the arrival of the steamer and decided where she should anchor, depending on weather conditions. On certain days passengers were landed at the north end of Staffa and had to walk along the shore path to Fingal's cave, presumably then having less time to admire it. One commentator mentioned (1894) that the path to the cave was slippery and that the footwear of many of the "sprightly young girls" was far from suitable, consisting as it did of "thin-soled and ridiculously high-heeled boots and shoes". A ladder of 150 steps led to the summit of the island, but only the most agile would have had time to climb it as well as visiting the cave. The same time was given at Iona, despite which some passengers tried to crowd the boats on arrival there, in a panic that they would not have sufficient time ashore. In 1898 the cabin fare, including the services of boatmen and guides, was 15/- (75p) and breakfast, dinner and a plain tea could be had for 5/- (25p). The steamer called at Carsaig in the south of Mull, an hour before arriving at or after leaving Iona. The area abounded with "valuable geological specimens and fossils of every kind" and there were also the Carsaig Arches, "a formation somewhat similar to that of Staffa". However, no time ashore was given. For this trip, without meals, a family of four would have had to pay £2/5/-, not including buying some sea-shell necklaces offered for sale by children on Iona.

In pre-1914 days, MacBraynes did not provide any short cruises out of Oban. In 1893 there were only full day trips, of which the cheapest were those to Tobermory (return fare 7/6d (37.5p) cabin, 4/- (20p) steerage), to Crinan (7/6d, (37.5p) cabin only) or to Loch Sunart (12/- (60p) and 6/- (30p)). Trips of a couple of hours were available, provided by Alexander Paterson, who came from Cumbernauld and started operations in 1892

6.1 A view of Oban about 1876, with *Pioneer* at the North Pier. (Glasgow University Archives)

6.2 *Pioneer*, as rebuilt in 1875, anchored off Staffa about 1880. (Author's collection)

6.3 *Grenadier*, in original condition, leaves Salen. (By kind permission of the Mull Museum)

6.4 Passengers being ferried to *Grenadier* by flit boat in 1908. The location is given as Iona, but it almost certainly Carsaig. (National Maritime Museum, Greenwich, London, neg.no.29984)

S. S. "PRINCESS LOUISE". *2 p.m. to 6.30 p.m. 14th September 1906* M. I. & R.

6.5 *Princess Louise* (1898) sets off for a cruise, c1906 (Author's collection)

with a little screw steamer called *Marchioness of Lorne*. She was soon replaced by a ship named *Princess Louise* and in 1898 by a larger vessel of the same name. A ship named *La Gloria* was chartered briefly before the latter came into service. Cruises were given to Connel in the morning and around Kerrara in the afternoon, both at a fare of 2/- (10p), and through tickets were available on the Caledonian Railway. A coach drive from North Connel to Glen Shellach was also possible. Clearly Paterson aimed at the less affluent end of the market and his sailings did not compete with MacBraynes. She seems to have been a happy little ship, but had one sad duty to perform in May 1927 when she carried the body of Captain N G MacAlister RN to be buried at sea. The two operators seem to have had an amicable relationship, but the short cruises were not mentioned in the guide.

The sailing from Oban to Gairloch was perhaps the most scenic of all the trips and certainly crammed more sightseeing into one day than did any of the others. It is not clear exactly when it was started, since it was referred to as "new" in various seasons in the 1870s, but it was certainly in operation by 1872, when it was worked by *Pioneer* and it was then given to the newly-modernised *Glencoe*. Her captain at the time was Angus Campbell, later of *Columba*, this being his first command. He was credited with introducing the side trip to Lochs Coruisk and Scavaig and it would seem that he remained with the ship on this service for about ten years. *Glencoe*, with her steeple engine, proceeded with "a definite and unhurried rhythm"[2], which must have made the long day more comfortable for her passengers than the later diagonal engine. *Grenadier* was actually built for this route and given what was by then obsolete but smooth-running oscillating machinery; she briefly worked on it in 1885, her first season, under Captain Donald MacCallum. However, the vessel most closely associated with it thereafter was *Gael*, acquired in 1891. The service ran thrice-weekly in each direction and having left Oban at 7am, the steamer called at Tobermory, Eigg and Arisaig (Mallaig after 1901), before

2   Letter from Donald MacPherson in Langmuir Collection, about a trip on this ship in 1921

heading across to Armadale, reached at 2.20pm on Tuesday or noon on other days. The reason for the late arrival on Tuesday was that a diversion was made to Loch Scavaig, where the steamer anchored to give passengers an opportunity to be rowed ashore. The route was then via the Sound of Sleat to Kyle, Portree and finally Gairloch, arrival there being at 8pm on Tuesday, or 6pm on Thursday and Saturday. On the latter days, it was also possible, by changing at Kyle, to reach Stornoway at 9pm. The return Oban-Gairloch fare (1898) was 37/6d (£1.88) in cabin and 22/6d (£1.12) in steerage, while the return fares to Stornoway were 43/6d (£2.17) or 25/6d (£1.27).

It is not known just how many tourists actually made the through Oban-Gairloch trip in one day, but in evidence to the royal commission on the west highlands in 1890, one Donald Darroch, obviously a local man, estimated that in summer 40,000 passengers landed from the steamers at that destination. While this would have included some who had come on the twice-weekly Glasgow-Stornoway through service, the majority would have disembarked from the Oban steamer and it would therefore seem that capacity loads were carried. Nor is it known with what degree of relief the tourists saw Gairloch come into view, but a day trip of this length certainly required some stamina. One commentator suggested that, while the scenery was no doubt magnificent, the people one met en route were infinitely more interesting. The writer instanced in particular the policemen on the piers – it was common for the local officer to go down to meet the boat – well-groomed and of imperial aspect, King Edward's highland satraps.[3] However, if they were tired, passengers could take comfort in the knowledge that carriages would be waiting at the pier to take them up to the Gairloch Hotel, a "comfortable building with superior accommodation and commanding an extensive sea view", according to the guide book. The hotel was a large building in the Jacobean style, which totally dominated the village. Designed by the architect Andrew Maitland, it was first opened in 1872, no doubt with an eye to the tourist

6.6 The Gairloch Hotel, about 1900. (Author's collection)

6.7 The steersman on *Glencoe*. The ship did not possess the facility of a bridge. (By courtesy of the Mitchell Library, Glasgow City Council)

3   Literary Tours in the Highlands and Islands. D T Holmes. A Gardner, Paisley, 1909.

numbers then arriving on *Pioneer*. It then became a focal point in the circular tours offered by Hutchesons / MacBraynes and the hopes of its proprietor, Mr R Hornsby, were certainly fulfilled, since it had to be extended in 1880, to plans of the same architect, and again in 1896, when the architects were Ross and MacBeth. As a result the original fairly plain three-storey building almost disappeared underneath the more florid extensions. By 1896 it offered 150 beds, suites of apartments and numerous public rooms and *The Times* in 1879 was moved to comment that "The comforts are undoubted ; the management is excellent". Apart from its indoor facilities, the hotel possessed extensive gardens with greenhouses, so that guests could enjoy the range of fruit and flowers to which they were no doubt accustomed. A bathing machine was also provided for their use and, along with other pastimes, "Sea bathing could be enjoyed to perfection". Whether taken as a marathon or spread over several days, the Oban-Gairloch sailing certainly gave tourists a chance to see some of the finest scenery on the MacBrayne network and it was a great pity that it was not resumed after 1918. Perhaps there had been a decline in numbers even before war broke out. During visits to the area, *Waverley* allows visitors to sample part of the itinerary in one day.

In the 1880s, the steamer continued to Lochinver, but this meant a very late arrival and an extremely early departure and, as these timings were too much even for the Victorians, the extended service failed to attract traffic. The main reason for continuing to Lochinver, according to the 1888 edition of the guide, was that it would allow tourists to drive to Scourie and hire a boat to visit the island of Handa, a noted breeding place for seabirds, including the elusive Richardson Skua. The geology of Handa was also stated to be of interest to visitors. Those who hankered after remote places could still reach that village once per week by changing on to the Stornoway steamer at Kyle or Portree. By 1914 Culag House, built by the previous Duke of Sutherland as a shooting lodge, had been converted into what was said to be a magnificent hotel. As there were 280 named lochs in the parish, fishing was clearly one of the local attractions, particularly for trout. A circular tour could then be made by coach either from Ullapool to Garve or from Lochinver to Lairg, in either case reaching Inverness by the Highland Railway. Perhaps the trains of the latter left something to be desired in the matter of creature comforts, particularly after a journey of 46 miles in a mail coach, since the guide concluded this section by saying that the journey from Lairg to Inverness was soon over and "the comforts of a good hotel await the traveller".

Perhaps David MacBrayne did have some thought for the less affluent, since in the early 1880s weekly tickets were offered for £3 and allowed a rather hectic six-day tour using the various tourist steamers. One could leave Glasgow for Oban on Wednesday on *Columba*, *Linnet* and *Chevalier*, take in Staffa and Iona on Thursday and go on to Inverness via the Caledonian Canal on Friday. From there Gairloch was reached on the Saturday by train and coach. Sunday, of course, was a day of no doubt welcome rest and on Monday the tourist was off to Oban on board *Glencoe*, to return to Glasgow on the following day. Those who thought that this would all be too hurried could, by paying an extra 10/-(50p), have a ticket which would allow travel on six individual days within a month while two weeks sailing could be had for £5.

The various other day excursions and services were followed by the timetable for the Glasgow-Stornoway and Glasgow-Inverness through services, by *Claymore* or *Clansman* in the former case and by *Cavalier* in the latter. With the spread of railway in the Highlands, both of these were by 1900 used mainly by cruise passengers. However, writing of 1889, the Glasgow author O H Mavor, (James Bridie) recounted a passage on the first of these ships, while he and his younger brother were en route to Skye, in the care of the family's maid Seonaid, who hailed from that island. The two boys shared a lower berth while Seonaid had the upper berth and, although it was not a particularly rough passage around the Mull of Kintyre, the poor girl was violently and dramatically sea-sick.[4] In the same year, Captain J T Newell, en route to a (relatively inexpensive) "shoot" on Lewis, found that, "by taking a deck cabin on *Claymore*, I got to Stornoway with far less change and worry than if travelling the same distance by land". His party had brought their own servants and were thus able to have their meals brought to their "airy cabin", saving them the trouble of descending into the

4   *One Man's Living*. O H Mavor (James Bridie). Constable, 1939

"hot, whisky- and food-stricken atmosphere of the regions below". Captain Newell was in fact paraplegic, following a riding accident in India, and it simply may be that he would have found the steep companionways too difficult, although he did not let his disability prevent him from going shooting when he reached Lewis.[5] Rather earlier, two (quite adventurous) young ladies travelling by *Clydesdale*, on the same service in 1872, complained of the stifling heat in the saloon and the atmosphere of whisky and toddy. They also complained that the steamer was five hours late.

A list of all the MacBrayne ships was given, with tonnage and horse power, and *Columba* and *Iona* received the prominence of a page to themselves. Otherwise little is said about the individual vessels. Generally MacBrayne did not exaggerate the amenities of his ships, probably leaving the reputations to speak for themselves, but in the guide in the 1890s there was one curious exception to this rule. The Glasgow-Islay direct service was then worked by the "splendid paddle steamer *Islay*", which boasted "superior sleeping accommodation". She had previously sailed between Stranraer and Larne as *Princess Louise* and her owners had sold her to MacBrayne in 1890, when she was deemed, by the Marine Superintendent of the London and North Western Railway, to be incapable of improvement for any further service at Stranraer. A circular tour to Islay was offered at a fare of 10/- (50p) cabin from Glasgow, going out by *Columba* and returning by *Islay* every Tuesday and Friday evening.

There were no advertisements in the book until after 1900, but a brief list of hotels was given on p31. This did not go into any details and for the larger resorts simply said "many splendid hotels" (Oban) or "various good hotels" (Rothesay). It is interesting to note that quite a few of those hotels, such as the Argyle on Iona and the Coll Hotel are still in business. A few, such as the Gairlochy Inn, were managed by women.

The guide was definitely aimed at visitors who had little personal knowledge of the Scottish Gaeltacht and who probably needed re-assurance. It is hard now to know who all these visitors were, but a brief study of

6.8 *Claymore* at an apparently deserted Gairloch pier. (Author's collection)

---

5   *Scottish Moors and Indian Jungles.* Captain T Newell, 1889.

the Oban Visitors' Register – a publication produced for some years in the 1890s – gives some indication. By 1894 there were 15 hotels in the town, together with numerous temperance hotels and 120 private lodgings. In the third week of August of that year, 800 visitors were recorded as being in residence in Oban. Of these, 407 came from England and Wales and 20 from Ireland. There were 71 from a wide range of overseas countries, although quite a few of these were British, some in the army or civil service in India, others, such as Lady Playfair, residing abroad (she gave her address as Algiers). Sixteen were from the USA. The domicile of 19 was not known. That left 283 Scottish visitors, of whom 100 came from Glasgow (this period did not include the Glasgow Fair holidays) and 70 from Edinburgh. A very few, usually single gentlemen, from nearby locations such as Strontian, Dalmally or from Glasgow, may have been in Oban on business, but at that time of the year it can safely be assumed that most were tourists. There is a marked divergence in the type of accommodation occupied. Of the 170 Edinburgh/Glasgow visitors, 112 were staying in apartments (66%), while of those 407 from England and Wales, 304 (81%) stayed in hotels, as did 56 (78%) of those from overseas. Not all the wealthier visitors opted for the hotels. Morven House had as guests General and Mrs Simson Buist and family, from Edinburgh. Sportsmen in knickerbockers and clergymen, the Register commented, were very numerous among the visitors at that time and "spooning" honeymoon couples were a common sight on the Corran Esplanade. Many visitors returned year after year. In that particular week of 1894, not a single resident in the Great Western Hotel came from Glasgow and only five from Edinburgh. A head porter in one of the big hotels later commented to his grand-daughter that he considered it a bad week if he had not been given three sovereigns in tips by its end. It was these wealthier tourists who would have purchased the MacBrayne guide prior to embarking on a series of tours.

(Note: This information is based simply on a snapshot, taken in one week of one year, but there is no reason to think that it is atypical, other than that it did not cover Glasgow Fair. It is an underestimate, since not all hoteliers and apartment owners responded to the request for information on visitors' origins and, even where they did do so, were often vague about exact numbers, merely giving "F Brown Esq and Family" or "J Smith and party". In these cases it has been assumed that a family consisted of four persons and a party of the same number. In some cases servants or maids were listed as such, but in most they are not mentioned separately, although, given the status of the guests, they must have been there. The number of visitors to the town would have been swelled by those on the steam yachts moored in Oban bay, belonging to people such as Sir Donald Currie of what was then the Castle Line of South African ships, with *Iolaire* (not the ship of the 1919 disaster). Presumably they would not have used MacBrayne steamers.

The guide also contained a list of pier- and ferry-masters and Company agents.

No author's name is given for the guide and it is possible that David MacBrayne himself wrote much of it. Whoever was the actual author, it is clear that MacBrayne intended the guide to be taken by readers on several levels. At its face value, it was a very thorough description of the places to be visited on the tours made possible by the Company's steamers. Thorough indeed it was; there were no sound-bites for Victorian travellers. Modern developments were not neglected. Travellers on board *Linnet* on the Crinan Canal were told to look out for the Argyle (sic) and Bute Combination Poor-house and Lunatic Asylum above Lochgilphead. By 1914 this reference had been dropped and perhaps tourists were in any case more interested in the Glenfyne Distillery, which had been passed shortly before this point. Fort William's appearance had been very much improved in recent years (the 1890s) by the new houses and villas which had sprung up. Geology was also featured in some detail, not only in places such as Fingal's cave at Staffa, but also in Glen Roy, where the work of Professor Tyndall was discussed at length.

Oban had, in 1898, nine churches and six banks, and three newspapers were published weekly. The rateable value had risen from £1,719 in 1847 to over £40,000. There were a number of large and splendidly-appointed hotels and a handsome hydropathic establishment, in the Scottish baronial style, was under construction. In stating this, the author was being economical with the truth.

In 1880 the Oban Hydropathic and Sanatorium Company published a grandiose scheme to

6.9 A party of passengers on board a paddle steamer at Oban in August 1913. According to notes made on the back of another view of the group, they had been staying in Craigror, presumably a guest house. The group includes several Roman Catholic priests and it would be most likely that they are on board *Grenadier*, en route to visit Iona. The names are:- Back row, l to r: J E Parvons, J P Brodnick, E V Carter, J F McGovern, J E Parsons, F Tryers SJ, C J Laycock. Front row l.to r: F Welling SJ, E M Swindells, G Swindells, B G Swindells SJ (Author's collection. The individuals were identified from other photographs by Margeorie Meikie, family historian)

6.10 The number of yachts anchored in Oban bay in the height of the holiday season must have made navigation difficult for the captains of MacBrayne steamers. In this view, taken in the 1880s, *Mountaineer* of 1852 threads her way through the maze to reach her berth. (Courtesy of the University of St Andrews Library, RNWS-14-173)

6.11 An early view of the Great Western Hotel in Oban. It was opened in 1863. (Author's collection)

6.12 To-day the hotel is little changed externally and is busy with coach parties, but the pleasant promenade in front of it is now a race track, thanks to Oban's one-way traffic system. (Author)

build an hotel of 137 bedrooms on the hill known as Torr a'chip, above the present Rockfield Road. This was to be fitted with fresh and salt water baths, in addition to all the amenities of a 19th century luxury hotel. As many of its expected patrons would be less fit than the tourists who crowded onto MacBrayne's steamers and connecting coaches in all weathers, a "hydraulic railway" (presumably of the cliff lift variety) would transport them from the town to the heights above. The contract was awarded to R MacAlpine of Hamilton, whose tender of £19,041 was the lowest received. Work began in 1881, when 300 men were employed and a railway line of some kind had been laid to bring the stone up to the site. The tender was probably too low and, as it was found that local stone was not satisfactory for the work, money had to be expended on bringing stone from further afield. In the aftermath of the failure of the City Bank of Glasgow in 1878, credit was scarce. The money ran out by the time the building had been completed up to the roof line in 1882 and it proved impossible to raise further capital, although attempts to do so continued for over ten years. To say in 1898 that it was "under construction", was only technically correct. The shell, which indeed suggested a building in typically Scottish baronial style (though perhaps overbearing rather than handsome), remained for many years, gradually being plundered for building stone, while items such as fireplaces were surreptitiously removed and installed in new villas being constructed nearby. Most of what remained was destroyed in the storm of January 1927, the storm which sent *Lochinvar* to seek shelter off Ardgour (qv. Ch.13), but some walls and a turret still stand to-day, a monument to one of the more intriguing "might have beens" in the history of tourism in Scotland.

The neighbourhood of Ullapool was also recommended for those with an interest in geology. Staffa, of course, called for much detailed information and no less than two and a half pages were devoted to its geological marvels, with (by the 1890s) one very fine whole-plate photograph and one smaller view. The information is both factual – "These columnar caves vary from 18 to 50 feet in height ; the depth of dark water within them from 36 to 54 feet." – and poetic – "The tremendous noise of the swelling tide mingling with the deep-toned echoes of the vault that stretches far into the bowels of the isle – form a combination of effects without parallel in the world!". However, the author seems to have thought that his efforts were not, on their own, adequate for the tourists, since, just to make sure that they were suitably impressed, almost half a page is taken up with a quotation from Scott's "Lord of the Isles", a poem to which repeated reference is made in the book. In early issues of the guide, the writer explained that, when rounding Arnish point on the approach to Stornoway, travellers interested in geology could see the line separating the conglomerates from the gneiss, which apparently ran right down the middle of the harbour. It is likely that, by the time Arnish was reached, many tourists would have lost any interest they once possessed in geology and would be grateful simply to see the harbour itself, never mind the dividing line, and this particular point was dropped from later issues.

One could be forgiven for thinking that the writer of the book was inclined to drop names, since scarcely a castle or large house was mentioned without the name of the present, and quite often the previous owners being given. This began when *Columba* had only reached Erskine – the house was built by Lord Blantyre who was accidentally killed in Brussels in 1830 – and continued to Inverness and all points west. On the north east shore of Loch Ness were Aldourie, the beautiful residence of Edward G Fraser Tytler Esq and on the opposite side, Dochfour House, a fine modern building in the Italian style, the seat of G E R Bailie Esq. At Lochaline was the mansion of T V Smith Esq, proprietor of Ardtornish. Eigg, which was stated to have about 2,500 inhabitants, was the property of R L Thomson Esq., while Canna was the property of A G Thom Esq. Sometimes, as in Islay, where five landowners are named in as many lines, this becomes positively indigestible. To a modern reader, it may be tedious, but it should be remembered that MacBrayne would have wanted to reassure passengers that, even in these remote and often wild shores, there dwelt some "respectable" people, such as one could have met in a London club at other times of the year. Given the rate at which estates were being bought up in the late 19th century, often by those who had made their money in industry or commerce, it must at times have been difficult to keep this part of the guide up to date. It should also be remembered that, even in the years between the two world wars, the local press would often list notables when they came back for a spell of residence in their Scottish properties, as well as giving the names of their guests.

Perhaps there were some who found it just too like life at home in England. As early as 1872, a writer in the St Paul's Magazine (Robert Buchanan) complained that the typical tourist seldom quitted the inland chain of mainland lakes (sic) and recommended that, to get away from it all, the tourist should go to the Outer Hebrides. Not many took this advice and generally the tourists continued to confine their explorations to the mainland lochs and nearer islands. They also seem to have fretted when unable to communicate with the outside world, much as do present-day travellers when deprived of their hand 'phones. This problem was particularly acute when travelling between Ardrishaig and Oban via Crinan, where there was no telegraph line available and no chance of wiring ahead to book accommodation in Rothesay or back to Oban to enquire about bags or gloves left behind in the hotel. To save his passengers from this anxiety, Hutcheson in 1876 paid for a private telegraph line between Crinan and Ardrishaig and telegrams could then be handed to the purser of *Chevalier* or *Linnet*, for onward transmission. There was also a suggestion that a telegraph instrument would be placed on board *Linnet*, but it is unclear if this was actually done.

It is more difficult to find information on the passengers who travelled for business rather than pleasure. An account of passengers on McCallum's *Saint Clair* in 1877 listed a bachelor party, a doctor coming to visit his mother in Coll, another doctor, from England on a fishing trip, a retired minister and his wife, the Fiscal of Tobermory (who had a farm in Tiree), a young Glasgow teacher and the Chief Constable and Sheriff Clark of Mull. A "humble highlander" who entertained them with Gaelic songs, completed the complement. No doubt the same type of passenger would have been found on the non-tourist steamers of Hutcheson at that time. Nor did the writer of the guide go into any details of what it was like to travel off-season, though D T Holmes enigmatically said that "When passengers are few, MacBrayne wisely economises on coal" and mentioned "dripping, top-booted seamen",[6] He was one of the few to give an account of what it was like to travel off-season, with a good description of meeting the ferry at Raasay on a stormy December day and, later the sad tale of his landing from *Fingal* at Tiree in a gale, when, after plucking up his courage to jump into the ferryboat, he found himself struck on the mouth by a sheep which was thrown in after him.

Of the accommodation of the poorer inhabitants, and of these people themselves, nothing at all was said; black houses were not of interest to the tourist at that time. The only very brief reference to the housing of the local people was made in connexion with that of tweed, in Harris. Apparently it would well repay the tourist's trouble to visit one of the "little cots" where the cloth was woven. At Ullapool it was mentioned that the houses were arranged in rows, suggesting that this was so unusual in these parts as to warrant a special mention, and villas, where they existed, were generally noted favourably. Tarbert (Argyll), though up and coming, had unfortunately to make do with some "nice cottages". In 1872 Mr T H Ismay, of the White Star Line of Atlantic liners, recorded that the natives around Loch Maree, were "very poor".

There was little about the fauna of the area, other than in context of shooting or catching it in the name of "sport". There are some references to ornithology, especially on the island of Handa (beyond Lochinver) and the Richardson Skua, which local boatmen apparently called "Dirty Allan". Ailsa Craig was mentioned in passing, though as MacBrayne vessels did not go anywhere near it, this was somewhat academic. More alarmingly, tourists on the coach from Loch Maree to Achnasheen station were told to look out, at the shooting lodge of Mr Bignold, for a great iron cage in which were two noble golden eagles. It seems strange that such birds would have survived in captivity. Fishing was clearly a pastime which would attract passengers and Loch Shiel is recommended as "abounding in fish" from the time of Saint Columba. There are occasional references to plants and flowers, but in general it would seem that readers of the guide were expected to be interested in nature only when it was on the grand scale.

6   D T Holmes. *Literary Tours in the Highlands and Islands*. A Gardner, Paisley 1909.

When it came to history, the author seemed to be on much less sure ground. A brief reference was made to the stones at Callanish in Lewis (written as Callernish), which were apparently of Druidical origin. Nothing else was said of other ancient sites or standing stones in the area. Ossian appeared from time to time and it seemed to have been expected that readers would be familiar with his doings. The reigns of some early kings, such as Kenneth I and Kenneth II, were covered briefly and MacBeth is dealt with in the setting of Iona. There were numerous scattered references to the Lords of the Isles (often in the context of Scott's poem), but no explanation of who these were and no suggestion of the scope of their rule, nor of why it ultimately ended. Burns was given the occasional quotation – the Falls of Foyers on Loch Ness and three stanzas of "Farewell to the Highlands" at the end of the book. Some minor poets were also featured. Whittier was quoted to tell the fate of two unhappy lovers at Loch Maree. Duncan Ban MacIntyure was mentioned in passing (in the section on Loch Awe) as the Highland bard but it is not stated that he wrote in Gaelic and the tourist no doubt went home assuming that he wrote in English. The late Professor Blackie, "our gay Grecian Gael" (!), had penned a stanza about Oban which was quoted:-

"For Oban is a dainty place
In distant or in nigh lands,
No town delights the tourist race
Like Oban in the Highlands."

He was also called on to praise the beauties of Inverness, at rather greater length, in a sonnet.

Clan feuds, as in Glencoe, Invergarry and on the island of Eigg, were covered from time to time, the more bloody ones receiving most attention, but there was no attempt to explain the clan structure, nor the position and status once enjoyed by the chiefs, nor of the complex structure of their households. Given that he wandered quite far in the course of 1745/6, it is unsurprising that Bonnie Prince Charlie made frequent appearances, usually when mention was made of a place where he slept or hid. However, Culloden was summarily dismissed in one line, as the place at which the Stuart cause was finally crushed in 1746.

When dealing with the 19th century, the writer became even more selective. The Clearances were simply not mentioned or glossed over in such cases as that of Muck (at that time uninhabited), whose inhabitants had all emigrated to America in 1828. Nor was any reference made to the part which Hutchesons' ships had played in taking people away from Lochaline or down to Campbeltown for onward transit to Canada or Australia. There is only one exception to this, in a quotation from John Bright MP about Glen Urquhart:

"In Highland glens 'tis far too oft observed
That man is chased away and game preserved.
Glen Urquhart is to me a lovelier glen –
Here deer and grouse have not supplanted men.".

Even Queen Victoria, in "*More Leaves from a Journal*", noticed with some regret that so many estates were being bought by English landlords, although it is clear that she thought this inevitable.

Likewise there was no reference in the guide to the agitation of the crofters, which was becoming a highly charged political issue just at the time when the first edition of the guide appeared, nor of the fact that *Clansman* had carried police reinforcements to Skye in 1882. Later both *Lochiel* and *Glencoe* were involved, the former transporting soldiers in 1884 and the latter police reinforcements in 1886. In the case of the former, her master, Captain Cameron, and his crew refused to sail with the military on board, and all had to look for alternative employment. No doubt MacBrayne did not want his passengers to think that the Scottish highlands might be going the way of Ireland, where the land question was then at its most delicate. That would not have encouraged tourists. It might have been thought that the work of Lord Napier and the Crofting Commission could have received a passing note – he was after all a peer of the realm – but it was likewise ignored. Explanations would have been too complicated, possibly compromising and run the risk of creating a wrong impression. Gladstone's Crofters' Holdings (Scotland) Act of 1886 ended the agitation, but again this was not mentioned.

The question of Gaelic is interesting. The language could not simply be ignored, as it had to be used when referring to place names and to occasional aspects of local history. Sometimes the spelling is, to modern eyes, rather strange, but then there was no Gaelic Orthographic Convention in the 1880s. But there was no reference to the current use of the language by most of the population served by MacBrayne steamers – probably over 200,000 at that time – and by most of the passengers in steerage. Nor is its use on board by most of the crews given any notice, although tourists must have been aware of this. If they travelled via Oban, they would also have heard it as soon as they set foot on the North Pier, since the Register of Visitors remarks that, over all the other tongues heard, was "the mellifluous accents of the Gaelic ".[7] Its then-current status was another of those topics which the writer of the guide thought it best not to mention. North Britons did not speak Gaelic. However, by 1914 a reference to the "plaintive sound of the Gaelic" had crept in.

In short, the MacBrayne guide was written to sell to the tourist the idea of a romantic, poetic country, with a marvellous landscape, steeped in eventful (but definitely non-threatening and none too accurate) history and peopled by upstanding citizens of North Britain. Its towns were being constantly improved with banks, villas, splendid hotels, asylums and (later, in Fort William) electric street lighting and almost-perfect sanitation, its countryside dotted with picturesque "cotts" where the natives wove tweed for the enjoyment of visitors. As the guide went through annual editions for many years, it would seem that the formula worked. Those who wanted to gain a broader understanding of the region, of its real history and of its current economic and social status, had to look elsewhere.

6.13 Soldiers of the Gordon Highlanders on board *Pioneer*. It is not clear where they were going but a board just visible behind suggests Rothesay and it is unlikely that these men were involved in the above repression. (Author's collection)

7   The 1881 census recorded that Gaelic was spoken by 60% of the inhabitants of Oban.

Having said that, and having stripped away the long purple passages of Victorian prose and the name dropping, what remained for the reader was a very good account of what was to be seen from the steamers and, assuming that they bothered to read it all, the 19th century tourist must have gone home much better informed about the natural features of the west of Scotland than does his counterpart to-day. It was good value for 1/-.

For those who did not require the full guide, a free booklet was issued containing a map, timetables, fares for tours and some illustrations. *Columba* appeared on both the front and back covers of this publication in 1905, in the latter case apparently anchored off Staffa. Since in her entire career of 58 years, this steamer did not leave the confines of the Clyde, this was curious, but no one seems to have noticed. A small pocket timetable was also issued by David Bryce and Son, Glasgow, containing times for services between Glasgow, Inverness and Gairloch, with a description of the route. A paperback version of the guide was available from about 1909, at the same price, and its cover was graced with a coloured illustration of *Columba*.

When post cards came into fashion early in the 1900s, the Company decided to enter this field and commissioned a set of a dozen cards, printed in colour from water colours, three of which are signed by J W Carey. The subjects are delicately drawn and are not in any way exaggerated. Steamers featured in two of the scenes. *Grenadier* is shown at anchor off Staffa, while ladies in what would probably have been called "walking dresses" picked their way over the basalt columns, followed by a gentleman in full highland dress. There seems to be quite a sea running and at a later date, in the late 1920s, some lady tourists who had come ashore from *Fusilier*, were swept off the path to the cave and drowned. The other ship shown on a card is, rather curiously, *Mountaineer* of 1858, which the Company had acquired as *Hero* from a Clyde owner in 1890 and renamed in 1892. Although quite a pretty ship, she was a minor member of the fleet and it is strange that she was thus honoured, in a view of Loch Leven. In view of their neglect in the guide book, it is strange to find two cards which depicted scenes of local life. One is entitled "A Highland Sheiling" and shows a man and a boy, both wearing glengarry bonnets, sitting talking outside what may be a black house, while some sheep graze nearby and a flock of geese flies overhead. The other is of a highland cottage, which is indeed a black house, with smoke coming out through a hole in the roof. A woman is coming home with a basket of peat on her back and an older woman and girl appear to be carding wool. There are some ducks roaming beside them and plenty of thistles. Even allowing for some artistic licence, these are a good representation of scenes which a tourist would have found in the islands. All the other cards depict highland beauty spots. Lochs Coruisk and Scavaig certainly appear gloomy and wild, much as described in the guide book, but all is tranquil at Staffa and Loch Maree looks inviting under a sunlit sky. The latter card also gives a good idea of the type of road which tourist coaches would have used. The series is completed by views of Eilean Donan Castle and Dunvegan Castle. Strangely neither *Iona* nor *Columba* appeared in this series, although they had plenty of cards of their own, particularly in the case of the latter. It is unusual to find used copies of these post cards, suggesting that most people who bought them did so to keep as a souvenir.

Of course many other firms began to publish cards, thus providing the company with a good deal of free publicity. The most prolific publishers of cards of MacBrayne's ships were the Kyle Pharmacy and Valentine's of Dundee, but local chemists and photographers also joined in and one of the earliest to put cards on the market, by 1902, was the chemist W J Tolmie of Stornoway.

There was little change in the format of the guide up to 1914. By 1912 chapters on Edinburgh and Glasgow had been inserted at the beginning. The number of hotels in Oban had risen to 17, in addition to which there were 13 temperance hotels[8] and the port was of such importance that, instead of the agent who looked after Company business in other places, Oban had a representative, Mr D Campbell Brown, one of the directors. A list of hotels, private lodgings and farmhouses to let could be obtained on application to Head Office in Glasgow. There were

---

8   One anonymous commentator was unkind enough to suggest that these were run either by people who had held a licence and lost it or by those who had no hope of being granted a licence.

now coloured illustrations in the guide, using the post cards mentioned above, and the black and white photographs had attained a very high standard. The first letter in each chapter was rendered in Celtic form and the text was enlivened with sketches of historical events, local people and animals. Perhaps the most significant change was that commercial advertising was included, much of this being for MacBrayne's suppliers. Thus it can be learned that the Company used Buchanan's jams and jellies ("absolutely pure") and Corry's lemonade, soda water and ginger beer. Meat was supplied by Brechin Brothers of Glasgow and fish and game by S L Neill of Duke Street in that city. On board these were enhanced by Royal Albert Sauce, made by Caithness Talbot, greengrocer, of Robertson Street, Glasgow. Pure and safe cream and milk, delivered in sealed bottles[9], were offered by the Glasgow Dairy Company, which also promoted the Bulgarian Sour Milk Treatment, a form of yoghurt. Modern forms of transport had begun to appear. The conveyance from Ardrishaig to Loch Awe was a motor and a charabanc featured in one of the little sketches, in the section on Ben Nevis. There was also an advertisement for Commer Cars, illustrated by a photograph of one of the ten vehicles which that firm had supplied to MacBraynes. Sailings to Lochinver had reappeared and occasional trips to Thurso were mentioned, but the sailings on Loch Maree had gone, although *Mabel* still featured in the fleet list. The new Glasgow-Stornoway ship *Chieftain* was "more like a yacht than a tourist steamer" and the guide enthused about her electric light, electric bells and silent electric cranes, but oddly there was no illustration of the vessel. Nor did the guide say that occasionally she might be diverted from her schedule to transport cattle, as happened in July 1914 when she had to double back to Kyle from Lochmaddy with these. Ossian had been banished from the text, but there was still plenty of Scott and Charles Edward Stuart, though Alexander II and Robert I also made various appearances. But overall there

6.14 *Mountaineer* in Loch Leven. (Author's Collection).

9 Milk was then generally delivered by pouring it into jugs brought by housewives to the milk cart.

6.15 *Grenadier,* in a choppy sea, waits off Staffa while her lady passengers, in the height of Edwardian fashion, negotiate the steps to Fingal's Cave. (Author's collection)

6.16 MacBrayne's slightly idealised view of a black house. (Author's collection)

6.17 The crew of the "flapper" *Mountaineer* (q.v. ch14). John Noble, who came from Tobermory, is on the extreme left, but no others can be identified. (By kind permission of the Mull Museum)

S.S. "PRINCESS LOUISE" SHIPPING CATTLE, ISLE OF COLL.

6.18 MacBraynes also used *Princess Louise* on cattle runs at sale times. Her shallow draft made her a useful acquisition for serving places such as Coll, which at that time did not have a proper pier and cattle had normally to be transhipped by ferry boat. (Author's Collection)

had been little change over thirty-four years. Having found a successful formula, there was no point in altering it.

The guide was not re-issued in its gilded form after 1914 and when it re-appeared in 1921 it was in paperback only and in a somewhat reduced format, there being now only 112 pages of text, rather than 131. However, the formula was exactly the same and the text unchanged. Rather oddly, there was no mention of the war which had just ended, although other operators of shipping lines made much of the part their ships had played in the conflict. Perhaps this was because it was difficult to sound heroic about the daily grind of keeping essential services going with minimum resources, and *Grenadier* had not had any stirring adventures during her time as a minesweeper, although *Plover* had had an encounter with a U-boat while on her normal run. A description of the route of the Outer Isles steamer had been added, suggesting that this was now considered to be a tourist service. At Oban, a bus from the Great Western Hotel now met steamers (and trains) and by 1926 no fewer than four operators in Portree were offering coach tours to passengers from *Claymore*. Two of those used 14-seater Fiat charabancs. In that year, *Columba* was at last displaced from her position on the cover, by a ship which was probably *Gondolier* and for the first time the price increased, to 1/6d (7.5p). Perhaps in acknowledgement to emancipation, there was now a photograph of a lady angler, but unfortunately the length of her skirt gave away that this was no modern miss but a lady of twenty years previously. In fact, this particular illustration summed up the stagnation which seemed to have affected the guide – the old images and text were still repeated year after year.

Passengers too were rather different from at least some of those pre-1914. MacBraynes had begun to offer short cruises out of Oban and continued these even during the first world war, using *Mountaineer* (1910). In 1916 she went to Loch Creran on Mondays and Fridays, at a return fare of 2/6d (12.5p). By 1935 there was quite a range on offer, still mainly by *Mountaineer*, though in that year *Iona* also cruised to the Isles of the Sea, while *Lochfyne* made evening trips. Forenoon cruises took one to Loch Sunart or Crinan, afternoon cruises to places such as Loch Creran or Loch Spelvie. These were ideal for holidaymakers with little time or, perhaps, less money in their pockets. *Lochfyne* gave evening cruises on Thursdays to Tobermory or Fort William and those who wished to sample two new ships in one day could, on Tuesdays, Thursdays and Saturdays, take *Lochfyne* as far as Tobermory, have an hour ashore and return on *Lochearn* at mid-day. The fare to Tobermory or Loch Sunart was now only 6/- (30p), a considerable cash reduction on those of 1893 and a great deal cheaper in real terms, while an evening cruise around Lismore was only 1/6d (7.5p). Less affluent passengers were now welcomed by MacBraynes. In 1930 those on board *Glencoe* from Mallaig to Portree were noted as elderly ladies encumbered with rags, bags and parcels, young men, some, with rather indeterminate legs, in plus fours and others bristling with golf clubs, apoplectic-looking men of military mien and commercial travellers.[10] Plus fours were very much in fashion in the years between the wars and another commentator mentioned that all the wardrobe that was needed for a tour was a suit of plus fours, a pair of flannels in case of a soaking and a waterproof.[11]

Paterson's *Princess Louise* also carried on her short trips until 1934, when he retired and sold his ship to MacBraynes. She had become more adventurous in her destinations, now including Loch Spelvie (Mull) and Loch Melfort, at fares of 2/- or 2/6d return. (10p and 12.5p)

MacBrayne's was not, of course, the only guide on the market. The various Scottish railway companies produced holiday guides and those of the Caledonian and the Highland Railways both covered MacBrayne territory, and there was also the excellent Miller's Guide. Post-war travellers could also, from 1920, purchase one of the first Ordnance Survey Tourist Maps, of Oban and district, with a most attractive cover, but at 3/-(15p) this was fairly expensive, even allowing for post-war inflation.

10   Mrs E Pickworth, *By Sea to the Isles*. Published by the author, Llandudno, 1953.
11   *Across Hebridean Seas*. Iain F Anderson, Chatto and Windus, London, 1937.

Clearly the new owners of the Company after 1928 thought that the guide was in need of a complete revamp, since by 1933 it had become a book of 72 pages, with soft covers. The front cover was illustrated by a picture of a somewhat emaciated and worried-looking highlander, wearing a kilt, but unclothed from the waist up. He was clutching a claymore and a small shield. Fortunately he was later replaced by a view with a group of better-built, or better fed, clansmen, likewise kilted but fully clothed. They supported a series of banners on which were the Scottish Saltire, the Lion Rampant, the Company's houseflag, the Red Duster and a MacBrayne pennant. The man in the centre, heavily bearded, brandished a claymore and shield, while in the background the almost-new *Lochfyne* sailed serenely on her way. Under the picture were the slogans "The Royal Route" and "the Isles of Youth", below a strip of Royal Stuart tartan. The latter description, taken from the Gaelic Tir nan Og, was used extensively after 1920 by the Company to promote the idea of a holiday away from it all, where "The measure of clocks and calendars will not trammel you . . . You will know another dimension.". It was also used by the BBC as the title of a broadcast on MacBraynes, on what was then the Scottish Home Service on 14 May 1936. (Some extracts from this are quoted in other parts of this book.) The artist responsible for the cover was Tom Gilfillan, who had also devised the figure of a highlander which adorned the Company's buses. With minor changes, this artwork was to be used as long as the Company retained its separate existence. By 1939 *King George V* had replaced *Lochfyne* on the cover of the guide.

The format in the guides post-1928 was still that of a tour beginning in Glasgow, on board *Columba* (in 1933) or later on the new (to MacBraynes) *Saint Columba* and other tours were covered in much the same order as they were pre-1914, although the Oban-Gairloch marathon was no longer available. The style of writing was, however, totally different, being no longer didactic but much more that of a conversation between equals. Clearly this guide was aimed at a different type of tourist than its Victorian predecessor, probably someone who had some, but not unlimited

6.19 A group of passengers on an inland loch steamer. Judging by the plus fours worn by the man on the right, the view was taken in the 1920s. The group is not necessarily on a MacBrayne steamer, but might well have been, and the view is included here for interest. (Author's Collection)

money and perhaps at most a fortnight at his/her disposal for a holiday. This tourist wanted to relax and unwind, after almost a year's work and would not have been interested in masses of detail about the landscape, long accounts of its (assumed) history or minute information about the improvements being made to the area. However, while the style of the 1933 guide is that of a straightforward description of the places visited, this had by 1936 changed to that of a tour guide (Donald R MacLaren) describing the routes to an obviously male passenger ("Your hot water, Sir.") and the tone was now distinctly chatty. "You and I had better get aboard" marked the beginning of the tour and the commentary continued in this slightly arch vein. The local population received more of a mention than it did pre-1914, and the reference to Gaelic – "like the cadence of a wind that skirts across the summer fields" – was much more appealing. At Ardrishaig, "we are on the verge of the *Celtic race*" from whom the visitor was assured of a grave courtesy and selfless hospitality. However, there was no mention of the asylum at Lochgilphead – although it was still there and would be for many years to come – nor of banks, villas and local newspapers. Instead the tone conveyed a relaxed description of the route, with the emphasis on enjoyment amid natural splendours. A little history was given now and then, but Ossian and the Lord of the Isles had been banished. Prince Charles Edward still made the odd appearance and now Cumberland was referred to openly as the "bloody Duke", a title unthinkable to the Victorians. The Butcher was, after all, the Queen's great-uncle. Motor coaches had also appeared, apparently like a modern parlour "walnut, cedar and kindly springs, upholstery bland and as inviting as your favourite armchair". The coaches "glide" – perhaps a slight exaggeration, considering that the roads were still somewhat primitive – and there was of course no question of appetites being sharpened by the air of a brisk drive. There were still references to life in London "not even at the Ritz or the Savoy does a mavis sing to you while you eat" (on board *Gondolier*), but the bird was at least given its Scottish name. At times the tone became somewhat twee, in

6.20/21 Tourists of the 1930s. The author's mother on Staffa and his mother and father on Iona in August 1939. (Author's Collection)

a kind of Christopher Robin way, "something to do with toys, Hans Andersen and the credits you and I brought over from childhood". At points, it is difficult to see any connexion between the narrative and the Scottish highlands.

The Loch Ness monster had by 1936 obliged with another publicity item, the crew of *Gondolier* being convinced "of its actuality", as they had seen it for ten minutes, travelling at a speed of fully nine knots an hour. It is unlikely that any MacBrayne crewman would have talked of "knots per hour" and the writer did not seem convinced, but the visitor was told to have his camera ready.

The individual ships received much more notice than they did pre-1914. En route to Stornoway, *Lochness* came in for some praise as "a buirdly (well-built) ship" and "seaworthy and equipped with every favour of comfort and convenience you can think of". The voyage was obviously made on a good day, as the tourists were relaxing in deck chairs, and once again Chris Fraser has a rather different take on it, having found that, when acting purser on board, it was often best to take to his bunk after passing Rona and thus manage to arrive at Stornoway in fit condition to enjoy high tea. *Lochfyne* – new in 1931 – received enthusiastic coverage in the 1933 guide. Nothing, the writer assured the tourist, had been spared towards ensuring the maximum of absolute ease. The furnishings were luxurious in the artistically-designed smoke room and dining room. The hot-water heating system was praised and no doubt many tourists were glad of it on chilly days, as were her winter passengers on the Clyde. Nothing was said of the rattling noise and thumping vibration which marked this vessel's progress – it was impossible to carry on any conversation in or near the gentlemen's lavatory – nor was the clutter on the upper deck mentioned. By 1936 the tone had become more personal – she was evidently a happy ship, "with a smile for every passenger". The Lloyd Loom chairs in the observation lounge provoked the writer into one of his more metaphysical bursts of enthusiasm "You and I are not too austere to know the inner meaning of armchairs in an observation lounge", but he does not go on to say what this inner meaning

6.22 A recent view of the Marine Hotel, now the Regent, in Oban. (Author)

actually was. Perhaps he simply meant that it was likely to rain. *Lochnevis* (1934), a comfortable enough ship, was "the last word in marine elegance". Captain Robertson's *Lochmor* was a sturdy boat – "polished, efficient, modern" and her accommodation provoked the thought that "a good bunk is a virtue and the sea air is full of sleep". Here also, the guide did not go into the question of engine noise. *Gondolier* was described as a toy ship, a thing of joy, "able and apt for a voyage away from the shape and umbrage of the ordinary".

A more detailed account was given of the accommodation on *Lochbroom*, the ship which in 1936 undertook the Glasgow-Stornoway service, which was now quite frankly described as a cruise. She had some single-berth staterooms in first class, as well as two- and four-berth rooms and a "gents" cabin. There were hot salt water baths, a music saloon and smoke room, a dining saloon and electric light was fitted throughout. At sea, passengers could enjoy such diversions as potato racing on deck. She was clearly an improvement on *Claymore*, but she did not last long enough to build a reputation among holidaymakers.

By the end of the decade, the style of the guide had reverted to a more factual account of what was to be seen from the Company's ships. There was a short account of the new *Lochiel*, "The last word in marine practice" praising her "elegance and seaworthiness". Most of her passengers would have agreed with only the second of these adjectives. *Lochgarry*, successor to *Lochbroom*, received even more enthusiastic mention. Her steam heating arrangements were of the most modern type. (No mention of heating had been made for earlier vessels.) There were six single- and forty-four two-berth cabins fitted with hot and cold running water. Cleanliness was doubtless helped by the salt and fresh water baths and showers. The large smoking room was decorated in pale blue and furnished with a cocktail bar, complete with ice-making equipment and tea- and coffee-making facilities in addition. There was a large writing room and a capacious dining saloon – in which passengers still sat at long tables for ten – and a sports deck. She was "complete with everything that matters on a sea holiday". Her itinerary now extended to Lochinver and, on alternate trips, to Lochinchard. It was a great pity that the enterprise shown by the Company in fitting her out to this standard was not to be rewarded, since she became MacBrayne's only war loss, in 1942. But her acquisition also gave a chance to show that the Company still had the London upper-class market in its sights:

"That's the Ridleys."
"The Ridleys?"
"Yes, I met them on the *Lochgarry*."

Glasgow-Stornoway round trip fares 1936

Single-berth cabin	£11
Berth in two-berth cabin	£10
Berth in four-berth cabin	£9
Berth in Gent's cabin	£6/10/- (£6.50)

To encourage an extension of the tourist season, a discount of 20% was given on voyages starting on 14 and 25 May and from 28 September onwards ; the final trip left on 19 October.

Lochgarry cruise fares 1939

Single-berth state-room	£15
Berth in two-berth state-room	£10

There was again a discount for early trips and for the last, which in the event did not run.

6.23 *Lochgarry* at Kyle. (© Duncan Macpherson Collection, Dualchas Heritage Service, The Highland Council)

6.24 Passengers disembarking from *Fusilier* at Oban on 25 August 1927, after a cruise to the Isles of the Sea. (National Maritime Museum, Greenwich, London, neg.no. N30772)

For anyone writing about the west highlands of Scotland, with a view to attracting tourists to visit the area, the matter of rainfall could be difficult. The sun did not always shine. At the beginning of July 1885, the Company was praised in the Oban press for allowing *Chevalier* to sail (to Staffa and Iona) with only six passengers on board and in September of the same year storms forced her to turn back on several occasions. The writer of the pre-1914 guide solved the problem simply by not mentioning it. Hardy Victorian tourists were clearly expected to wrap up, put up and shut up. They would no doubt have taken the precaution of visiting the Clydesdale Rubber Company when passing through Glasgow, to invest in some "waterproof and showerproof garments" and perhaps also a sou-wester. Such a cavalier approach was no longer suitable for the more pampered visitors of the inter-war years and the writers of the contemporary guides did mention the weather and the chance of rainfall. However, this was done in such a way as to suggest that it could not be a problem. Sometimes it is simply stated that it had (most conveniently) rained in the night. On other occasions the showers are described so poetically that no one could possibly complain – "a drift of rain from Glen Loy passes like a jewelled curtain on a new scene". Nothing in the guide would prepare the unsuspecting traveller for days of continuous downpour or the Oban landlady who would habitually greet drenched visitors with the innocent question "Did ye get wet?"

Publication of this guide ceased with the outbreak of war and was not resumed when peace came again. Post-war material was much simpler, a combination of guide and time-table, but the former was now contained, in 1948, in a fairly brief introduction. The accent was still on a combination of history and relaxation, using the slogans of "the Edge of the World" and "The Land that Time forgot", although the theme of the Isles of Youth was still featured. By 1959 colour photography had become an economic possibility for a publication of this kind and MacBraynes made full use of it. The timetable/guide for that year contained some excellent views of both the ships and places served. The introduction was now a good deal longer and, as before, featured the appeal of the history of the area. But now there was also much more about the inhabitants and the visitor is urged not to miss a chance to watch Highland Games or to take part in the "jolly uproar of a village dance". The wheel had come almost full circle from Victorian times. Pocket timetables were also issued. All these publications ceased with the creation of Caledonian MacBrayne and it is only recently, with its annual full-colour "Explorer" book that that organisation has produced anything to equal MacBraynes.

The coming of the motor bus and, to an extent, the motor lorry opened up another opportunity for publicity, one of which MacBraynes made full use. The number of places where its ships might be seen was, after all, limited, but lorries and buses penetrated town centres and might appear on many main roads, where they would ensure that visitors to the area would be aware of the Company's existence. Until 1936 buses were painted a dignified crimson lake, with off-white roofs. In that year, co-inciding with the entry into service of the first buses with a streamlined style of bodywork, MacBraynes devised one of the most attractive and eye-catching liveries ever to grace the roads of Scotland. The lower panels were painted post-office red, the window surrounds cream and the roof and rear panel apple green. The highlander with his claymore graced the side panels and, on some vehicles, also appeared in cut-out form on the radiator. The red Scottish lion rampant appeared in a blue rectangle behind the rear wheels and again sometimes on the radiator. On the rear panel were the slogans "MacBraynes for the Highlands" and "Royal Mail Services". Lorries were latterly red with a cream band below the windscreen and cab doors carried the slogan "The Royal Route". When containers came in, they too were prominently lettered "MacBraynes". Buses were always kept in immaculate condition, even in winter, when slush and salt on the roads made this difficult. These vehicles carried the Company name all over the west highlands and on many islands and no "corporate livery" dreamt up by design consultants has ever had the publicity value which they brought.

6.25 Bus no.79 was a Throneycroft Nippy, new in 1948, and latterly used as a mobile booking office and advertising hoarding, in which capacity it is seen in Somerled Square, Portree, in the 1960s. On offer were tours to Dunvegan at 10/6d (52.5p) or 11/- (55p) and to Elgol at 13/- (65p). This bus has been preserved. (Chris Orchard, Online Transport Archive).

6.26 Detail of the splendid livery, as seen on a coach at Inverness. (R L Wilson, Online Transport Archive)

6.27 The narrow roads and pinch points such as this bridge gave motorists plenty of time to contemplate the MacBrayne message, and perhaps to wish that they had travelled by bus. The vehicle in question is no.41, an AEC Reliance of 1959, allocated to Fort William in 1962 and the location is the bridge over the Caledonian Canal at Banavie. (R L Wilson, Online Transport Archive).

R.M.S. "IONA."

Iona featured on only one cigarette card, no.26 in Mitchell's series. It dates from the 1920s and refers to her use on the Lochgoilhead and Arrochar services, but the ship is depicted as she appeared before 1891, when the gaff was removed from her mast. (Author's Collection)

Catering

All this sightseeing made a tourist hungry and MacBrayne took pains to remind readers of the refreshment facilities on board the ships. An excellent lunch was to be found in the airy cabin of *Lochawe* (on the loch of that name) "and truly the sharp drive through the crisp air (from Ardrishaig) makes travellers fain to satisfy the wants, as well as to feast their eyes on the beauties of nature". On *Columba* meals were served at any time, while on other ships meal service was clearly at fixed times. On *Chevalier* it was apparently "a dinner fit for a lord". Dinner was also served on the Islay steamer immediately after leaving the pier at West Loch Tarbert at 12.5pm and passengers were re-assured that they could do full justice to it, the loch being quite calm at all times. What might come afterwards was not mentioned. Strangely, early editions of the guide do not mention herring, a dish about which later editors became very enthusiastic. A great epicure of the 1920s, Colonel Newnham-Davies had apparently commended the breakfast herrings (sic), placing them high on the list of the world's famous dishes. But not everyone was so keen on MacBrayne's herring. In the novel "Eliza for Common" by O Douglas, sister of John Buchan, an elderly lady, Mrs Service, remarks, "I'll never forget the boat from Mallaig – the fresh herring to breakfast and me so sick-like. I've never been able to endure the smell of herring since . . ." D T Holmes,[12] on the other hand, enthused about the breakfast served on *Lochiel*, on leaving Portree on a December morning, with excellent ham, eggs and sausages, the meal being enlivened by the genial talk of the captain and his colleagues. After such a repast, a pipe on deck was a necessity and, on a sunny morning, the scenery was incredibly beautiful.

After 1919, afternoon tea became a feature of the catering and is remembered as a silver service of tea with scones, pancakes and strawberry jam on board *Iona*.

In 1888 and 1905 meal charges were:-

	Cabin	Fore cabin
Breakfast	2/- (10p)	1/6 (7.5p)
Dinner or hot lunch	3/- (15p)	1/6 (7.5p) (1888), 2/- (10p) (1905)
Tea (with Meat)	2/- (10p)	1/6 (7.5p)
Plain tea (1905 only)	1/- (5p)	

In 1888 these charges included the steward's fee.

Rather curiously, meals cost 6d less on *Iona*, *Columba*, the Crinan steamer and the Sound of Mull mail steamer. Hot breakfasts were served on all steamers immediately after leaving port in the morning, thus allowing passengers to snatch a few more minutes in bed before rising, a practice still carried on by Caledonian MacBrayne. No doubt many welcomed and welcome this – as mentioned above, some of the tours involved a very early start.

The food served seems to have been of good quality, but somewhat standardised and for very many years the menu did not vary. In the 1890s breakfast for cabin passengers was clearly quite a substantial meal, since in addition to the choice of herring, white fish or salmon, ham and eggs, mutton chops, Irish stew, sausages and cold meats were on offer. These main courses were followed by rolls with tea or coffee and preserves. Luncheon consisted of cold meats and biscuits or oatcakes with cheese. Hot soup could be obtained only on *Lochawe*. It may be that this meal was intended for servants or for those who wanted nothing more than a snack. Dinner, in the years before 1914, was the main meal of the day and on the menu were soup, white fish or salmon, chicken, various roasts, hot or cold, tongue and corned beef. To conclude there were again biscuits or oatcakes with cheese. Those with a sweet tooth could indulge themselves only on *Columba*, *Claymore*, *Clansman* and *Cavalier*, since these were the only ships on which deserts were served. For tea, there was again fish or cold meats, with the alternative of boiled eggs, to be followed by

---

12   D T Holmes, op.cit.

toast, fancy bread, biscuits and preserves. The plain tea consisted only of the toast etc. Tea or coffee and biscuit could be had for 6d (2.5p), sandwiches for 4d (2p) or 6d (2.5p). Organising the delivery of provisions to the steamers must have called for careful planning.

No accounts of a meal on board *Columba* seem to have survived, but there is an excellent description of breakfast on *Iona* in 1876, between Greenock and Kirn – "Cutlets of salmon fresh from the water, sausages of a tenderness and delicacy of which the benighted Cockney . . . can have no idea, coffee hot and aromatic and suggestive of Arcady the blest, marmalade of all kinds with bread and butter and toast, all equally good and served up by the cleanest and most civil of stewards.".[13] Others were less enthusiastic. In the early 1890s Miss Ada Goodrich Freer – a lady much involved with the supernatural – travelled on *Fingal*, from Oban to Coll and was so put off by the offer of roast beef and bread and butter pudding for lunch that she gave the meal a miss altogether, not because she felt seasick but because it was just too commonplace. She also regretted the practice of taking afternoon tea, which had by this time spread even to North Uist. *Fingal* was also criticised by Holmes for her stuffy cabin and its greasy odours.

By 1936 less information about the actual content of meals was given to the prospective traveller and only a scale of charges appeared. Luncheon had now replaced dinner as the main meal and the charges were:-

	First class	Third class
Breakfast	3/- & 2/- (15p & 10p)	2/6 &d 2/- (12.5p & 10p)
Luncheon	3/6 & 2/6 (17.5p & 12.5p)	2/6 (12.5p)
High Tea	3/- & 2/- (15p & 10p)	2/6 & 2/- (12.5p & 10p)
Plain tea	1/3 (6p)	1/3 (6p)

However, by this date tea-rooms had appeared on excursion steamers and those who wished to sample Scottish baking at its best could, at any time, indulge on a variety of scones, cookies, French cakes and fancy biscuits. A "cookie" was then still a kind of sweet bun, not the US name for a biscuit.

Inflation took its toll and by 1953 and 1959, prices were rising rapidly, though there was now no difference in the prices charged to passengers in first and third class.

	1953	1959
Breakfast	4/6 (22.5p)	2/6 (12.5p) (plain) 6/- (30p) (cooked)
Luncheon	5/- (25p)	7/- (35p) (coffee 6d (2.5p) extra)
High Tea	4/6 (22.5p)	6/- (30p)
Plain Tea	2/- (10p)	3/-.(15p)

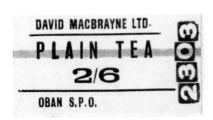

A ticket for Plain Tea, dating from about 1955.

---

13   J E Ritchie, *The Cruise of the* Helena.

7 Fresh Water Services

T HE NAME OF MACBRAYNE is primarily associated with sailing on the open sea and it is interesting to remember that sailings on inland lochs formed an important part of the Company's activities until 1914 and again briefly from 1953 until 1967.

Loch Awe

The first venture into inland services was taken in 1875, when Hutchesons bought a little wooden steamer named *Queen Of The Lake*, which had for some time been plying on Loch Awe. This steamer had been sailing on the loch since at least 1865, when a circular tour, described as a "New Extension Tour" had been advertised from Oban, at a fare of 18/- (90p) Travellers left the town by coach at 8am and the route was via Bonawe and the Pass of Awe (now known as the Pass of Brander) to Brandor (sic). From there tourists sailed in *Queen Of The Lake* to Ford, from which they returned via the Pass of Melfort, the whole trip taking eleven hours. The route could be reversed.

In the year following her acquisition by Hutchesons, the vessel was replaced by the much larger *Lochawe*, built by A & J Inglis in Glasgow, then taken to pieces and re-erected on the lochside. With a length of 100ft (30.5m), she was large for a Scottish loch steamer and in appearance quite unlike any other. Her machinery and funnel were located aft and a large saloon, with a distinct resemblance to a greenhouse, was on the main deck. There was also accommodation on the lower deck. Her hull was painted white, to give her some resemblance to a private yacht, but even this could not disguise her rather tubby lines and the fact that she was no yacht.

Intended as an alternative to the Crinan Canal/Crinan-Oban steamers, the route via Loch Awe allowed those who were not too keen on an open sea voyage to enjoy more sheltered waters and still reach Oban from Ardrishaig before bedtime. Passengers holding tickets via Crinan could change to the route via Loch Awe on payment of an extra 6/- (30p) to the purser on board *Columba*, a fairly expensive supplement. A coach awaited passengers at Ardrishaig and left there at 12.50pm. After a "sharp drive through crisp air" of about 14 miles, it deposited them at Ford pier, at the south end of the loch, at 3pm. The 30 mile sail to the pier at the Pass of Brander took until about 5.15pm and the connecting coach arrived in Oban at about 8, a good deal later than the steamer from Crinan. After 1880 a train connexion from a pier at Loch Awe station brought the passengers to Oban at 6.30pm. Prior to 1880, southbound passengers left Oban by coach at a very early hour and arrived at Ford about 11, where they then had almost four hours to admire the beauties of the locality, since the coach did not start for Ardrishaig until 3pm, with an arrival of 5.10. It was therefore not possible to do the southbound Oban-Glasgow trip in one day. However, the arrival of the railway in Oban altered these times and after 1880 passengers left that town at around 8am and Loch Awe pier at 9, to reach Ford at 10.40 and Ardrishaig at 12.40pm, in good time to connect with *Columba* on her southward sailing. A day excursion from Oban to Ford was also available at (pre-1914) 7/6d (37.5p) first class and cabin or 5/- (25p) third class and cabin. It was also possible to take a day tour to Ardrishaig, going out by the Crinan-Oban steamer at 8am and *Linnet* on the Crinan Canal, then returning via Loch Awe, or the route could be reversed. The timings of the Crinan steamer, the guide book assured passengers, "can be relied on", in contrast to the train times, which might not be in force during part of the summer. This tour cost 7/6d (37.5p) and only a cabin fare was quoted. MacBrayne's Loch Awe service ran only in the summer months and calls were made at intermediate piers,

Ford Pier, Loch Awe

7.1 The (relatively) great size of *Lochawe* can be seen in this postcard view of Ford pier. The ship on the other side of the pier is *Countess Of Breadalbane* and both are awaiting passengers for the 3pm sailing back to Loch Awe pier. She was in fact almost the same length as the MacBrayne vessel, but narrower and clearly sat lower in the water. (Author's collection)

Pass of Melfort

Valentines Series   11265

7.3 A coach traversing the Pass of Melfort. (Author's collection)

7.2 Passengers on board *Lochawe*. Perhaps there was a lack of seating on deck, since the gentleman with a distinct resemblance to Edward VII, complete with Homburg hat, seems to be perching on a step ladder. Small the ship may have been, but she still flies proudly the Royal Mail pennant. (By courtesy of the Mitchell Library, Glasgow City Council)

presumably to cater for local traffic. When not employed on these service runs, *Lochawe* was available for charter. In 1912 the Ardrishaig-Loch Awe coach was replaced by a "motor".

The guide book enthused over the quiet loveliness of the "lake" and went into some detail on its islands, twenty-four in number. Many of these harboured stories of love and revenge, pious labours and daring deeds. The monument to Duncan Ban MacIntyre – "the Highland Bard" had a brief mention, but nothing is said of the subjects of his poetry, or that he wrote in Gaelic. The sailings of *Lochawe* were suspended during the first world war and not resumed thereafter, the vessel being scrapped in 1925. As no replacement road service was provided, it may be that the service had latterly not attracted many passengers. Loch Awe was one area where MacBrayne had to face a degree of competition, in this case from the steamer operated by Duncan Fraser of the Loch Awe Hotel Company, *Countess Of Breadalbane*, whose afternoon return trip from Ford almost exactly duplicated MacBrayne's return sailing. Steamers were also operated by Thomas Cameron of the Port Sonachan Hotel. However, as guests at the hotel who held MacBrayne's tickets were allowed to use these on the hotel steamer *Caledonia* without additional charge, it would seem that there was peaceful co-existence rather than outright competition on the loch. The Port Sonachan Hotel was advertised as the leading hotel for anglers on Loch Awe. Experienced boatmen were employed, with first class boats, not only on Loch Awe itself but also on various smaller lochs and the Sonachan "hill lakes", which were kept stocked with trout. For those of a less sporting nature, there were "lovely walks and drives".

Touring around Loch Maree

One isolated part of the early MacBrayne empire which has not since been accessible by water was Loch Maree, in what was then Ross-shire. It featured in the round trip from Gairloch to Inverness and the steamer trip on the loch was suggested as a refreshing alternative to a long coach drive. (The distance by road was 30 miles.) Tourists from Gairloch, had to be careful to reserve seats in or on the coach on the previous evening, since priority was given to booked seats in order of application and those intending to do the trip in the reverse direction had to wire to the Gairloch Hotel in advance for places. The operator was Mr McIver of Achnasheen, with, in 1905, over half a century's experience. In that year, the coach left the door of the Gairloch Hotel at 9am and, having en route noted the Established Church Manse, tourists arrived, after a drive of six miles, at Tollie pier.

There they would find awaiting them the steam launch *Mabel*, probably the smallest unit of the MacBrayne fleet at that time, being only 45ft (13.7m) long. However, she did possess a saloon, no doubt appreciated by passengers on wet days, but this was not decked over and thus deck space was somewhat limited. She had been built about 1880 by T B Seath of Rutherglen to act as a private estate yacht for a landowner in the Outer Hebrides. In 1884 she was acquired by Mr R Hornsby, owner of the Gairloch and Loch Maree hotels, the latter being a "charming summer resort for sportsmen, tourists and families". Queen Victoria stayed at the hotel from 12 to 18 September 1877 and described it as a nice little house, neatly furnished. Despite weather which was unpleasantly close and wet, and a plague of wasps, she was so impressed that she declared that she wished to return one day, a wish which was to remain unfulfilled. Her visit was commemorated by a stone with a Gaelic inscription. For Mr Hornsby, *Mabel* was sailed over the Minch by one Roderick MacIntyre, who had operated a sailing smack on cargo services in the Uists. She crossed safely to Poolewe but disaster almost struck while she was being taken on to the Loch, as the road collapsed under her weight and she was stuck fast for a week. Mr MacIntyre remained on board to look after her and holes were knocked in two nearby walls to allow the mail coaches to go past. She then went on to Loch Maree and was bought by MacBrayne in 1887.

Mabel ran between Tollie, at the western end of the loch and Rhu Nòa, calling en route at Talladale for the hotel. Initially she was based at the hotel and in the 1890s the timetable provided a sailing from there to Tollie at 10.30am. She was then coaled and left on a trip for the full length of the loch at 11.15, this taking two hours. She was due back at 4pm and then sailed back to

S.S. "Mabel". at Tollie Pier   Valentines Series

7.4 *Mabel* at Tollie pier. (Author's Collection)

Talladale for the night. By 1900 the hotel was owned by Mr T MacAllister of Inverness and managed by his daughter. *Mabel* now gave two return sailings for the length of the loch from Tollie. She was manned by a crew of three and in 1900 these were John MacLean (captain), Mr Barr (of Glasgow) (engineer) and Mr MacIntyre (Fort William) (purser). A small guide book for tourists, entitled "*The Voyage of the* Mabel", was written by A. Resident, of Tollie presumably, but there was also a much larger guide to Gairloch and Loch Maree, written by J H Dixon, a native of the area, and published in 1886. The coach connecting with the morning sailing brought passengers from Rhu Nòa to Achnasheen station – nine miles – at 2.30pm, having stopped for twenty minutes to allow for a rushed luncheon at the Kinlochewe Hotel. Passengers could travel all the way from Gairloch to Achnasheen by coach, arriving about 11.30. In either case, arrival in Inverness was at 5.15pm. The loch sail cost 4/- (20p) in 1898 and 5/- (25p) in 1905. The Gairloch-Inverness coach and rail fare was 38/6d (£1.92.5) in first class and it is not clear if a reduction was offered to those who took the steamer. Round trip fares of 52/6d (£2.65) first class rail and cabin or 38/9d (£1.94) third class and steerage, were available from Oban, but these did not include the above coach or steamer fare. Special coach rates, not quoted, were available to excursionists and private coaches could be hired in connexion with all trains at Achnasheen. At the height of the tourist season an earlier departure from Gairloch at 6.30am allowed connexion with the 12.35pm Inverness train at Achnasheen.

The tour from Oban required three days (and some stamina) and a fair amount of money. While it has not been possible to find a record of charges at the Gairloch Hotel, in 1905 a night in Inverness staying at McGilvray's Temperance Hotel at 58 Church Street would have cost 2/- (10p) for a single or 3/- (15p) for a double bedroom, plus 1/6 (7.5p) or 2/- (10p) per guest for breakfast and from 2/- (10p) for dinner. According to the Highland News, it was really a very comfortable house and charges were exceptionally low. Mrs McGilvray had done much to popularise it during her tenancy.

Without counting the cost of lunches, one had clearly to reckon on spending at least about £5/10/- (£5.50) per person on this tour if travelling in first class and about £1/4/- (1.20) less if prepared to use third class and steerage. Even that was hardly cheap by contemporary price levels.

S.S. CLANRANALD II., LOCKSHIEL.   *D.B. Series.*

7.5 *Clanranald II* as a steamer on Loch Shiel. (Author's Collection)

"CLANRANALD II" LOCH SHIEL STEAMER AT THE PIER, GLENFINNAN.   B.5132.

7.6 The same ship after conversion to a motor vessel, seen at the pier at Glenfinnan in post-1945 years. The monument to Price Charles Edward is behind the ship on the right. (Author's Collection)

This interest in the area began to wane even before 1914. Perhaps Loch Maree was too remote to attract the hardiest of 20th century tourists, or perhaps these charges were just too high even for the well-off, since *Mabel* was taken out of service after the 1912 season. By that date touring by car had become well established – the Great Western Hotel in Oban advertised a motor garage (with resident mechanic and inspection pit) as early as 1905 - and those who first took to private motoring would no doubt be those who could previously have afforded the fares for trips such as those on Loch Maree. The steamer was laid up on the loch shore and gradually rusted away, being still there in 1937. It was a pity that this piece of MacBrayne enterprise was not better rewarded, since from the little steamer, tourists had an incredible panorama of the range of Munros – Ruadh Stac Mòr, Sail Mòr and others – which surround the loch and could also enjoy weaving in and out among the many little islands. Apart from steamer calls at Gairloch, MacBraynes showed no further interest in the area after 1918. A private operator tried to run a motor launch on the loch in the inter-war years, but it did not fare any better and was soon taken out of service.

Loch Shiel

The MacBrayne Company was involved with sailings on this loch at two different periods of its history.

About 1889 MacBrayne took over, apparently on lease, an hotel at Shiel Bridge and installed a manager to run it. The hotel was then extended by the purchase of an old church of corrugated iron in Govan, which was cut down into sections, transported to the wilds of Moidart and re-erected as an annexe to the hotel. Probably to cater for guests at the hotel, a small steamer named *Maud* was bought in August 1889. Her origin is uncertain but she had been built by T B Seath in Rutherglen. She gave a service to Glenfinnan at the other end of the loch once a week, but her main occupation on most days was to tow the boats of anglers to the part of the loch where they wanted to fish, and bring them back to the hotel at night. This lasted until 1897, when the entire estate was bought by one Rudd, who had made a fortune in the diamond diggings in Cape Colony and intended to invest the proceeds in a new hotel on the same site. He turned MacBrayne out of the hotel and proceeded to build a new one beside it, but on its completion in 1900, both were burned down after a fire started when workmen held a dance to celebrate the completion of the new hotel.

When MacBrayne ran the Loch Shiel service, a circular tour was offered in connexion with the service which then operated from Oban to Loch Sunart. Timings were however, rather awkward, since the Sound of Mull steamer ran to Salen (Loch Sunart) only on Tuesday and Friday, arriving there at 7pm. Tourists would then go on by coach to Acharacle, where they would on the next morning sail on *Maud* to Glenfinnan, take the mail coach to Fort William and return to Oban on the afternoon steamer. The guide book contained a warning that times of sailings on Loch Shiel had to be checked by "special inquiry" before travelling, as *Maud* sailed only on one day per week, unless notice were given beforehand, and it would seem that this was not always on the same day. It was all rather problematic. To those who had more time at their disposal, the guide book recommended extending the tour by taking the mail coach at Glenfinnan "on a magnificent drive through scenery of the wildest description" to Arisaig, where on the next day they could join the swift steamer (on the Oban-Gairloch service) either to go north at 11.15am on Thursday and Saturday, or return to Oban on Monday, Wednesday or Friday at 12.15pm. Passengers were warned that, as the landing place was four miles from the village and hotel, those joining at Arisaig had to telegraph in advance to arrange a conveyance to meet the steamer. Fares for Loch Shiel sailings are not given, but the round trip Oban-Fort William-Arisaig-Oban cost 11/- (55p) in first class and 7/6d (37.5p) in steerage. To this had to be added the coach fare of "about 11/- (55p)", payable to the driver and of course lunches (probably about 2/6d), overnight accommodation at Arisaig and the conveyance to meet the steamer there. This two-day tour would therefore have cost about 30/- (£1.50) per person in first class, or the wages of a tram driver for one week. It seems that the sailings of *Maud* ceased in 1897.

7.7 *Lady Of The Lake* at Acharachle. The card was posted in the reign of Edward VIII, but the actual date of the photograph is not known. (Author's Collection)

HEAD OF LOCH SUNART, STRONTIAN

7.8 The head of Loch Sunart, "a fine place for a very quiet holiday" according to the writer of this card, posted at Strontian on 30 August 1904. The steamer is most probably *Handa*, bought from Martin Orme in 1887 and by 1900 used on the service from Glasgow via the Crinan Canal to Loch Leven and Loch Sunart. (Author's Collection)

7.9 A Bedford VAS bus, no.77, at Ardgour on the service from Acharacle. (Chris Orchard, Online Transport Archive)

7.10 A ticket for the Loch Shiel tour from Fort William, issued at the Steam Packet Office (S.P.O.) in that town in the 1950s. MacBraynes continued to use that abbreviation long after most of the "steam packets" were diesel vessels. Allowing for inflation, it would seem that the round trip was cheaper than in the pre-1914 years. (Author's Collection)

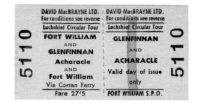

In 1898, Lord Howard de Walden had placed his small steam launch, *Lady Of The Lake*, on a regular daily mail service on the loch. This seems to have been so successful that in 1899 a larger steamer, *Clanranald*, was built for the service. Unfortunately she had too deep a draught for the loch and in the next year a similar steamer, *Clanranald II*, replaced her. Though only 70 ft (21.3m) in length, she was quite a commodious vessel and boasted a dining saloon. Remembering her many years later, a writer in the Scots' Magazine complained of feeling sea-sick when she went down for breakfast on board the ship. In 1926 she was converted to diesel propulsion and *Lady Of The Lake* at some date was also re-engined as a motor vessel. In 1951 what was by now the Loch Shiel Steamboat Service Co Ltd announced that it could no longer continue the service and it passed to MacBraynes. *Lady Of The Lake* sank during the following winter and *Clanranald II* made her last run in 1953, being scrapped at Acharacle in the following year. MacBraynes introduced two launches for the loch service, *Loch Shiel* and *Loch Ailort* and it remained in their hands until it ceased on completion of a new road through the area early in 1967. In later years the timetable provided for a year-round mail service leaving Acharacle at 8.45am and, calling en route at six piers, arriving at Glenfinnan at 10.45. The launch left on her return sailing at 1.15pm and again the trip took two hours. In summer a further express sailing, taking 90 minutes in each direction, was given for tourists, leaving Acharacle at 4pm and arriving back at 8. A return fare from Glenfinnan to the upper end of the loch cost 11/5d (57p) in 1959. Tickets of the type used on the bus services were issued on the Loch services. As in coaching days, the loch sailings were also incorporated into circular tours from Oban and Fort William. Cruises are still given from Glenfinnan in summer by a private operator.

Bibliography

Black's Guide Book Advertiser, summer 1865.

CASTLEBAY AND HEAVAL FROM THE STEAMER

8 Captain Duncan Robertson

"THA NA *SHEILA* AIR NA CREAGAN" (the *Sheila* is on the rocks). On New Year's Day 1927 the Robertson family in Kyleakin was about to sit down to dinner when one of the young waitresses from the hotel next door ran in, breathless, to tell them of the accident to the Stornoway mailboat. Thus, by telephone to the hotel, Captain Robertson was deprived of his dinner, as he had to return to his own ship forthwith and take her up to Applecross to pick up the passengers who had been landed near there. (qv Ch.4)

Although he did not command any of the larger tourist steamers, one of the best-known captains in the MacBrayne fleet in the inter-war, wartime, and immediate post-war years was undoubtedly Duncan Robertson, master of *Lochmor* from her appearance in 1930 until shortly before his retirement in 1949.

Duncan was born in 1884 at Sasaig in Sleat on the Isle of Skye, the youngest and last of a family of eight children. His father had a croft in the area, not far from the present Gaelic college of Sabhal Mòr Ostaig and Duncan attended the local school, where he received, through the medium of English, a very sound basic education. He grew to be a man of 5'8" (1.72m) in height, with light blue eyes and dark hair. As was the case with so many young men of his time in the islands, there was no future for him on the land, as the croft would in the course of time pass to his eldest brother and, as many did, young Duncan looked to the sea for a career. Even as a child, he was used to going out in his father's boat and had already come to know the waters around the island before he was grown up.

The early years at sea were spent as a crew member of various yachts and it was not until 1905 that he became a merchant seaman. In the summer of that year he worked on board the turbine steamer *Queen Alexandra* on the Clyde, under the command of Captain Angus Keith, who found him attentive to his duties and strictly sober, that last word being underlined in his reference. Presumably some of the seamen known to Captain Keith were not always as sober as he would have wished. On board this new turbine ship he would have met many tourists from England and further afield and would have begun to learn the skills in dealing with them which would later make him so popular as a captain.

He returned to yachts in the following summer and served on board *Albatross*, where he was found to be obliging, civil and attentive and, once again, strictly sober. In 1907 he served on the yacht *Mavis* belonging to Colonel Campbell of Knock in Skye, who was so impressed by his capabilities that he recommended him to Mr R H Nelson who bought the vessel in 1908. *Mavis* was a small yacht, but in 1909 Duncan Robertson experienced something larger when he served on the motor yacht *Star Of The Sea*, to which he would return in 1914. In 1910 and 1911 he was on the steam yacht *Iolaire*, owned by Lady Currie, widow of Sir Donald Currie of the Castle Line and predecessor of the vessel lost at Stornoway in 1919. The yacht was a frequent visitor to Oban. Thereafter he went "deep sea" for two years. He was employed by Bell Bros. and Co. and sailed with them to South America on board *SS Bellardo*. That company found him "steady, energetic and thoroughly reliable". In the winter of 1914/5 he was on board *SS Tourmaline*, owned by Robertsons of Glasgow.

His first contact with MacBraynes was in April 1917, when he joined *Chieftain*, serving briefly before being moved to *Claymore* as second officer. The ship was still sailing on her normal route from Glasgow to Stornoway, the only concession to the war being the replacement of her handsome livery by a coat of camouflage. However, the usual cruise passengers would not have been on

8.1 Captain Robertson on the bridge of *Plover*, between 1927 and 1929. His two sons are with him, Norman behind and Neil in front, but the identity of the other man has been lost.

8.2 *Plover* at Kyle pier in the late 1920s. (© Duncan Macpherson Collection, Dualchas Heritage Service, The Highland Council)

board and the ship would have been sailing mainly as a cargo vessel. He served in this capacity until 17 December 1917 and he returned to the ship as Mate from 19 June to 4 September 1918 and then from an unknown date until 27 May 1919. According to Captain MacFarlane he was obedient and attentive to his duties, trustworthy and strictly sober. During the summer of that year he was Mate on *Columba* and returned to her during each of the two following summers. In these winters he was on *Devonia* (October and November 1919). In the winter of 1921 he briefly transferred to MacBrayne's friendly rival MacCallum, Orme and Co and was on *Dunara Castle*. He came back to MacBraynes in 1922 and spent that summer as Mate on board *Cygnet*, on the Inner Isles mail service to Barra. From her he transferred to *Plover* in October 1922 and remained on her until May 1924. It was then that he came to know the route with which he would later be so closely associated, from Mallaig and Kyle to the Small Isles, North Uist and Harris. He had a brief spell on the Islay run aboard *Pioneer* from May 1924 to February 1925 and then returned to *Plover* as Master in 1925. It was on this ship that he gained the reputation of being a captain who could and would without risk put to sea in all weathers and come back to port safely, if sometimes rather late, the ship's funnel caked in salt and sometimes with some accessories missing from the deck.

Duncan Robertson married in 1918. His bride was Jane Nicholson, whom he had known since his schooldays and who had most recently been in domestic service in Greenock. The couple settled down in Glasgow, in a flat in 64 Exeter Drive, Partick, a street developed only in 1905. He also sat for his master's ticket in the autumn of 1919 and was successful in obtaining this. His family grew to three – two sons and a daughter. The eldest son was Norman, born in 1920, and his second son, Neil, later to be well known in Gaelic circles as proprietor of the West End Hotel in Edinburgh, followed eighteen months later. In 1924 his daughter Ishbel arrived. The family now moved from Glasgow back to Skye, to a council house in Kyleakin, next to the King's Arms hotel. From the jetty, Captain Robertson would row himself over to Kyle at an early hour in the mornings on which he was to sail.

However, it was not only *Sheila* which was on the rocks but the MacBrayne company itself and these years could not have been altogether a happy time to be working for it. The reconstruction in 1928 (qv Ch.14) brought fresh capital and much of this was used to build four new ships, one of which, *Lochmor*, was duly assigned to Captain Robertson's service in place of *Plover*. There could hardly have been a greater contrast between his old and new commands. *Plover* was a relatively small ship, powered by simple steam machinery and with accommodation of a standard that by 1928 had caused questions to be asked in parliament. Although she was a good sea-boat, in that she could cope with the worst that the Minch could throw at her, she rolled badly and was rather wet in heavy seas. *Lochmor* was totally new in concept, with diesel engines and vastly improved passenger accommodation but she was, to the Company's disappointment, rather slower than the ship she replaced. Nor was she a particularly good sea-boat and when heading into a storm, was inclined to put her head down and her tail up, to the point where she would be making virtually no headway at all. Nonetheless she represented progress of a kind which had not been seen in the islands for many a day and Duncan Robertson must have been a proud man when he took her out of Kyle on her first voyage, her hull then painted a light grey instead of the usual MacBrayne black.

Thus began a partnership of skipper and ship which was to last for almost nineteen years and to become something of an institution, even in an area where associations of such a kind were not uncommon. Both were an integral part of local life, in a way which, to a lesser extent, survives to-day and it is hard for anyone who has not lived on an island to appreciate the significance of this. Even with to-day's car ferries, giving a service of a frequency never dreamed of in the 1930s, this link still survives. Local people and visitors alike had a high opinion of Captain Robertson's abilities and some showed this in tangible form by gifts. One of his most treasured possessions was a pair of binoculars presented to him by Earl Cawdor. Other gifts could be shared by all the Robertson family, who had now moved over to Kyle of Lochalsh and settled in a house from which ships coming from the south could be seen long before they reached the port. When *Lochmor* hove in sight, the children would run down to the pier, where the staff would tease them by saying

"Och she's delayed at Eigg" or some such nonsense. They knew better – they had seen her coming up the Kyle. And so they were there to welcome their father and to see what he had brought, for it was seldom that the Captain returned from a trip empty-handed. Even for a skipper, pay in MacBrayne's service was not generous, but thanks to these gifts from grateful locals in many a port, the family could enjoy a good standard of living and a fine table. From April 1940, when a boom closed off the channel at Kyle Rhea, *Lochmor* was based at Mallaig and the Robertsons had to move into rented accommodation in that town. By that date, however, the two boys were on active service and Ishbel was first at school in Inverness then at college in Glasgow. Captain and Mrs Robertson returned to Kyle when the war was over.

The Captain's command of *Lochmor* was to be remarkably free from incident. Given the nature of the coasts which she served, this was highly creditable, especially when it is remembered that this period included the war years. The only grounding took place very early in her career, when she ran on to a sandbank at Kyle in 1931. Attempts by her sister *Lochearn* to pull her off were unavailing and she was in due course rescued by the veteran paddle steamer *Glencoe*, then all of 85 years of age. The incident was captured on camera and the managers in Glasgow were not amused. As these sandbanks often shifted, no blame was attached to the Captain, whose seamanship was superb. A tale recounted by a retired doctor on the BBC programme (discussed in detail later) made this clear.

"It was in Dunvegan in Skye, many years ago now ("now" was 1949 and it seems that the incident happened in 1937). A terrible night, you couldn't see your hand in front of you and the air was full of rain and flying spray. The boat was due to sail to South Uist, to Lochboisdale. A lot of people on the pier begged him not to attempt it. But for some reason or other Duncan Robertson felt it had to be done. He had made up his mind and that was that. I've never known such a night. Sometime in the early morning I heard the telegraph going and then the anchor chain running down. That sounded ominous to me, so I got up and dressed, putting on oilskins, and struggled up to the bridge. Here was Duncan, wet, almost exhausted, his eyes streaming with tears with the effect of the wind and driving rain. "Where are we?" (the doctor asked). "If I am right", (said the Captain), "we are at the mouth of the harbour." If it had been a nice sunshiny day like this, he couldn't have been righter. He was where he said he was to a yard. To me, it was like magic." This incident so impressed another (anonymous) passenger that he or she wrote a poem about it, of which the first stanza ran:-

"'Twas a dirty night at Dunvegan
The waves were mountains high,
When Robertson in the ship *Lochmor*
Sailed down the coast of Skye."

Unusually Captain Robertson's command was featured in not one but two radio programmes and he also took part in a third. The first went out on what was then the Scottish Home Service of the BBC on 24 March 1937 and was entitled "Bu Mhath leam a rädh" (I would like to say). It is a travelogue, with a good deal of history and was spoken by Captain Robertson himself. It gives a vivid description of a voyage, in fair weather, on the Inner Isles run, from Mallaig back to Kyle, and shows how he regarded those places at which he called so often. There are many interesting sidelights, such as that on Rum, then inhabited only by Mrs Bullough, widow of the man who had built the fantasy of Kinloch Castle, and her servants, and inaccessible to anyone else. Although he was far too much of a gentleman to criticise a lady, his comments suggest that he did not approve. Being in Gaelic, this programme was clearly aimed at an audience who knew the regular travellers and the ship herself and therefore there was no need to say much about these. Perhaps his partiality for the ship came through in his comments on the rarity of sea-sickness, and some listeners no doubt gave a wry smile when they heard them, for *Lochmor* and her twin could be very uncomfortable in bad weather. Chris Fraser, in his autobiography "*Christy Boy*", gives a

8.3 *Lochmor* loading a variety of goods at Kyle in the 1930s. From the bridge the captain supervises the operation.

8.4 As can be seen in this photograph, taken at Kyle in the 1930s, cargo handling was very labour-intensive. The pier staff who dealt with it were known locally as "lumpers" and in their work they had the help of a large Clydesdale horse, looked after by one Duncan Matheson. The man in the uniform cap with his back to the ship is Mr MacWilliam, station master at Kyle at the time. Captain Robertson seems to be fairly relaxed about the operation and clearly has time to talk to some passengers.

convincing, almost harrowing account of the ship's behaviour when heading into a south-easter en route from Harris to North Uist and its effect on him, as a young purser, who had still to issue tickets, dividing his time between the ticket office window and a convenient bucket. Other regular passengers remember too what happened to pupils from Inverness Academy returning home for the holidays, in the days when Harris and North Uist were off-shore colonies of Inverness County Council and the idea of a secondary school in the southern Hebrides was unthinkable. On the Wednesday or Friday run, these youngsters, who travelled steerage, would board at Kyle on the previous evening and often go ashore again, the girls in full finery, to a dance in the village hall, returning to the ship not too long before she sailed at 6am. Once the Minch began to have its effect, their finery suffered. But a man is entitled to defend his ship's reputation. Children who were attending high school in Portree were catered for by special calls there at holiday times.

The script of the programme is given in full, with a transalation, as an appendix.

The scene of a young boy leaving North Uist for secondary education was recently re-enacted in the BBC television series "Gruth 's Uachdar" ("Crowdie (cheese) and Cream") in which the preserved motorship *Balmoral* took the part of a MacBrayne vessel and (perhaps with inward pleasure) resumed her original red funnel for the occasion.

The second programme, made to commemorate Captain Robertson's retirement was "*Professional Portrait – The Skipper's Last Trip*", broadcast on the Scottish Home Service in the Spring of 1949. As *Lochmor* was at that date in dock to be re-engined, the trip was actually made on *Lochearn*, which had already undergone that process. The programme would nowadays be called a "docu-drama", since professional actors took the part of the Captain and other characters who appeared and the whole had a distinct flavour of the then-current BBC weekly comedy "The MacFlannels". The part of the Captain was played by W H D Joss, otherwise know to listeners as the adenoidal Uncle Mattha, and Meg Buchanan (Sarah MacFlannel) played the part of a lady passenger. Rikki Fulton also appeared. The narrator was James McKechnie and a Mr Jackson (?Gordon) accompanied him.

The programme took the form of a trip on a Wednesday or Friday sailing from Kyle on the Inner Isles run, and began at about 3.30pm on the day before sailing, when *Lochearn* arrived back in Kyle. There was a description of the unloading process, with the Captain keeping an eye on things from the bridge:-

"Alastair, do not be troubling about that piano yet – get that calf of Mistress MacPherson's ashore!"

There followed a brief reference to greetings in Gaelic and the Captain explained that, out of a crew of 29, all but three had the language. The narrator followed up with "it is a fact that, as far as the working of the ship is concerned, practically everything is in Gaelic. About the only thing which is quite certainly English is the ship's telegraph." The travellers were then taken to their cabin, the starboard one on the promenade deck, beside the Captain's own cabin and he explained that he would have liked to invite them up to his house but they were packing up to leave and "It's worse than crossing the Minch in a gale". They went off to what was clearly the Lochalsh Hotel instead and the Captain recommended the whisky.

The clatter of the engines obviously had no effect on McKechnie, since he did not waken up on the next morning until eight, by which time the vessel was well into her voyage. The pair joined Captain Robertson on the bridge and he warned them that, when they cleared the coast of Skye, they would feel the current coming up the Minch. This led on to an exposition of his seamanship "Out here you get to know by the feel of the ship where you are . . . Och, we don't go much by lights. The point about a light is that it can go out . . . Of course, they're useful, but out here you have to work a lot by instinct. Maybe it's something you get by long experience, maybe it's something you are born with – I don't know – but it's true . . . Charts are all right, but there are things you can't put in a chart – what it means when the sky looks like that down the Sound of Raasay – or what it means when the sea birds are doing different things. If a stranger tried to navigate these islands in all weathers with charts and lights, he would soon be on the rocks. You get to know things by other ways. Just over there by that point there are some nasty shoals. I've never seen them in the chart – they'll be in the chart of course, I'll show you after breakfast – but I know they are there another way – because my father told me when I was a boy. My father was a Skyeman too and he had to do all this without engines. My father would not be telling me that if it was not true."

In due course they reached Scalpay and then on to Tarbert, where they had time to visit the hotel, in company of the Captain. They had no fear of missing the boat. Then on to Rodel, where goods were transhipped by rowing boat, a big heavy boat with two long, old-fashioned sweeps. (This was one of the two calling point at which there was no pier.) They came alongside and the skipper rang "Slow Ahead". In ten minutes they put on board that heaving boat so much stuff – crates, bales, mail-bags and even the driving cab of a lorry (Lot 227, it was called) – that the crew were doing tight-rope acts on the gunwhale. At Rodel also, Jackson managed to procure a large basket of eggs (rationing was still in force in 1949) "one suspects, but cannot prove it, with the aid of Captain Robertson".

Having reached Lochboisdale, they went up to the hotel, where the landlord recounted the story of two good men. "A gentleman was coming over to fish. The weather was very bad, but he sent a telegram from the mainland – "With the help of God and Captain Robertson, will be with you to-morrow night". Well, the time came and so did the *Lochmor*. The Captain came up to see us, as he always does. I thought I'd show him the telegram. And his comment "Ay, ay, two good men." The landlord concerned, Mr F S MacKenzie, was referred to in another contemporary commentary[1] as being one of the outstanding men of the west and the hotel itself was by 1936 thoroughly up-to-date, with electric light, a sun lounge and hot and cold running water in the bedrooms.

After calling at what Captain Robertson called the cocktail islands – Rum and Eigg – they reached Mallaig and, with the Captain, went up to the hotel on the hill for lunch. He pointed out to them the house in which he was going to live (at Teangue on Skye) and "the weather-beaten red face widens into the widest of wide grins, and the blue eyes shine". And so back to Kyle, where the ship came alongside sweetly with the gentlest of bumps, and the derricks are were swinging with a caution from the Captain, "Alastair, you will be very careful with that loom that is coming from Mrs McGregor". When they heard the telegraph signal "Finished with Engines" they wondered to each other what his views on retirement actually were, whether he was blissfully happy or profoundly sad; but they did not ask. Perhaps that was just as well, since Captain Robertson did not want to retire and deeply resented being obliged to do so. The days when MacBrayne captains could stay at work until they were well into their seventies had now passed.

In an epilogue, Captain Robertson himself spoke, evidently after he had actually retired. "I have never been so busy in my life as I am now, and I am supposed to be retired. I have a house and a few acres of arable land, and a few more acres that will carry a few sheep. A cow and some hens – what more could a man want? A boat? Well, I have a boat too. And if my wife or daughter says "We could be doing with some fish" I know where I can get some fish. I knew something about that almost as soon as I could walk . . . Or if it is a rabbit from the hill that is wanted, maybe I know where I can get that too. And soon there will be electric power . . . I belong to Skye and I have come home".

"Is mòr mo ghradh don Chuain	("Great is my love for the sea
Is mòr mo ghradh do Eilean m'àraich,	Great is my love for the Isle which reared me,
Ach is motha gu lèir mo ghràdh do mo dhaoine.	But greatest of all is my love for my own folk.
Soiribh leibh uuile..."	Farewell to you all...")

---

1   *The Lure of the West.* Duncan MacPherson. E Mackay, Stirling, 1950

The programme ended with a verse of the Skye Boat Song, with an accompaniment on the clarsach. In these days of reality television, a programme such as this might to some seem rather folksy, but it does convey an idea of the esteem in which the man and his ship were held in the communities which he served so well, for so long.

The programme in which Captain Robertson played a small part was a broadcast with the title "*The Isles of Youth*", on 14 May 1936. It seems to have been made to commemorate the withdrawal of *Iona* and *Columba*, but other ships featured in it also. His contribution follows as a second appendix.

Sadly Captain Robertson was not given much time to enjoy his new home, his fishing trips and his animals. In the autumn of 1949 he and Mrs Robertson set off happily to spend some days at the Mod, that year being held in Inverness. They had only reached Kyle when he became unwell and it was thought that he had suffered a stroke. He was taken to Raigmore Hospital in Inverness, then on to Aberdeen Infirmary, where he died on 26 November. He was buried at Kilmore in Skye and sixty years later, he is still well remembered in the Hebrides. He was replaced on *Lochmor* by Captain Donald MacLeod of Harris, who commanded her until October 1958 and was known as a great raconteur in both English and Gaelic. In the early winter of 1955/6, he achieved fame as the man who blacked out Skye, although the incident reflected no discredit on his seamanship. It was rather the opposite and it happened in this way. One stormy evening, when *Lochmor* was moored at Kyle, the Captain became concerned that she might be damaged in the gale blowing from the west and he decided to take her over to the more sheltered waters off Skye. However, she made little headway and, when there seemed to be a danger that she would be blown back on to the rocks at Kyle, he dropped anchor. Unfortunately the anchor then cut the cable which supplied electricity to Skye and the Sgitheanachs had to do without power for three weeks. *Lochmor* escaped unharmed. In October 1958 he was succeeded by Captain J MacKinnon. It was good to know that in later days the Company did not forget Duncan Robertson and in 1964, when the new car ferry was being shown off to the people of Skye at Armadale, Mrs and Miss Robertson were invited to the party held on board.

Of course it required a crew to run a ship and, while individual members of the crew of *Lochmor*, came and went, many stayed for years with the ship and with Captain Robertson, creating almost a family atmosphere on board. As mentioned above, most were Gaelic-speaking, something which lasted on board MacBrayane ships as long as the company itself lasted – most of the crew of *Claymore* (1955) still used Gaelic on board in 1973. Many also hailed from Skye. Successive Chief Stewards were A MacDonald of Staffin and N MacLeod, from the same part of the island ; the former left the sea to own a drapery business in Kyle of Lochalsh. Of the crew, Calum Robertson[2], D MacKinnon, J Anderson and Dan MacGillivray (stevedore) were all Sgitheanachs, from Ferrindonald, Sasaig, Sasaig and Aird respectively. John Harvey, Second Officer and later Mate, was from Kilbeg in Skye. The wireless operator was J D MacRae and for many years the purser was Alastair Cummings. Other seamen in the 1930s included Donald Robertson (Aird), and from Teangue, Alan Campbell, Jackie MacColl, Duncan Robertson and Alastair Nicholson. The ship's carpenter, Alastair Anderson, came from Isleornsay and was known as "Saor Ruadh" (the red carpenter). In the engine room, the Chief was Charles Cullen and the Second, T Moore – engine room business was conducted in English. The only woman to work on board was the stewardess, who in the 1930s was Emma Matheson, remembered by Chris Fraser for her kindness to the sea-sick young purser. Six seamen shared a compartment in the lower deck forward, with tiered bunks, and six stewards had similar quarters forward of this, but in this case the bunks were all on one level. Living in such close quarters, it must have been essential for men to be able to get on with each other. The crew's galley and a cabin for the carpenter and his mate were right forward on the main deck. The Chief Steward, Second and Third Engineer and the Mate all had individual cabins on the port side of the main deck, while the Captain and Chief Engineer had rather larger cabins forward on the same deck, beside the motor casing. Work for those on the bridge was

---

2   Not Calum Robertson of *Grenadier* and later *Lochinvar*.

LOCHBOISDALE, SOUTH UIST.

8.5 *Lochmor* arriving at Lochboisdale, a card written on board the ship at Kyle in December 1936 and sent as a Christmas card. (Author's collection)

8.6 Captain Robertson (left) and purser Alistair Cummings relaxing in the lounge of the Lochboisdale Hotel.

8.7 Captain Robertson with two visitors on board *Lochearn*, in the last months of his career.

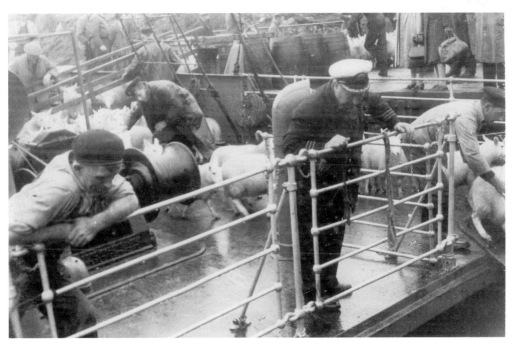

8.8 Sheep being embarked at an island port. A fair number of barrels also await shipment and Captain Robertson and a crew member assess the position in the hold.

made more comfortable by the fitting of a wheelhouse, in which radar was fitted in the late 1940s. Curiously it was only after that date that the ship had two grounding incidents, at Lochboisdale in 1957 and off Rum in 1962, neither serious.

And what of *Lochmor* herself? Despite some of the comments in the broadcasts, she was no beauty, although she and her twin had something of a businesslike air about them. The unraked masts and original small funnel gave them a stiff appearance and in looks they were no replacement for *Plover*, which had a racy elegance. The original grey hull was perhaps meant to make the ship and her contemporaries look like miniature Union-Castle liners, but the colour scheme was completely impractical for ships battling with the Minch in all weathers and was soon given up for the traditional and very smart black, still used to-day on Caledonian MacBrayne vessels, despite several attempts by design consultants over the years to change this. Passenger accommodation for those in first class was concentrated in the midships area with a degree of cosiness. Hot and cold running water was provided in the cabins, with reading lights over the bunks. There was an attractive dining saloon with small tables for three or four, to a total of 27, and a smoke room and lounge on the promenade deck. Unfortunately she had her drawbacks. The original engines were extremely noisy and occupants of the cabins beside the engine room would be rudely awakened from sleep when these started up at Lochmaddy at an unearthly hour of the morning. It was unlikely that they got much sleep thereafter. The two cabins on the promenade deck were slightly quieter. In earlier vessels, such as *Plover*, first class was aft and subject to more discomfort in bad weather. That facility was now enjoyed by steerage passengers, who had at their disposal a smoke room, a small saloon with a pantry and a general room with 14 berths. This was adequate at most times of the year, but became hopelessly overcrowded when filled with returning islanders at holiday times. Alastair MacLean in "*Night fall on Ardnamurchan*" gives a vivid and depressing account of steerage conditions on *Lochearn* and those on her sister were no doubt identical. But at least it was all under cover and there was no question of having to share this space with animals, as was still the case on vessels such as *Glencoe*. The cattle or sheep were all penned safely on the main deck forward.

Despite their drawbacks in the matter of speed and sea-kindliness, both the *Lochs* served the Hebrides well and ended their careers in a blaze of glory in 1964, by standing in on the new Oban-Craignure car ferry service, in place of the new *Columba*, whose delivery was delayed by two months. They then went off to Greece, unusually still together, and, as *Amomoni* (*Lochearn*) and *Naias* (*Lochmor*) served the islands of the Cyclades as well as they had done those off Scotland for another ten years before going to the breakers in 1974. They had done well.

8.9 The officers of *Lochmor* about 1931. In the back row (right) is purser Cummings. In the front row are Calum Black (Mate), an unknown man, Captain Robertson, the Chief Steward and J D MacRae, the wireless operator. Neil (left) and Norman Robertson are sitting on the deck.

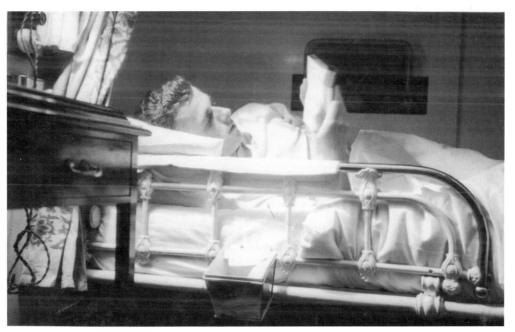

8.10 An interior shot of cabin B on *Lochearn* – the name of the occupant of the berth is not known. One of the innovations on the two ships which commanded much attention was the provision of reading lights above the bunks and the wiring for this can be seen on the left. (Author's collection)

8.11 Stewardess Emma Matheson and a Chief Engineer (?Charles Cullen) on board *Plover*. (© Duncan Macpherson Collection, Dualchas Heritage Service, The Highland Council)

8.12 A regular passenger was Dr Flett of Edinburgh, a keen angler, who fished in the lochs around Lochboisdale. He is seen here forward on the promenade deck with the Captain. Class distinction is maintained by the notice behind the latter's head.

8.13/14 The handling of cars was a source of interest to bystanders and concern to the crew. In the first view, a touring car is off-loaded at an island pier, possibly Tarbert (Harris) and much of the male population seems to have come down to watch the operation. In the second, a slightly later model of car is carefully placed on the forward deck after being slung aboard.

Appendix I
Retiral of Popular Sea Captain – May 7th 1949

From a report in *The Oban Times*

The Captain of the steamer the *Lochmor* is home to Skye
And still in storm and quiet shall his good ship cover
The wild ways of the Minch where the grey fogs fly:
But Captain Duncan Robertson, sometime of the *Plover*,
The Master of the Mail Route to the Outer Isles,
The captain of the ship *Lochmor* – the faithful, the great,
The forty-five years seaman – leaves the bridge and waves to Kyle's
Haven of long friendship, from his own away in Sleat ...

Fumed a minister, rowed out to her when the weather was rough:
"You could have come alongside, they were saying ashore,
You could have reached the pier there easily enough".
"The same ashore, there, were telling me you should
Have preached a better sermon, the other Day of Rest-
It's the same people there were telling me you could –
But like myself, no doubt you were doing your best".

He said, "We had some bad spells, we had some good days too" –
Now, as a crofter-fisherman, may the seas be yet
A joy-ride for the Captain, and the waters calm and blue,
And all go well for him who never fishes with a net.
But the Minch is a battle where the breakers plunge and rear
"And what's the worst experience of everything you know?"
"The income tax" said the Captain of the good ship *Lochmor*...
So, peace be to the Captain, where the calm, blue hyacinths grow.

Author's note. It has been impossible to trace the author of this poem, who modestly signed her- or himself "W.M.C.". It is reproduced here by kind permission of *The Oban Times*. The difference of opinion with the minister took place at Scalpay in the 1930s.

Appendix 2

Bu Mhath Leam A Radh – I Would Like To Say

Bu Mhath Leam A Radh, le Captein D MacDhonnaachaidh
Air a chraobh-sgaileadh air an 24mh de'n Mhairt, 1937, 6.15-6.30pm

A chàirdean, chan 'eil fhios agam an cuala sibh riamh me "Sheòras an eich bhàin". Sean 's mall gun robh an t-each, cha rachadh Seòras coir thaobh am bith ach air mharcachd. Latha bha sud, bah e ag gluasad an coin cladaich le ceum 'san uair aig an each mar a bh'àbhaist. Thàinig iad gu bàgh far an robh sogth bheag air a tarraing suas is bodach a mhuinntir an àite gu trang 'ga tearradh. Sheas Seòras agus ag geur amharc air a' bhodach car tacain ars' san "Carosn a tha sibh ris a sin?"

"Oh" fhreagair an seann dhuine, "tha mi 'n dùil gu'm fàg e nas luaithe i".

"Saoil am fàgadh e an t-each bàn nas luaithe?" thubhairt Seòras.

"Chan abrainn nach fhàgadh" ars' am fear eile, "faodaidh sinn fheuchainn co-dhiù." Is thug e deagh sguab air a 'phrias mhòir a bha goil ri taobh is chàirich e sud le grad bhuille air deireach an eich. Mu'n robh fhios aig Seòras gu dè a thachair, sud an t-each bàn a-mach ris a'mhonadh, agus air m'facal dhuibh, ma's fior an sgeul rinn e suas ann an leth uair an t-astar a chaill e ann am fichead bliadhna. Tha astar fada romhainn an nochd fhathast, oir bu mhath leam na'n tigeadh sibh còmhla rium air a'bhàta a tha fo'm chùram – an *Lochmòr* is gabhaidh sinn cuairt air eileann na Gàidhealtachd. A chionn nach 'eil an ùine ach goirid bithidh e cho math dhuinn deagh sgriobahd do theàrr a'bhodaich a chaidh air each Sheòrais a thoirt dhith, feuch an ann a's luaithe a theid i.

Tiugannibh matà, tha 'n ùpraid air ceidhe Mhallaig cha ghasda shunndach air bòrd is mar sin fuasglaidh sinn na ropan is cuiridh sinn ar n'aghiadh ris a'chuain.

Tha latha briagha sollier ann le speur liath ghorm os ar cion le breachadh de neòil bhàna a'seòladh gu mall bho dheas gu tuath. Tha gluasad mheanbh air agaidh na fairge agus currachd geal a'togail a cinn an sid 's an seo. Tha a'ghrian 'gar failteachadh is a'sgaoileadh leacan air a h-uile a tha null fo'r comhair gu ruig Tir nan Og. As ar dèidh tha smùid an ludheir 'ga chall fhéin 'san astar. Faiceabh cuideachd an fhaoileag no dhà a tha a'snàmh gu h-aotrom os ar cionn a'feiteamh ri spruidhleach na cuinneige. Chan eil faoileag na droch chladaich a tha seo idir. Tha mi cinnteach gur h-i an dearbh thè leis am miann a bhi air mullach a'chruinn – an t-e a bha leinn bho'n a chaidh mi gu muir an tosieach. Tha sinn mar sin 'nar seann luchd-eòlais is cha bu mhath leam s bhi 'ga h-ionndrainn.

Chan fhada an ùine gus am bi sinn am fasgadh Eige far an faic sinn an Sgur. Tha a'Charraig iongantach so mìle troigh ann an àirde is ag éiridh suas ann an cumadh a tha gu math coltach ri cailleach chrom chrotach is i fo eallach trom. Tha i cho dubh ris an t-suith' is cho lom ri a dhà bhois ; gun aon ghas feòir no fraoich a' fas oirre. B'e sin a cruth bho'n dhealbhadh an saoghal. Coltach ri bean Lot dh'fhan i an sud ag amharc sios ai bailtean a'chòmhnaird. Tha bàt'aisig a'freasdal oirnn an so, is feumadih sinn sùil a thoirt ai muinntir an àite agus orrra-san a bhio a'dol ait tìr.

Ann an uair an uaireadair an déidh cùl a chur ri Eige, tha sin fo bheanntan ghrumach Rum. An ám a bhi a'dlùthachadh air saoilidh sibh nach 'eil ann ach aona bheann mór uile gu léir. 'S gann gu bheil mir cinneis ri fhaicinn. 'S e fàsach a th'ann, seilg a tha an t'eilean. Chan 'eil tuath no tuineachadh ; treabadh no tìreadh an sud. Chan 'eil ceo-cgailt as am beagan thighean a tha aca-san a tha 'freasdal air an uachdaren. Tha duine a'faireachdainn samhcair an eilein a'dridheachd air intinn, agus tha sinn, mar gu'm beaach, a'mothachadh gu bheil spioral na laithean a dh'aon ag iathach mu'n cuairt dhinn ann an ciùineas an àite. Chan 'eil cat fhéin air fhulang air an eilean so, air eagal gu'm bi iad a'sealag air isean eòin. Is beag na tha againn ri lainneashadh an so is mar sin tha sinn a'togail oirnn agus a chionn is gur fada bhuainn ar ceann uidhe fhathast, cha dean sinn ach ligeadh is lionadh aig ceidhe eilean beag Chanaidh.

Am mach fo'r comhair tha Uidhist a a Deas agus ann an fhuarahd chì sinn Barraidh MhiNeill. Tha eirisgeidh an sud cuideachd agus a'tighinn 'na chòir cò e an Gaidheal nach urrainn a bhi ag cuimhneacadh gur air an tràigh an eilein sin a dh'fhàg Prionnsa Teralach a'cheud lorg air a'chuiart chiurramach an Albainn. 'S ann an sud cuideachd, gu h'àrd air rudha biorrach, a tha caisteal a'Bhreabadair far an do chuireadh a'Bhan Tighearna Grange mun tugahd i Hiort is an déidh gu Heisgeir – ach 's e naigheachd a tha sin. A'dol seachd air Rudha na h'Ordaig, is a steach gu bun Loch Baoghasdail sgaoillidh sinn ar bratach s chum modh cuimhne a chur air cliù Fionghas a'Prionnsa. Is ann 'san eilean so a chluinnear seann eachdraidh is sean òrain a tha meas air ceòba. 'S ann aca tha na seannachaidean gleusda an so, agus is mór an déidh air a bhi deanamh luaid air eachdraidh na dùthcha, a bàrdachd is a ceò,

Air feasgar dhi-coadoan tha ùin' againmn sgriob a ghabhail troimh au dùthaich àghmhor so far a bheil beanntan àrda is còmhnardan réidh. Tha na beanntan sin air an taobh an ear a'falach o'n chuan Sgitheanach maise na farsuinneachd a tha sgaolite eadar iad 'san cuan Siar, far a bheil machraichean toamanach uaine dà fichead mìle de thràigh réidh ghil bho Phollachara an Uidhist a Deas gu Griminnis an uidhist a Tuath. Tha croitearan an seo aig am bi fichead cruach arbhair, ceithir eich agus mòran spréidhe.

Ach ruigidh sinn Airdh-mhuillin, far an d'rugah 's an do thoghiadh Fionnghas nighean Raoghail 'Ic Aonghais Oig. Ged a bha baile choig peighinn aige, cha robh a'dhachaidh ach mar a bha aig a'chuid eile 'san ám – tigh fada dubh, le còmhnuidh an aon cheann is crodh 's a'cheann eile. Chan 'eil ann an diugh ach làrach lom. Tha ciethir mìle tuath air an làrach so far am faic sin Hiort air feasgr soilleir – tha tobhta mór Ormacleit, an caisteal a chuir Mac 'ic Ailein suas do'n mhnaoi a thug e as an Fhriang, 'is e a'fanaid ai tigh tugaidh. Seachd bliadhna, bhàtar 'ga thogail, agus seachd bliadhna bha iad 'ga mhealtainn. Chaidh e 'na theine an latha thuit Mac 'ic Ailein aig Sliabh an t-Siorram. Cumaidh sinn oirnn ged tha gu Houghbeag a tha trì mìle tuath air so, far an d'àraicheadh Niall MacEachainn, athair an Diùc Tarrentum a choisinn mór chliù dha fhèin mar cheannard-airm aig Napoleon. Anns a'bliadhna ochd ceud fichead is còig thar fichead, thàinig an Diùc air long-choghaidh Bhreatunnach a choimhead a chàirdean, agus dachaidh a shinnsireachd; thug e leis ùir a'chladaich e à starsuch athar, ann am poca de chlò-bàn a rinn baineach an Hoghbeag. Ach tha an t-ám gainn a nis a bhi fuasgaladh. Fàgaidh sinn Sassanuch no dhà aig Fionnladh, 's greim bàis aig gach fear aca air slait-isagaich.

Bithidh seòladh thrì uairean againn gu Loch nam Madadh. Chì sinn air an làimh chlì Beinn Chorrodail far ma bheil uamha anns an robh am Prionsa trì seachdduinean am falach ; Taigh-soluis Uisinnis gu h-àrd air an rudha, geal mar bodach sneachd, is a'seasamh cho stolta ciùin, is a toirt dubhlain do bheuchdaidh na fairge, agus e sìor choimhead a null air an Eist is air an Aisgeach : sud sgiobart cuideachd far a bheil Bòrd a'Phrionnsa ; agus Buidheidh air taobh an ear Pheighinn-na-Faoghla, far an robh a tacan fo'n choill mu'n d'fhuair e teicheadh.

Ach feumaidh sinn cabhaig a dheanamh, 's cahn urrainn sinn ach Uidhist a Tuath ainmeachadh. B'e so mar a bhios fios agaibh dachaidh MhicCodruin, aon de shàr bhàird na Gàidhealtachd.

Tha sinn ag cumail oirnn chun na Hearadh, far an d'rugadh Màiri Nighean Alasdair Raudh anns an t-seachdamh linn deug, agus Iain Gobha dà cheud bliadhna 'na déidh. Ann an Roghadal chì sinn Eaglais Chlimain, le uaighean cinn-chimidh Chlann Leòid 'na h-ùrlair. A sin chun an Tairbeirt, agus air ar tilleadh a mach as an lochd sin tadhaillidh sinn an eilean creagach Scalpaidh.

Togaidh sinn a nis cùrsa an ear 'san ear-a-dheas a' stiùradh air caol; Rònaidh 's a'deanamh air Caol-Loch Ais, ar ceann-uidhe. Air an làimh dheis tha cladach uamharr' àrd an Eilean Sgitheanach agus seallddh de mhórachd a'Chuireang. Air an làimh chlì beanntan mór na Comraich agus farsuinneachd na Mórthir ag cur fàilt oirnn.

Nach móra a nis an t-atharrachadh a thàinig air an t-saoghal O'n a bha Phacaid beag thaphaidh le h-aodach a'ruith eadar uidhist is an t-Eilean Sgitheanach. Bha iongnadh dhith 'na latha fhèin. Faodaidh gu'n cuala sibh mu'm fear shocharach a Cairinnis a chasidh am mach gu Loch na Madadh a d'aon gnothach 'ga faicinn. Chaidh e air bòrd is bah na chunnaic e fo a clàr ag còrdadh ris cho math 's nach d'thàinig e uisge fhèin gus an robh i gu h'aotrom a'snàmh air bhàrr thonn air a turus do Dhunbheagan. An ám tillidh co bh'aig a' cheidhe gufoighidneach a' feitheamh air ach a mhathair. 'Niaair aa chunnaic i e, ruith i le luath cheum 'ga ionnsuidh ia a'tilgeil a làmhan mu ambaich, is 'ga phògadh, ars' ise, "O ghràidh an t-saoghail is thill thu; tha mi icnnteach gur iomadh aghaidh choimheach a chunnaic thu bho'n a dh'fhàg thu'n tigh."

Tha an saoghal air fàs beag o'n uair ud leis na innleachdan a tha againn an diugh air muir air tìr agus 'san iarmailt. Nach fhaod sin a radh gu bheil an saoghal air a thoirt do leac an teinnntean againn. Is mór n t-adhartas a chuinnaic mi 'nam latha fhéin ann an goireasan is an comhfhurtaachd bho'n a chaidh mi gu muir an toiseach 'nam sheachd bliadhna deu 's chan 'eil mi air hor sam bith 'nam sheann duine. Tha aon nì a bu mhath leam a radh riutha-san leis am bu mhath sgrìob a ghabhail do na h'eileannan ach air a bhaile eagal roimh tinneas-mara, agus is e sin gur ann fìor ainneamh, gu sònraichte anns an t-samradh, a chithear neach a'fulang leis an tinneas mhosach so. Tha sin a'toirt 'nam chuimhne balachan a chunnaic mi aon uair is e 'na sheasamh air a chorra-bid aig an taobh, grein bais aige air 'a chlliathaich, is e cho geal ri cailc.

Bha mi duilich air a shon is chaidh mi null far an robh e. Dh'fhaighnich mi dheth an robh e tinn. "Chan 'eil a nis" fhreagair esan "Chan 'eil an còrr ri tighinn a nuas mar tig sàil mo bhrogan."

Tha móran air am bu mhath leam iomradh a thoirt, ach tha mi air mo cheangal teann ris an uaireadair an so isnach urrainn mi a'bheag tuille a radh, ach mu'n sguir mi, is miann leam mo mhìle beannachd a toirt do na h-Eilean aich air son am modh an deagh-ghean, an co-chomunn is an càirdeas. Agus mo làmh-sa dhuibh-se a tha air tìr-mór, ma thig sibh leam gu Innis Gall gu'm faigh sibh fàilte is furan, slàinte is fallaineachd. Chì sibh cuideachd maise is grinneas nach 'eil a leithid 'san Rinn Eòrpa. Is tuigidh sibh an sin gur ann le dùraachd mo cridhe a tha mi ag ràdh:-

Na caochlaidhean a dh'fhaodas teachd,
Le aiteas no le bron,
Chan fhuaraich iad gu bràth mo thlachd,
Do'n tìr a chleachd mi òg:
Gach doire, cuairteag agus glac,
'S an dh'fhuair mi'n toiseach treòir,
Tha dùrachd blàth mo chridhe steach,
An Eilean a'cheò.

I Would Like To Say, by Captain D Robertson
Broadcast on the Scottish Home Service on 24 March 1937, 6.15-6.30pm.

My friends,

I don't know if you have ever heard of "George of the white horse". As the horse was old and sluggish, dear George always went along by the sea when he went anywhere. One day he was going along by the shore with the horse going at a steady pace as usual. They came to a bay where a skiff had been hauled up and one of the old men of the place was busy tarring her. George stopped and with a keen look at the old man, after a short while, said "Why are you doing that?"

"Oh", answered the old man, "I expect that she will go more quickly."

"I wonder if this white horse of mine would go more quickly?" said George.

"I think it might", said the other, "we can but try". And he took a good brush load from the brass pot beside him and swiped it with a quick stroke over the horse's rump. Before George knew what was happening, the white horse jumped out on to the moor and, on my word to you, he covered in half an hour the distance he had covered in twenty years. There is still a long distance in front of us to-night and I would like you to come with me on the boat which is my charge – the *Lochmor* – and we'll take a trip around the islands of the Gaeltacht. Since we have only a short time, we will need a good scrape of the tar that the old boy applied to George's horse to try to make her go more quickly.

Let's get going, there's hustle and bustle on Mallaig pier but it's great to be on board when they cast off the ropes and we head out to sea. It's a fine clear day, with a grey-blue sky overhead and a scattering of white clouds sailing slowly from south to north. There's a slight swell on the sea and white horses raising their heads here and there. The sun is there to welcome us and sheds its beams in the direction of Tir nan Og. Behind us the smoke from the funnel loses itself in the distance. A seagull or two is to be seen flying just over our heads waiting for crumbs in the water. This is not the seagull of the evil shore at all. I am convinced that it is the one with a well-developed appetite – the one that has been with us since I first went to sea. That's why we are old acquaintances and I would not like to be without it.

It isn't long until we are in the lee of Eigg, where we see the Sgur. It's amazing how the Cliff is a thousand feet high and rises up in a form which is very like that of a hump-backed old woman bent beneath a heavy burden. It as black as soot and as bare as your two palms, without a single blade of grass or heather growing on it. That's been its shape since the world was formed. Like Lot's wife, it tarries and looks down on the villages of the plain. The ferry boat is waiting on us and we ought to look on the people of the place and on those who are going on land.

An hour after turning our backs on Eigg we are under Rum's gloomy mountains. In times to come, you will wonder that there was but one single great lady (living) on it. There is scarcely a single person to be seen. It's an empty place, this island, with never a farmer or ploughman around. There is no sign of any chimney smoke, save that from the house of the great lady and from the few houses there are for those who attend to her. People feel the silence of the island penetrating their inner being and we, like the bee, are conscious of the spirit of days that are gone, weaving itself around us with the quietness of the place. Not even a cat is allowed on this island, for fear that it will hunt the birds' chicks. There is not much for us to do here and with that we get a move on and as our destination is still a long way off, we do no more than tie up and take on cargo at the pier of the little island of Canna.

Out there in our view is South Uist and on the weather side we see Barra of the Mac Neills. Eriskay is there too and, as behoves anyone who is a Gael, we cannot but remember that it was on the beach of the island that Prince Charles left his first footprint on his agonising journey around Scotland. Here too, high up on a sharp headland, is Breabadar Castle where Lady Grange was held before she was taken to St Kilda and after that to Heisgeir – but that's another story. Passing Rudhnaordaich, we come in to the entrance to Loch Boisdale where we shall unfurl our flag to keep alive the legend of the Prince. It's on this island that you can hear old stories and old songs, distilled in great esteem through the music of the pipes. These are in tune with the antiquity of the place and have greatly enhanced the history of the land, its poetry and its music.

On Wednesday evening we have time to have a walk through this happy country with its high hills and smooth plains. The hills on the east coast hide from the Minch the beauty which is spread out between them and the Atlantic, where there is green machair and twenty miles of smooth beach with narrow glens from Pollachar in South Uist to Griminish in North Uist. There are crofters here who have twenty stacks of corn, four horses and many cattle.

But we will reach Ardamullan, where Fionnghas, the daughter of Ronald MacAngus was born and brought up. Although it is a township of five land-groats, there were only the kind of houses that were in many other places at that time – long black houses, with the inhabitants at one end and the cattle at the other. Today it is just a piece of empty ground. Four miles to the north of this site, where we can see St Kilda on a clear evening, there is the great ruin of Ormacleit, the castle which MacAlan built for the lady he brought from France, since he had a low opinion of the thatched houses. As the years passed, he accumulated possessions and as the years passed, they had a good life. It was burned down on the day on which MacAlan fell at (the battle of) Sheriffmuir. We will carry on, however, to Houghbeag, which is three miles north of this point, the home of Niall MacEachan, father of the Duke of Tarrentum, who won great renown as a commander with Napoléon. In the year 1825, the Duke came on a British warship to see his relatives and the home of his ancestors ; he took with him some dust which he dug from his father's grave, in the bag of white cloth which a woman in Houghbeag made for him. But our time is running out. We shall leave a Sassenach or two at Lochboisdale, each man of them with a morsel of bait on his fishing-rod.

We'll sail for three hours to Lochmaddy. We'll see on our left-hand side Ben Corrodale, where there is a cave in which the Prince was hidden for three weeks; Uisinnis lighthouse is high on the point, white as a snowman, radiating defiance to the roaring of the sea and perpetually looking over to Eist and Aigeach. There's Loch Skipport too, where there is the Prince's Table ; and Buay to the east of Benbecula, where he had to hide in a wood for a short time until he could make good his escape.

But we must get a move on and we can but glance at North Uist. As you people may know, it is the home of MacCodrun , one of the great bards of the Highlands.

We keep on course for Harris, where, Marie, daughter of Alastair Ruadh was born in the seventeenth century, and Ian Smith two hundred years after that. At Rodel we'll see St Clement's church, with the graves of the chiefs of Clan Mac Leod on the floor. After that, on to Tarbert and on our return out of the loch, we'll visit the rocky island of Scalpay.

Now we'll set course east south-east, steering for Kyle Rona and making for Kyle of Lochalsh, our destination. On our right is the fearsomely high coast of the Isle of Skye and a sight of the majesty of the Quirang. On our left are the great mountains of Kintail and the wide spaces of Morthir welcome us.

Hasn't much changed in the world since the smart little sailing packet was running between Uist and the Isle of Skye. It was the wonder of the very day. Maybe you have heard of the well-off man from Cairnis who went out to Lochmaddy to see to some business. He went on board and looked under the planks of the deck and he was really pleased to see that the water was not coming in, since she was skimming so lightly on the crest of the billows on the trip to Dunvegan. On the return trip, who should be patiently waiting for him but his mother. When she saw him she ran with a quick step towards him and, throwing her arms around his neck and kissing him, she said "Oh my best love in all the world, you're back; I'm sure that you've seen many a foreign face since you left the house".

The world has grown small(er) since that time, with the devices which we have to-day, at sea, on land and in the heavens. You may say that the world has become a flagstone for our hearth. Great is the advancement I have seen this very day in gadgets and comfort from the time when I first went to sea at the age of seventeen and I am by no means an old man. There is one thing I would like to say to those who would like to take a tour to the islands but who are afraid of sea-sickness and that is that it is very seldom that one sees anyone suffering from this horrible malady, especially in summer. That brings to mind a lad that I saw once standing on tiptoe at the ship's rail, looking like death and as white as chalk. I felt sorry for him and went over to where he was. I asked him if he was sick. "Not any more", he replied, "The rest will not come up as salt water is on my shoes".

There is much else I would like to mention, but I am pressed for time and so cannot say much more, but before I finish I would like to wish a thousand blessings on the folk of the islands, for their well-mannered kindness, their sense of community and their friendship. And my hand to you people on the mainland, if you come with me to the Hebrides, where you will get a greeting with a welcome and a toast to your health. You will see too beauty and grace which has no equal in Europe, and you will understand that it is from the depth of my heart that I say:-

Changes may be in store
Bringing gladness or sorrow.
But the love I have for the land
Which I knew when I was young
They will never extinguish.
Every grove, every turn, every hollow
Where I first found life's energy,
Still bring warmth to my heart
On the Misty Isle.

Appendix 3

"The Isles of Youth" broadcast

"I have come here from my ship the *Lochmor* at Mallaig to tell you something about the outer Islands and the places we sail to.

South from Tarbert, Harris to Lochboisdale is just a mass of islands. Their coasts are so indented that the sea looks like the land and the land looks like the sea. They would do fine for stepping stones for the likes of a giant or some of the ancient heathen gods that are buried about Rodel, if they were feeling playful.

It is like a sad farewell to leave the islands but when you come back again, they make you more than welcome.

Some say that Barra is the most majestic and splendid and I know Barra. Others that the little group of islands grouped around the Traigh Mòr channel are the most wonderful in their colours, the enclosed water at Scalpay, the run up the east coast of Skye and across to Tarbert the most surprising and beautiful. They all have their different qualities, just as Canna differs from Rum and Eigg from them both.

I have sailed in all kinds of ships, some of them that looked like a wheelbarrow and others running across to France when the submarines were about especially, so slow that they seemed to be going astern when they were going ahead.

I have been commanding a ship in the MacBrayne service since 1917. I have sailed in the *Cygnet* and the *Plover*, both able vessels, but for comfort, seaworthiness and handiness, the *Lochmor* and her sister ship the *Lochearn* are just about the best ship that could be designed for the island services.

Now if any of you don't feel like your breakfast or your dinner and if you feel that your spirits are getting down and you would like to be young again, let me tell you that we have the finest air in the world and we'll have you at the reels before they have time to tune the pipes.

Man, we have plenty of sport and entertainment – splendid mountains, bird life on hill and shore you never see on the mainland. There is no need for any angler to add a bit pound or an inch or two, for every basket and every fish just looks like a dammed lie.

Thigibh air Cuairt a dh'amharc eillanin na h'arda n'iar agus cha dichuimhuich sibh an sealladh ri air beo. (Come and look around the panoply of islands high in the west and you will not forget the sight while you live.)

8.15 *Lochmor* dressed overall at Tarbert on VJ day in August 1945.

Appendix 4

Captain on *Lochmor*.

Seirm:Togaibh fonn le sund 's caithream
De Caiptain an *Lochmor*, am fiurain fearail.
Togaibh fonn le sund 's caithream

Rann :'S e Slète gorm a dh'araidh og thu
Tir nan seid lòn thar mara.

Air long nan sèal an làithean t'aige
Thug thu eòlas air gach cala.

'S tu nise ceannard an *Lochmoire*
Tha seòladh null gu Loch nam Madaih.

Ged bhitheadh am fairge leum 's sgaoileadh
Thaghaileadh tu an Rum 's Canna

A' dol timcheall Rudh na h'Orduigh
'S tu a' seòladh i triomh 'n cathadh.

(Chorus. Raise a tune with a joyful shout
 To the captain of *Lochmor*, a strapping laddie.
 Raise a tune with a joyful shout.)

(Verses)It was sea-blue Sleat that you knew as a youngster
A land of plenty by the sea.

On a sailing vessel in those early days
You got your knowledge of every harbour.

And now you are skipper of *Lochmor*
Sailing out yonder to Lochmaddy

Though the scattered seas may be leaping
You'll get through to Rum and Canna

And when rounding Rudh na h'Orduigh
It's you who sails her through the spindrift.

(It is not known who composed these verses, nor to what tune they were sung.)

8.16 Captain Robertson played host to some distinguished travellers during his service and here he enjoys a crack with Sir Harry Lauder.

8.17 Captain Robertson wearing his "cold weather" uniform. This consisted of a very long scarf, knitted by his daughter Ishbel when in primary school – it could be wound round the neck several times and thus kept out the worst of the winter's gales.

In this chapter, photographs not otherwise credited are from Miss I Robertson's collection and I am greatly indebted to her for so kindly placing it at my disposal. This collection has also made it possible to use broadcast material, with her permission and the co-operation of BBC Scotland. Thanks are also due to the Librarian at Sabhal Mòr Ostaig for allowing access to copying facilities.

Telephone: Central 9956.
(Private Branch Exchange.)

ALL PASSENGERS AND THEIR LUGGAGE, AND GOODS AND LIVE STOCK, ARE ONLY CARRIED SUBJECT TO THE
CONDITIONS SPECIFIED ON BACK OF SAILING BILLS.

GLASGOW & HIGHLAND ROYAL MAIL STEAMERS.

Telegraphic Address,
"MACBRAYNE, GLASGOW."

IN YOUR REPLY REFER TO

DAVID MACBRAYNE, L??

ALL COMMUNICATIONS TO BE ADDRESSED TO THE COMPANY,
AND NOT ON ANY ACCOUNT TO BE ADDRESSED TO INDIVIDUALS.

INITIALLED BY

ALL CHEQUES AND MONEY ORDERS TO BE MADE PAYABLE TO
DAVID MACBRAYNE L??. AND CROSSED.

S.S. "Claymore"   119 HOPE STREET,

GLASGOW, 6th September 19 19

TO ALL WHOM IT MAY CONCERN.

This is to certify that the bearer, Duncan Robertson, has sailed with me on board the steamer "Claymore" of Glasgow as 2nd Officer, from the 26th of April, 1917, till the 17th of December, 1917, and as Mate from the 19th of June, 1918, till the 4th of September, 1918, and as 2nd Mate from the 4th of September, 1918, till the 27th of May, 1919.

During all this time I have found him very obedient and attentive to his duties. He had full charge of a watch for twelve hours each day, and I have the greatest pleasure in recommending him to anyone who may wish his services, as he is trustworthy in every respect and strictly sober.

Colin McFarlane

Master.

A testimonial for Duncan Robertson, written by Captain Colin MacFarlane of *Claymore*.

9   A Bus Conductor with David MacBrayne Ltd

FTER DISEMBARKING FROM *COLUMBA*, *"You will be agreeably surprised to find yourself being escorted into a MacBrayne De Luxe Motor Coach, the last word in comfort and modern equipment. Having seated your self at your ease, you find that you have entered on a stretch of road unequalled by anything throughout the world; the city, with its smoke, its noisy chaos and contaminated atmosphere is forgotten ... Climbing the famous Kintraw Hill, without apparent effort, the motor coach rapidly brings you to the summit, 700 feet above sea level. Smoothly the coach proceeds downhill until it comes upon the road which skirts the shores of beautiful Loch Craignish. Just when you have come to the conclusion that you will never see anything to compare with it, as if by the touch of a magician's wand, Loch Melfort, with the mystic islands of Shuna, Luing and Scarba rising beyond, appears from afar like a sheet of shimmering glass ... The road runs through pleasant meadows. These in turn gradually give place to naked crags, until high above the sea, you get your first glimpse of Oban ... "*
(Oban to Ardrishaig (by Motor), as detailed in the MacBrayne guide for 1933.)

The Oban-Ardrishaig service had its origin in a coach service from the latter to Cuilfail, a distance of 24 miles. This connected with the steamer and left at 12.50pm. The return journey set out at 8.30am. The single fare was a fairly expensive 6/6d (32.5p) and it seems that the journey took about three hours. The coach was replaced by a through motor service from and to Oban on 28 February 1914. As this took four and a quarter hours for the through journey, it was only a little faster than the coach, but no doubt more comfortable. By 1933 the bus service covered the distance in a little over two hours, although the morning run out of Oban was allowed three, no doubt because of the need to deliver mail and other items. There were then two through services, with an additional summer-only tourist service. The buses used on that service at the time of the extract given above were Maudslays, with bodywork by Hall, Lewis, seating 31 passengers. From what has been said of them it is unlikely that they climbed Kintraw Hill without apparent effort.

Duncan MacTaggart was brought up in Campbeltown, where his father was in the police force. On his 18th birthday in April 1945 he was conscripted into the army and was not demobilised until December 1947, by which date his father had become a sergeant in Oban. Duncan went there to live with his parents and soon found work as a grocer's assistant. Having heard in 1952 that MacBraynes were looking for a conductor, he applied and was accepted. He was assigned to the Oban-Lochgilphead-Ardrishaig service, the only service actually based in Oban. Over the next seven years, he would come to know this road in all weathers and conditions rather less poetic than those envisaged by the writer of the guide.

In 1954 there were two daily departures in each direction. The bus based in Oban left at 9.45am, for which duty the crew had to report at 9. It was due in Lochgilphead at 11.43 and Ardrishaig twelve minutes later. The bus awaited the arrival of *Saint Columba* or *Lochfyne* or, in winter, the bus which had connected with the steamer at Tarbert, and left again at 1.10pm. On this journey there was a long break until 2pm in Lochgilphead, to allow the conductor to hand in mail which had been brought by the steamer and to collect mail for distribution on the way back to Oban, which was finally reached at 4.05pm. Having handed in his takings and cleaned the inside of he bus, the conductor would normally be free to go home by 5pm. In summer time there would be several duplicate buses on the service and quite often Oban passengers would be put on one which

187

9.1 Duncan MacTaggart (on right) and driver Gordon MacPherson. pose in front of No.143, GUS933 at Oban, North Pier, in 1958. (Duncan MacTaggart)

9.2 A scene at Ardrishaig pier head with buses awaiting passengers from *Columba*, probably in the summer of 1935. That for Glasgow is nearer the camera. It is one of the Maudslay Meteor ML6A vehicles, of which four were bought in 1929. These had front and rear doors and very comfortable coach seats. The Oban bus is that nearer the pier; it is not possible to identify it definitely, but it is likely to be one of the AEC coaches bought in 1934. On the right is the bus giving the connexion to Campbeltown. *Columba* is at the pier and the shed carries on its gable wall an advertisement for the services of Clyde Cargo Steamers Ltd, in which MacBraynes had an interest from 1915. (Courtesy of St Andrews University Library, JV A2740)

would run express, arriving much earlier and giving them additional time in Oban. This journey formed part of a circular tour from Glasgow, the Tour Majestic, by which passengers returned to the city by train leaving Oban at 6.05pm. The fare in 1954, 3rd class and saloon, was 39/7d. (£1.96). Connexions to and from Campbeltown were available at Lochgilphead, leaving at 12.42pm and arriving at 4.10. The corresponding Ardrishaig-based bus left Lochgilphead at 8.50am and returned from Oban at 5pm, again giving a connexion through to Campbeltown.. On Saturday evening there was a short working to Ardfern, leaving Oban at 8.45pm and returning by 11pm. This gave local people the chance to come to shop in Oban, have tea and perhaps see a film before returning home. Others used this service to sample Oban's pubs and one Saturday regular was usually quite unconscious by the time Ardfern Road End was reached. The crew obligingly placed him in a sitting position in the 'phone box there, propping the door open to allow room for his feet. He seems to have stayed there until he came to at some point in the week-end, since he had always gone by Monday morning, none the worse of his night out. In the 1950s a dam was being built at Kilmelford and three Irish lads who were working on it and living in caravan accommodation were regular passengers on the return working of this service, having spent the evening enjoying themselves in the Culfail Hotel in Kilmelford. Three other young farm workers would cycle down to meet the afternoon bus at Cuilfail Hotel and go on with it to enjoy an evening in Oban. They returned on the late departure, but by the time the Cuilfail was reached at 9.15, they were generally in no condition to cycle home. They stayed on the bus and the conductor stowed their bikes in the mail compartment until they reached the end of the road to the farm. There was sometimes a problem when a vehicle without this facility was on the run and in such cases the bikes were placed in the gangway alongside the other passengers.

Occasionally Oban crews would be asked to work duplicates to the normal Alexander's service to Glasgow at peak holiday times. This was a common practice at the Glasgow autumn holiday (the last week-end in September) when many people came to Kintyre and mid-Argyll from Glasgow, all wanting to return on the Monday evening. They would work the 5pm Oban-Ardrishaig service then go on to Glasgow via Inveraray, returning from the city empty in the dead of night. Clearly tachometers were unheard of in those days, when bus crews were expected to work all the hours MacBraynes sent them! Very often there would be six buses on this special working.

On their normal journeys, the MacBrayne bus carried out many different functions. It was not simply a conveyance to take passengers between places on the route. Before leaving Oban, the conductor collected mail, newspapers and parcels for distribution en route. The bus concerned was fitted with a mail compartment, which reduced its seating capacity from 35 to 27. Mail was handed in at post offices in the villages served, such as Kilmelford and, from Ardfern Road End southwards, mail was also collected to be handed in at Lochgilphead post office. Newspapers were thrown out as the bus passed their destination, and there must have been times when they landed in a puddle, but it seems that no one ever complained. Parcels, which contained a wonderful variety of articles, were delivered to their recipients and others would be collected for distribution in Oban or Lochgilphead. Strictly speaking these were to be charged according to weight, but as there were no on-board scales, conductors became expert in guessing an approximate weight and sticking on the corresponding parcels tickets. Generally the contents were personal items such as a new pair of shoes or medicines from a chemist, but the bus also carried lobsters on the first part of their journey to Billingsgate market in London. Not many shellfish have begun their journey to the market on what was until 1952 referred to as a "De Luxe Motor Coach". All these were carried "at owner's risk". It was clearly a very personal service and enabled people living in remote cottages and villages to take advantage of the shopping potential of Oban or Lochgilphead without actually having to go there. The local population much appreciated these facilities and at Christmas time bus crews were snowed under with presents. Hand-knitted socks were a popular item and they often received more of these than they could ever have worn out in a lifetime.

The bus also functioned as a school run, in the days when taking a child to school by car was unheard of. Two children boarded at Soroba to go to school in Kilmore and three were picked up between there and Kilmelford. Conductors would see them across the road at the school, there being no such person as a lollipop man or lady then. There was no problem with their behaviour on the bus and indeed no problem with passengers at all, except for those who had drunk more than they could carry and sometimes made a thorough mess of the interior. When the bus returned to the garage, the conductor had the unpleasant task of making everything clean again.

In summer, tourists formed a substantial part of the passenger load and they likewise appreciated the personal service given by the crews, to the extent that they would insist on tipping a conductor at the end of a journey, although that was not supposed to happen. Many of these visitors were from England, a very few from overseas. As the service still formed part of the Royal Route, these often brought a fair amount of luggage to be stowed in the boot at the rear.

An unusual service given by MacBrayne's conductors was the collection or renewal of road licences for private cars. This was done through the tax office in Lochgilphead, the necessary documentation and fee being handed in on the outward journey and the tax disc collected in the afternoon. Unlike all the other services performed by conductors, this was not done purely on a voluntary basis, since conductors were paid 5/- (25p) per licence handled.

The through fares were, in 1954, 8/6 (42.5p) single, 12/6d (62.5p) return, but the former also counted as a day return. Tickets were issued using a Setright machine, the first of which had come into service in 1949. These were pre-printed, but blank at the end and were inserted by the conductor into a slot in the machine. By turning dials on the machine, the day, month, stage boarded and fare paid (in shillings and pence) could then be stamped on the ticket. Returns were cancelled by simply punching a hole in the ticket. The machine could not print fares which contained an odd halfpenny, such as that from Lochgilphead to Ardrishaig in 1960 (41/2d (2p)) and for these a surcharge ticket was used. Weekly tickets were also available, but were seldom used on this service. As mentioned above, parcel and newspaper labels were affixed to the items concerned, corresponding to the weight of the package. After returning to Oban, the conductor handed in the day's takings, to be checked against the machine's register by the depot staff. In winter this was sometimes a very easy job, as less than £1 would have been taken in fares.

The usual bus on this service was one of the Maudslays, then still fairly new. These were supremely reliable and breakdowns on the road were rare. Likewise they could be trusted to get through in all but the very worst of weathers. In the seven years from 1952 to 1959, there was only one occasion when a bus had to turn back, at Ardfern Road, since the driver was afraid that he would not make it up the hill beyond that point. Chains were carried to be attached to the wheels in icy conditions and crews often in winter had to turn out to affix these en route when the going became difficult.

Crews were quite well paid and three weeks leave were allowed each year. However, discipline was strict and en route visits by inspectors very common, to the extent that a conductor might have four such inspections in the course of a week. The inspectors travelled by car and of course word did often get around that they were on their way, this information being conveyed by one driver to another by a flash of the headlamps. However, this warning was not likely to be available on a run on which there were only two buses in all. Not wearing the regulation uniform cap was one misdemeanour which was likely to provoke the wrath of an inspector, but that would lead only to a lecture about the wearing of one's uniform. There were more serious offences. Having reached Kilmelford one day, a conductor went in to the post office to hand over and collect mail. While he was gone, a wee old man boarded the bus and made for a seat near the back. Now the bus concerned had very comfortable, high-backed coach seats. In due course the conductor returned, cast a quick glance over the passengers and, seeing no one whose fare he had not previously collected, rang the bell to start. They had not travelled beyond the village when an inspector arrived and proceeded to carry out a ticket check. He soon found the ticket-less old man and the conductor was given a day's suspension without pay for failure to carry out his duties properly.

Despite this strict discipline, crews remained with the firm for many years and often remained on the same workings, with the same driver or conductor, for many years. In seven years on the Oban-Ardrishaig service, Duncan MacTaggart had only three regular drivers, Alastair MacFarlane, Sandy Livingstone and Gordon MacPherson, with reliefs at holiday times or to cover illness. Sandy was by then quite near retirement and very definitely from the Gaeltacht. If the office needed to contact a bus crew while they were on the road, a call would be made to the post office at which they would next call, with a request that the driver should 'phone back, reversed charge. One day this happened to Sandy, who was heard to ask for the Oban number and say firmly that he wanted the call "carriage paid". During this period, the driver of the inward 8.50am working from Ardrishaig to Oban was James Potter and his conductor was John Fletcher.

It was a pleasant and interesting job and certainly very worth-while. But in 1959 Duncan married and decided that he would enjoy family life more if his work did not involve travelling away from Oban. He therefore applied for and was given a transfer to the pier service and the Ardrishaig bus had a new conductor for the first time in seven years.

9.3 Awaiting departure from Oban North Pier with a capacity load for Ardrishaig is no.135, another Maudsaly of 1949 with Park Royal bodywork, but in this case without a mail compartment. It was based at Ardrishaig garage and worked the opposite runs to those on which Duncan MacTagggart conducted. (Author's Collection)

No bus tickets for the Oban-Ardrishaig service have come to light, but this combined road and steamer ticket is for an Ardrishaig- Fort William journey about 1955. The coach portion would have been exchanged by the conductor for a bus ticket. (Author's Collection)

10 The *Grenadier* Disaster

S THE PASSENGERS RETURNING FROM A TRIP to Staffa and Iona disembarked from
Grenadier at Oban just after six o'clock on the evening of Monday 5 September 1927,
tragedy and the lovely ship on which they had spent the day must have seemed worlds
apart. It was almost impossible to associate sudden, horrible death with one of the Clyde's loveliest
creations, or with the beauty of Oban bay. Some would probably have spent some of their time on
board chatting to Captain Archibald MacArthur and would have wished the old gentleman well for
his retirement, due to begin at the end of the week.

Despite her looks and apparently delicate appearance, *Grenadier* was more than a pretty
summer butterfly boat. She was tough, and, until that night, lucky. Although employed all the year
round – mainly on the Ardrishaig mail run in winter and on cruising in summer - she had had
nothing worse than a minor grounding off Gourock in 1907. Even when employed as a North Sea
minesweeper (HMS *Grenade*) from July 1916 until the end of the war she had led a charmed life.
The nearest to tragedy that her passengers ever came was a bout of sea-sickness off the Treshnish
Isles in summer or Ardlamont in winter. Yet within eight hours of her return to Oban that night,
she would be lying partly-submerged on the bottom of the bay, her midships section a mass of
burnt wood and twisted metal, and three of the crew who had tended to the passengers would
have died a painful death, two of them being burned almost beyond recognition. Though loss of
life in comparable on-board fires, as in New York, had been far greater, this disaster shook the local
community to its core and would be talked about for years to come, a yardstick against which other
awful happenings would be measured. The cause of the fire has never been clearly ascertained and
no convincing reason for it has ever been put forward.

Grenadier was built in 1885 and was intended for the Oban-Gairloch tourist service in summer
and for the Ardrishaig mail run on the Clyde in winter. As, on the former, some passengers would
be spending a long day on board, she was fitted with compound oscillating machinery, already
obsolete but smooth in operation and not likely to become tiring, even after ten hours of continuous
sailing. She could accommodate 1150 passengers on a steam 5 certificate and had a crew of 20. She
was furnished to a high standard and had unusually wide plate glass windows in the main deck
saloons, to ensure that tourists would have a good view of the scenery, no matter the weather.
According to a newspaper report of her trial trip, her interior fittings were "a model of economical
and harmonious arrangement". She was given a clipper bow with a bowsprit embellished with
the letters GR, which is thought to have started life on some other ship. She did not serve on
the Gairloch run for very long and became much more closely associated with the cruise from
Oban to Staffa and Iona as her summer duty. She continued on the winter Clyde sailing for almost
all her life and, one day in the autumn of 1891, took the author's grandfather from Rothesay to
Tighnabruaich, where he started work as a lamp boy in the hotel. It was a messy job and he was
glad to leave it when he was old enough to begin an apprenticeship as a joiner, in Glasgow, but he
always had an affection for *Grenadier* thereafter. She also figured occasionally in Neil Munro's Para
Handy stories and that good captain was wont to claim that his own tubby vessel bore more than
a passing resemblance to her, a resemblance not evident to the rest of Clydeside. By the 1920s she
was known and well regarded throughout the western isles and, by the accounts of the tourists she
had carried in summer, her fame had spread much further afield.

Once the last passengers had disembarked on that September evening, the crew made the ship
tidy and were then free. Most went off into Oban, some to go home, some perhaps to meet friends

and enjoy a dram or two in one or other of the town's pubs. There was, however, no suggestion that any had returned to the ship the worse for drink. Captain MacArthur and others remained on board and in the course of the evening one of the local Customs officers joined them for a crack, one topic of conversation being his forthcoming retirement. He had commanded the ship since at least 1903, if not earlier and had earned a reputation for kindness and courtesy to passengers, as well as that of an excellent navigator. In summer he had made a habit of coming down from the bridge when all was running smoothly and meeting his passengers face to face. His kindliness was illustrated on occasions such as that when he put the ship back to Tobermory pier to pick up a poor old woman from Skye who was most anxious to travel to Oban but who had become confused about the departure time of *Grenadier*. He said that he would not have turned back for someone who was well-off, but as she was clearly poor and not used to travelling, it was another matter. As he was now almost 80, he should have retired at the end of the previous summer, but the Company had allowed him to stay on as an "adviser" to his successor, Captain Alex. MacLean. The latter, a fully competent officer who had been in their employment for thirty years, needed no adviser and the creation of this special post was probably a reward for many years of good service. Although the Company was by this time experiencing some financial problems, it still could find the money for such a scheme. Having two captains on one ship could have caused problems, but Captain MacLean seems to have been happy to work under such an arrangement and to have done his best to make the older man's last year at sea a happy one.

The ship was now under the charge of Angus Nicolson, a 24-year old seaman, who reported to the Second Officer and who seemed to be fully aware of the duties of night watchman. He had been with the Company for two years. He did not smoke and he had not been drinking on the day or evening in question. The sailor designated for this duty was allowed time off in the afternoon to have a sleep and he appears to have taken advantage of that arrangement. When he took over his watch, he had talked with Angus MacKinnon, First Officer, and there were no problems recorded. During the evening he went ashore for a short time and about 10pm made a meal for himself in the galley, situated admidships on the main deck. The last crew members to return to the vessel did so shortly after midnight and peace descended on *Grenadier* and on Oban town. There was no suggestion that anything was amiss. Some of the men slept in the dining saloon, others were in the forecastle, located right forward on the lower deck and separated from the steerage forecabin by an iron bulkhead. The two captains had adjacent cabins at the foot of the companionway leading down to that apartment. Nicolson made a round of the ship just after midnight and found everything in order. A paraffin lamp was burning in the galley, where the cooking ranges had been banked up ready to prepare meals the next morning. The galley door was probably left open.

At 12.40am, Nicolson went down to the focsle to get a kettle, a cup and some bread to make a snack. On his return to the main deck, he found the galley well alight with a sheet of flame. He immediately ran back to the focsle and shouted to those asleep there to warn them of the danger. He thought that all had heard him. He also roused Captains MacLean and MacArthur, and when the former went to see to the latter, he had already left his cabin. Meanwhile, D Baldwin, Chief Engineer, whose sleeping quarters were by the starting platform in the engine room and therefore near to the galley, had wakened about 12.30 with what he described as a "suffocating feeling" and, on leaving his cabin, also found flames shooting out from the galley into the passageways on either side. He ran down to the dining saloon aft on the lower deck, where John Ralph and Robert Riddell, chief cook, were asleep, and awoke them. He then went up to the bridge, where he had the foresight to pull the cord of the ship's whistle, which was soon sounding the alarm over the whole town. Having done that, he tried to go back down below decks, but, finding his way blocked by the fire which had now spread considerably, went ashore by the gangway and threw stones to smash the windows of the after saloon on the main deck, in case any should be trapped there.

Captain MacLean, having been awakened by Nicolson, at about 1am, he thought, and having seen to Captain MacArthur, went, still in his night attire, into the forecabin to rouse others but, there being no reply to his shouts, he then went up to the main deck. Seeing the extent of the fire, he turned down again and found a jacket in his cabin to protect his head. Back on the main deck, he realised that there was now no way by which he could reach the upper deck and so forced his way through the fore saloon and, by breaking a window, out on to the open deck forward. When he reached the open air, his clothing was beginning to burn and he jumped over the side into the water, extinguishing this fire before it had really taken hold; he was not actually burned. By this time also some crew members and others from the shore had taken a small boat up to the side of the ship and they fished Captain MacLean out of the water almost as soon as he had jumped in. He was rather dazed but soon recovered. Dugald Cameron from Millport, a deck hand who was quartered aft with the Second Engineer, was trapped on the upper deck and threw a life raft over this side, but was then saved by jumping in to the same boat. He reported that the fire had "spread like wildfire".

A crew member who was meanwhile taking a main part in the rescue operations was seaman Calum Robertson, who also commented on the flames shooting out of the galley. He woke the second cook and a steward who were asleep in the forecabin, on the port side, the side nearest the pier. He then saw Captain MacArthur standing just outside his cabin, apparently putting on a jacket. He urged him to hurry and received a reply which he thought was "I'm coming". He then shouted "Up the stairs, boys, it's about ablaze" and tried to break through the bulkhead to the focsle, but was driven back by the smoke and heat. At this point it was realised that there was still one person trapped in it, steward Albert Horsburgh, whose head and arms were now thrust through a porthole; he was crying out, "I'm burning now, shoot me, Captain, shoot me". Robertson went ashore to find some tools, with which to break through the deck from above. Having found only an axe and a sledge hammer, he tried with these. Some others joined him, all stripped to the waist in the heat, and they pulled out one of the ventilators, but were unable to go down into the focsle because of the heat and fire. They then went ashore with a length of the ship's hose and Nicolson connected this to a hydrant, but unfortunately did not realise that the hydrant concerned was there only to supply domestic water to the steamers and there was insufficient pressure to make any impact on the fire. Even if there had been, it is unlikely that it would have made any difference to the fate of Albert Horsburgh. In any case, the fire brigade arrived at this point, connected their hoses to the appropriate mains and quickly brought the fire under control. By means of a rope fixed to the bow, the ship's stern was swung away from the pier and very soon sank under the weight of water which was being pumped aboard. By 2am it was all over. Despite what had happened, damage was confined to the middle and fore parts of the ship and it seemed that salvage might be possible.

The prompt arrival of the brigade was entirely due to the forethought of Baldwin in sounding the vessel's whistle and by the coincidence that two night-duty policemen, Sergeant Dewar and PC MacMillan, were just at that moment on patrol in Tweeddale Street, only about 200 yards inland from the North Pier. Dewar ran to the police station in Albany Street and set off the rocket which was the signal to the fire brigade to turn out, while MacMillan went to the scene of the fire and did his best to help with the rescue efforts. Police Inspector MacCallum was also quickly on the scene and was instrumental in controlling the crowd of interested spectators who had meanwhile assembled and who were by now hampering operations. MacBrayne's agent, Angus Kerr, also arrived quickly at the pier and played a major role in the direction of operations. The entire episode lasted for about 20-25 minutes, but to those who had feared themselves trapped aboard, it had seemed like an eternity.

When the fire had died down, it became apparent that Captain MacArthur was missing and his body was found on the port sponson forward. He had suffered some burns, but was still fully recognisable and it was not clear why he had not been saved, or saved himself. Calum Robertson went on board again, to try to salvage some of his belongings and then had the horror of finding the charred body of the young pantry boy, Kenneth MacRae, at the foot of the companionway on the main deck forward. With considerable difficulty, a diver recovered Horsburgh's body the next day; he was found kneeling right at the front of the focsle and had been burned almost beyond recognition. Some made their escape by dashing through the spreading flames and crew members

J Kirkness and J Stewart also received what were at first thought to be serious burns, while their colleagues R Heferman and D Green suffered slight burns. David Graham had burns to his neck and arms. Others, not named, had broken limbs and many lost all their clothes and other possessions in the rush to escape. As one man put it "I didn't save any of my belongings, but I'm glad to get ashore with a whole skin". Crew members were taken in the first instance to the Marine Hotel, some in the boats into which they had jumped, and there they were cared for by Miss Nan MacLeod of Gilmore Buildings and a local doctor, Dr Currie. The manager of the Columba Hotel, Mr Gill, kindly opened up his tearoom to provide refreshment for those who had escaped unharmed and for the rescue teams. Four of the men who had suffered burns were then moved in the "ambulance waggon" to the MacKelvie Hospital in the town, Heferman and Green being allowed home the next day and the other two some days afterwards, their injuries having proved not be as bad as had been feared. Graham's burns were not serious enough to require hospitalisation.

Captain MacArthur's body was taken to Glasgow, where his home was, by the 12.00 train on Wednesday 7 September and he was buried on the Friday. A very large number of mourners, including Captain MacLean, accompanied his body to the cemetery. On the same day *Lochinvar*, her flag at half-mast, took the body of Kenneth MacRae back to Salen. There was a great deal of local sympathy for his mother, as she had lost her husband, who was piermaster at Salen, in March of the same year and had now lost a son, who had only recently left school. After a service in the pier house, the coffin was carried by the villagers in procession to the cemetery, located three miles from the village. At intervals people exchanged places with the pall-bearers. In this way, the people of the community showed their feeling for Mrs MacRae in her sorrow, in a way which a procession with a hearse could never have done. Albert Horsburgh's body was also taken back to Glasgow and buried on the following Saturday. Touching letters of thanks later appeared in the *Oban Times* from Mrs MacArthur and Mrs Horsburgh. Mr D H MacBrayne also wrote to thank publicly all who had helped with the rescue operation and Mr A F MacQuisten MP sent a kind and thoughtful letter expressing his condolences, both to those who had lost loved ones and to the Company.

There was no sailing to Iona on the next two days after the fire, but *Fusilier* came down from Fort William and resumed the service on the Thursday. It finished for the season on the following Saturday, when she moved south to the Clyde to take up *Grenadier*'s normal winter duty on the Ardrishaig mail run. She did not find great favour on this duty and there were complaints in March 1928 that she had been late on twelve occasions in the previous six weeks. She carried on these services in the next three years, but it was not until *Lochfyne* came out in 1931 that there was an adequate replacement for *Grenadier*. She herself was soon refloated and pumped dry, then languished at her berth at the North Pier, her saloon windows boarded up, until 12 April of the next year, when she was towed away to be broken up at Ardrossan. As the photographs show, she was not so badly damaged as to be beyond repair, but her age told against her.

Under the chairmanship of Sheriff D M Wilson KC and with Deputy Procurator-Fiscal P A C Milne leading, and before a jury, a public inquiry was held in Oban in October 1927 and much of what has been written above is based on the evidence presented to that inquiry. After hearing all the evidence, the Sheriff directed the jury to return a formal verdict, as there seemed to be no way of arriving at any conclusion as to the cause of the outbreak of fire. This they did without even retiring. No kind of detailed examination of the ship was carried out, as would be the case to-day and after more than eighty years, it is impossible to know what actually happened on that night. It seemed that Horsburgh had tarried too long after the alarm was given, perhaps to collect personal belongings and had he left when the others did, he might have lived. No one could account for MacRae's movements and he was clearly trapped by the time he tried to make it to the upper deck. It was more difficult to account for Captain MacArthur's death. He had been warned in time and could have gone with one or other of the crew who saw him after he had left his cabin. Perhaps he fainted, overcome by the excitement, or perhaps he had a heart attack. Or perhaps, as an editorial in the *Oban Times* hinted, it was emotion which overcame him and, not wishing to face life without his beloved ship, he chose to die with her.

All that can be said with certainty is that the fire originated in the galley and started very suddenly. It would now be referred to as a fireball and the speed with which the flames took hold would suggest that some inflammable liquid ignited and spread rapidly. Had something been smouldering there, someone would surely have noticed it, perhaps when they came back on board from time ashore. Robert Riddell, the head cook, testified that the galley had been left clean and tidy and that there had been no fat or dripping lying around. Other than Angus Nicolson, no crew member would have had any occasion to visit the galley during the evening. He had made his meal "about ten" and no one noticed anything out of order after that. All was clearly well until some time after midnight, perhaps about half past. There was some discrepancy in the times given as to what happened thereafter, although of course it could not be expected that tired men, abruptly roused from their first sleep, could give an accurate estimate of what happened when. Baldwin said that he had wakened about half past twelve and, of those asleep, he seems to have been the first to have noticed anything amiss and to have awakened himself, rather than being aroused by others. His berth was close to the galley and he mentioned "sheets of flame", suggesting that matters had become very serious in a short time. Captain MacLean said that Nicolson had wakened him about one o'clock, but this does not agree with Nicolson's own account and would seem to err on the late side, as the fire was almost over by then. Nicolson himself said that he found the galley alight at twenty to one, on his return to the main deck from the focsle and Sheriff Wilson picked on the accuracy of his timing, which was in total contrast to the estimates given by everyone else involved. He explained that it had reminded him that he had forgotten to wind up his watch and the Sheriff did not pursue this point.

One report in the Glasgow press mentioned that "poisonous fumes" had also spread and made the task of rescue even harder. These were not mentioned in the inquiry and it is difficult to see how such fumes could have originated.

Other writers who have tried to explain the speed with which the fire spread have mentioned that, with heavy saloon furnishings and layer upon layer of varnish on old woodwork, the ship was a tinder box waiting to explode. But the varnished woodwork was in the saloons and on deck, and, though the fore saloon was badly burned, damage to the main after saloon was limited to windows broken by the stones thrown from the pier by rescuers. As an old ship, she was certainly highly combustible, but the varnish, paintwork and furnishings would seem to have played little, if any part in the origin and spread of the fire.

Unfortunately any records of the disaster made by members of the Oban fire brigade seem not to have survived. It does seem strange, however, that there was no attempt to learn any lessons from the accident. It had taken place when the ship was conveniently moored alongside a pier in a town which had alert police and a good fire service and when the only people on board were crew members who knew the ship intimately and could find their way around even when the interior was filled with smoke. It was agreed by all that the crew had kept their heads, saved themselves quickly, done their best to ensure that there was no one left on board and then attempted a rescue operation under dangerous circumstances and with great risk to their own lives. Even with all their knowledge and skill and with cool heads, they would not have been able to do the same if the accident had happened when she was in service and well out to sea. However, prominent red boxes of hose reels appeared on other steamers of the fleet soon after the disaster.

A rather unpleasant postscript to the tragedy occurred some weeks later, when a woman named Elizabeth Brown was found guilty at Greenock sheriff court of misrepresenting herself to a minister as a relative of Captain MacArthur, now destitute as a result of his death. She was sentenced to nine months imprisonment. An agent commented that drink had been the cause of her downfall.

Calum Robertson went on to have a distinguished career with MacBraynes and this is dealt with in the chapter on *Lochinvar*. For many years after the tragedy, he had difficulty getting to sleep at night.

An epitaph for Captain MacArthur.

The name of the author is not known and the poem is reproduced by courtesy of the *Oban Times*.

Steadfast in service, to life's purpose true,
No blemish stained thy record, nor 'tis rue
Thou lenst adornment to an honoured post
And gave for courtliness a name to toast.

Though the inevitable hour has come at last,
And Death has claimed thee in its fiery blast,
Green as the bay tree we thy memory keep,
Loved and revered around the rolling deep.

10.1 A group of passengers and crew around a paddle box in happier times. The ship has her original funnels and the photograph was taken before 1902.

All photographs by courtesy of the Mitchell Library, Glasgow City Council.

All information on the fire and the subsequent inquiry, and the photograph of Captain MacArthur are taken from various issues of the *Oban Times* and the *Glasgow Herald* in September and October 1927.

10.3 After the fire, *Grenadier* lies partly submerged at the North Pier, with *Fusilier* behind. The North Pier was being rebuilt at the time.

10.2 Captain MacArthur

10.4 At Ardrossan, the superstructure has been removed but the fine lines of the hull and the beautiful clipper bow and figurehead can still be appreciated.

11 Working for the Goods Service
As told by Donnie MacKinnon

I WAS BORN IN SLEAT. There was a certain amount of seafaring in my family, since my grandfather had worked on yachts in his youth and my father had followed him in this. However, he had then come ashore, learned to drive and set up a haulage business at Camus Cross in Sleat, where he also worked a croft. When I left school, I went off to Inverness as an apprentice motor mechanic. After I had completed this, I returned to Skye and, having heard that MacBraynes were looking for staff on the Island, I applied for and was given a post in Armadale garage in 1969. In the following year, I obtained my PSV licence. At that time, the buses allocated to the garage were all Bedfords, of which there were five in summer, fewer in winter. The goods vehicle fleet comprised four lorries, three of which were also Bedfords and one an Albion Chieftain. The local manager was Danny MacLean, who had operated his own fleet until it was taken over by MacBraynes in 1948[1]. He was responsible for both the road services and the pier and remained with the Company until the formation of Caledonian MacBrayne in 1973. As the car ferry service was now in operation – worked usually by *Clansman* – Armadale pier was busier than it had ever been. There were five crossings to and from Mallaig each day and on the first run of the day, at 8am from Mallaig, there were often passengers on one or other of the new circular tours, who had slept aboard. Tour P, for example, offered six days in Skye, Harris and Lewis for (in 1969) £34 from Glasgow and Armadale garage was responsible for providing the coach to take these passengers to Uig.

Some of the timetable for the goods vehicles was based on delivering the weekly cargo unloaded by *Loch Dunvegan* at Armadale.on a Wednesday, quite often in the late evening and staff had to be available to load some of the cargo directly on to the lorries. Cargo consisted of asbestos slates and general building materials for the Department of Agriculture stores in Broadford, Dunvegan and Uig. In the Spring time, cargo included fertilisers and basic slag, which was nasty to handle as it was very dense and dirty. They were contained in bags of 1cwt (51kg) capacity. You were never sure what you might have to unload as the cargo was very mixed – food stuffs, furniture, machinery, hay, animal feeds, etc.

The main cargo being exported from Armadale was whisky and its by-products, which went to Glasgow via Kyle and Stornoway. *Loch Dunvegan* used to pick up bales of wool in Kyle which had been delivered by lorries from the Glasgow depot. Other work for the Ardvasar lorries was hauling building blocks and lime from Torlundy and Torrin, empty whisky barrels from the rail head at Kyle to Carbost, and in the spring and autumn, cattle and sheep floating.

About that time, a new service was started, called The Glasgow Express. It was a nightly service; the goods were loaded in ships containers and the larger lorries would carry four and the smaller lorries two. The containers were offloaded in Mallaig and brought to Armadale by *Loch Seaforth* in the winter and *Clansman* in summer, and their contents delivered to all parts of Skye, including Uig where they were loaded onto trailers for delivery to the Uists by the car ferry *Hebrides*. As road transport got busier, a lorry service was started from Ardvasar to Glasgow and I was a frequent driver on this run. It was worked either via Kyle or via Mallaig, depending on the times and seasons.. The down journey was made on Tuesday and Thursday, usually loaded with whisky, or sometimes sheep fleeces to Griegs of Bonhill, and the return left Glasgow on the Wednesday and Friday afternoons, to catch the last ferry from Kyle at 11.30pm. Latterly it was all night shift, starting on a Sunday night. I

---

1 The firm traded as MacLean and MacDonald. When MacBraynes took over the business, there were three buses and five lorries in the fleet. The former joined the MacBrayne fleet, but the lorries were either sold off or scrapped.

COACH SERVICES ON SKYE

ARDVASAR - KYLEAKIN (SKYE)
Daily except Sundays

	G	H	E			G	H
	a.m.	a.m.	p.m.	p.m.		a.m.	p.m.	p.m.
Ardvasar - dep.	7 45	8 0	1 55	2 0	Kyleakin Pier - dep.	9 40	3 15	3 30
Armadale Pier „			1 0		Armadale - arr.	11 0	4 43	4 55
Kyleakin - arr.	9 30	9 30	2 25	3 10	Ardvasar „	11 5	4 50	5 0

G—Daily, except Sundays, during school holidays at Xmas, Easter and Summer.
H—Daily except Sundays, except during school holidays at Xmas, Easter and Summer.
B—Daily except Sundays, May to September.
Fares—Ardvasar - Armadale - Kyleakin Single 3/1 Return 13/1. Day Return 10/3.

ARMADALE - PORTREE (SKYE)
Daily except Sundays

	B	J			B	J
	a.m.	p.m.	p.m.		a.m.	p.m.	p.m.
Armadale - dep.	10 30	1 0	5 30	Portree - dep.	9 0	3X 15	5A30
Broadford „	11 20	1 50	6 50	Sligachan „	9 22	3 37	5A55
Sligachan „	12 10p	2 40	7A35	Broadford „	10 10	4 25	6 55
Portree - arr.	12 30	3 0	8A 0	Armadale - arr.	11 0	5 15	7 55

Departure times from Armadale subject to arrival time of ferry from Mallaig.
A—Change at Broadford. B—18th May to 7th September.
J—17th June to 7th September only.
X—From 9th to 14th September, departs at 2.30 p.m. and runs 30 minutes earlier throughout.
Fares—Armadale - Broadford Single 7/- Return 10/9
Armadale - Sligachan Single 10/3 Return 16/7
Armadale - Portree Single 10/10 Return 17/3

PORTREE - KYLEAKIN (SKYE)
Daily except Sundays

				A		A
	a.m.	a.m.	p.m.	p.m.
Portree - dep.	8 35	11 15	3 0	5W30
Sligachan „	9 0	11 40	3 25	5 55
Broadford „	9 45	12 25p	4 10	6 40
Kyleakin - arr.	10 5	12 45	4 30	7 0

	MO	B	C	D	E	F	
	a.m.	a.m.	p.m.	p.m.	p.m.	p.m.	p.m.
Kyleakin - dep.	7 20	10 25	11 45	1 30	4 45	6 30	9 15
Broadford „	7 40	10 43	1 5	2 50	5 5	6 50	9 35
Sligachan „	8 25	11 30	1 50	3 35	5 50	7 35	10 20
Portree - arr.	8 50	11 55	2 15	4 0	6 15	8 0	10 45

A—From 19th May till 28th September only.
B—Monday till Saturday from 18th May till 28th September and Fridays only from 4th October till 15th May, 1964.
C—From 1st July till 31st August.
D—Or 20 minutes after arrival of train.
E—18th May to 15th June and 9th to 28th September only.
F—17th June to 7th September only.
*—Or 10 minutes after arrival of steamer if later than 5.30 p.m.
MO—Mondays only—operates when required.

Fares—Kyleakin - Broadford Single 2/7, Return Fare Double.
Kyleakin - Sligachan Single 5/6, Return Fare Double.
Kyleakin - Portree Single 8/-, Return Fare Double, Day Return 12/7.
Portree - Sligachan Single 2/11, Return Fare Double.
Portree - Broadford Single 5/10, Return Fare Double, Day Return 9/8.

KYLEAKIN - DUNVEGAN
Daily except Sundays—29th April to 28th September.
Mondays, Wednesdays, Fridays and Saturdays until 27th April and from 30th September.

	a.m.		p.m.
Dunvegan - dep.	7 30	Kyleakin - dep.	2 30*
Sligachan „	9 0	Broadford „	2 50
Broadford „	9 45	Sligachan „	3 35
Kyleakin - arr.	10 5	Dunvegan - arr.	5 5

*—Or 30 minutes after arrival of Boat and Train.
Fares—Kyleakin - Dunvegan Single 10/9 Return Fare Double, Day Return 18/7.

PORTREE - KILMALUAG

	A	C		B	D
	a.m.	p.m.		a.m.	p.m.
Portree - dep.	9 30	5 30*	Kilmaluag - dep.	6 45	1 0
Staffin „	10 30	6 30	Flodigarry „	7 0	1 15
Flodigarry „	10 45	6 45	Staffin „	7 15	1 30
Kilmaluag - arr.	11 00	7 0	Portree - arr.	8 15	2 30

A—Saturdays only October to May—Tuesdays, Thursdays and Saturdays, June to September.
B—Mondays and Saturdays only, October to May—Daily except Sundays, June to September.
C—Daily except Sundays and Wednesdays, October to May—Daily except Wednesdays, June to September.
D—Tuesdays, Wednesdays, Thursdays, Fridays and Saturdays only, from June to September.
*—Or 10 minutes after arrival of steamer.
Fares—Portree - Kilmaluag Single 7/1. Return Fare Double, Day Return 10/3.

PORTREE - PEINCHORRAN
Fridays only

	p.m.	p.m.		p.m.	p.m.
Portree - dep.	1 0	5 15	Peinchorran - dep.	1 35	5 55
Peinchorran - arr.	1 30	5 50	Portree - arr.	2 15	6 25

Fares—Portree - Peinchorran Single 3/7. Return 5/2.

All Passengers and their Luggage, Goods and Livestock carried subject to Company's Conditions of Carriage as specified in Sailing Bills, Notices and Announcements.

J. H. Ltd.

11.1 A leaflet describing the coach services on Skye, summer 1963. (Author's collection)

enjoyed this, as the pleasure of driving through Glencoe on a frosty moonlit night, with snow covered hills, made up for any fatigue. There were also trips to Inverness with sheep and cattle at the times of livestock sales. Containers, of which I have a preserved example, were in use by this time and four could be taken on the larger lorries. Glasgow drivers also came up to Kyle with wool.

There were occasional spells of driving on the buses in summer – duplicates, or tours via Portree and Dunvegan under contract to Granville Tours of Grimsby, and tours from local hotels to Elgol. The service buses went to Broadford, Kyleakin and Portree, although the frequency did not match that of the present services on Skye. The year-round service left Portree at 8.45am, returning from Armadale at 1pm, but there were two additional workings in each direction in summer. Buses awaited the arrival of the ferry from Mallaig – they were all Bedfords and considered to be great wee buses.

The atmosphere at the Ardvasar garage was a very happy one, but with the arrival of the Scottish Transport Group as owners of MacBraynes, changes were in the air from 1970 onwards. The garage was closed in 1971 and the lorries and drivers were transferred to Kyle. The bus services were transferred to Highland Omnibuses and, as part of the Scottish Bus Group, began to be affected by the industrial relations problems of the companies in the Lowlands. Although the lorry services continued for a time under the MacBrayne name, it was feared that these might also be disposed of in the future. In the event, under the auspices of MacBrayne Haulage Ltd, these were to survive and prosper until forced by the Thatcher government into private ownership in 1985.

Just immediately to the north of Armadale pier there is a filling station. This had been built by Shell in 1964, to coincide with the inauguration of the car ferry services, and had been leased to MacBraynes. It was to be the only one they ever operated. Naturally the STG were not interested in running filling stations and gave up the lease. In their place, I moved in as lessee and later owner, and remained at the garage until retirement in 2007.

11.2 One of the "great wee buses", Bedford OLAZ no.151, awaits ferry passengers at Armadale pier. It was new in 1952 and sold by MacBraynes to a local operator on Skye in 1967. The destination display "DUPLICATE" was one of the Company's idiosyncrasies and was useful only if you knew what service was running in duplicate. (Chris Orchard, Online Transport Archive)

11.3 Drivers Donald John Morrison (left) and Donnie MacKinnon awaiting passengers at Duisdale Hotel for a tour to Elgol, c1970. Donald John, from Glendale, was a driver in the goods service and alternated with Donnie on the Glasgow run until he became a full-time bus driver. (D MacKinnon)

11.4 Farquhar J MacInnes (left) and Danny MacLean load up the van for Uig at Ardvasar in 1970. Farquhar was from Teangue and became the alternate driver on the Glasgow run after Donald Morrison joined the buses. The lorry is L121, a 7.5 ton Bedford, new in 1967. (D MacKinnon)

11.5 The gentleman on the left is thought to be the Company's Catering Superintendent. He is at Ardvasar, outside the hotel, with Danny MacLean. The bus driver is Angus Nicolson and the bus is a Bedford with Duple body, from the series 179-186. (D MacKinnon)

MacBraynes Garage at Ardvasar, c 1955

11.6 Ardvasar depot c1955. MacBraynes had in 1962 29 depots, none of which were very large. With 25 buses, Fort William was the busiest and Ardvasar was well down the list. (D MacKinnon)

11.7 A scene outside Portree bus and lorry depot in the mid-1960s. The lorry at the head of the line, L114, was a Bedford 5 ton S type, acquired in 1960. It was used on the Kye-Portree-Uig mail run. The first bus, bound for Dunvegan, is no.211, a Bedford VAS1 with Willowbrook body, delivered in 1966 and the last one, which has just left the depot (out of sight on the left) is of the same type, while the two intermediate vehicles are Bedford/Duple coaches. The depot is still used, by Stagecoach, who took over operations on Skye in 2008. (The Omnibus Society)

11.8 On what is clearly a thoroughly dreich day, Bedford CSZ1 no.18 awaits passengers for Portree on the ferry slip at Kyleakin, while a large van is manoeuvred off the CSP turntable ferry *Broadford* and buses of two other local operators wait further down the slipway. After a mercifully short passage huddled in the cramped covered accommodation on this ferry, passengers no doubt appreciated the comfort of the Duple Midland body. At this time there were in summer five services connecting the two places, but only two in winter. (Harry Luff, Online Transport Archive)

11.9 *Loch Dunvegan* in Oban bay. (Laird Parker, courtesy of Frank Walton)

12 The Sound of Mull – *Lochinvar* and *Lochearn*

T
HE FIRST MACBRAYNE STEAMER to be permanently associated with the run from Oban to Tobermory was *Carabinier*, a former Isle of Wight ferry. She was bought in 1894 and served until *Lochinvar* came out in 1908.

To many people in Mull, *Lochinvar* was always associated with toothache and a visit to the dentist. There being then no one of that profession on Mull, any dental matter could be dealt with only by going to Oban and that could only be done by boarding *Lochinvar* on her morning sailing and taking advantage of the two hours which would, with luck, be available before she set off on her return trip, to arrive back around 4 in the afternoon. If the patient was in pain, they were no doubt glad to spend whatever time was needed to have the problem molar dealt with, but it was a long day if only a small filling were all that was required. In winter, sea-sickness might combine with toothache to make matters almost unbearable. On one occasion in the war years, when a certificate of residence was required by Mull residents when travelling to and from Oban, one lady, Connie by name, had the misfortune of arriving in Oban and being then prevented, by a bayonet-wielding soldier, from leaving the ship. In her misery and haste to catch the morning sailing, she had forgotten the certificate and therefore seemed a suspicious person to the authorities. Only when Captain MacDonald intervened, loudly and forcefully, from the bridge, was she permitted to come ashore and was then marched, still in agony and at bayonet point, through Oban's streets to the surgery, and back again when all was over. It was a relieved Connie who stepped on to Tobermory pier that night. There were no other medical facilities on the island at that time and surgical cases had also to be taken to

12.1 *Carabinier* makes a fine sight in the Sound of Mull. Coal and labour were cheap then.

12.2 The crew of *Carabinier* on deck at Tobermory.

Both views by kind permission of the Mull Musuem.

12.3 An annotated photograph of *Lochinvar* post-1949.

12.4 A group of passengers (with dog) on the promenade deck of *Lochinvar* in the 1950s.

Both views by kind permission of the Mull Museum.

hospital in Oban on board *Lochinvar*. When such cases were travelling, the forward seat in the saloon was curtained off, to allow them some privacy. In bad weather, being passed on board on a stretcher was not a pleasant experience.

Of course local people used *Lochinvar* for other reasons. Some did not want to entrust their business to a local lawyer and preferred to deal in the anonymity of an office in Oban. Any trip to Glasgow began and ended with *Lochinvar*. As there was then no high school on Mull, any pupils who wanted to progress beyond third year had to attend Oban Academy and live in one of the attached hostels, one being provided for each sex. It was exile for a term at a time, though parents sometimes came down for a brief reunion on a Saturday. At the end of term, the sight of the little red funnel at the North Pier was more than welcome. Farmers who were both customers of MacBraynes for the shipment of animals and passengers to and from livestock sales in Oban had a very close relationship with the Company. A good lunch in the ship's dining saloon, served on departure from the port, was just the thing to crown a successful morning at the sales. One farmer often extended his stay in Oban after the sales, but sent his dog home on board *Lochinvar*. The crew looked after it and put it ashore via the Craignure ferry, from whose landing place it made its own way home. Newly-married couples generally spent their honeymoon away from the island and a pleasing custom observed by the crew was to dress the vessel overall when such a couple were coming home to Mull. Local children would then exclaim "Here comes *Lochinvar* full of flags".

If a Mull resident did not want to spend a whole day going to Oban simply to collect something such as some new clothes which had previously been ordered, all they had to do was to have a word with a member of the ship's crew and the item would be picked up and brought back to Mull for them to collect at the pier in the evening.

When a day in Oban was being planned, it was best to avoid a Wednesday if at all possible, since on that day, *Lochinvar* diverted to call at Lismore on her return journey and this could cause delays. It also meant that she did not reach Tobermory until after 6pm, making it a very long day indeed. The crew were compensated by an extra 2/- (10p) per week (c1946) in their pay packets, but passengers had to pay the normal fare. The main reason for the Lismore call seems to have been to take horses and heavy cargo to the island. Over the years the Mull schedule altered little. In 1954 *Lochinvar* left Tobermory at 7.30am (Wednesdays) or 7.45 and arrived in Oban at 10.30. Wednesdays excepted, she left again at 1.15pm and was back at Tobermory exactly three hours later. En route she called at Drimnin, Salen, Lochaline and Craignure. There were piers at Salen and Lochaline, but at the other places, goods and passengers were transhipped by flit boat. A signal from *Lochinvar*'s hooter would warn the ferrymen in advance if one or two such boats were going to be required. Of course the amount of cargo to be handled had a very direct bearing on whether or not she kept to the timetable and cattle who did not want to come aboard could upset the schedule to a considerable extent. If they could be persuaded to jump straight into the ferryboat, so much the better.

Lochinvar was the third motor vessel to be built for David MacBrayne, in 1908. She was also the first large motor vessel, designed for open sea service, to operate in British waters. She was, however, only 145ft (44.2m) in length and everything on board was on a small scale. The purser's office, outside which passengers queued to buy tickets, was virtually only a large cupboard. The first class saloon was comfortable enough and below there was a dining saloon, where excellent breakfasts were served on leaving Tobermory. These may have been some consolation for the early rising necessitated by the 7.30am departure. Steerage accommodation was spartan, consisting of two small saloons, and in 1928 was described in Parliament as "not entirely adequate". It also lacked heating. At least until the 1950s, class distinctions were rigidly enforced on board. As cargo space was limited, steerage passengers often found themselves sharing the after-deck space with a flock of sheep, or some horses. At sale time, there could be 1,500 sheep on board and on

12.5 *Claymore* approaching Tobermory when acting as a car ferry. She could take eleven cars, which seemed ample accommodation when she was new in 1955, but very soon became insufficient. *Loch Carron* waits off-shore on the left. (National Maritime Museum, neg. no.N33707)

12.6 Loading a car by sling on to the Inner Isles steamer at Tobermory in 1936.

If road and air travel both appeal, then this picture must be very satisfying. A 1936 scene at Tobermory with an airborne Austin 7 taking off for the Inner Isles ferry. In the foreground an Alvis waits with trepidation for the same treatment. Dr J. Euan Dawson of Hampshire sent this photograph.

12.7 Mr Peter MacNab driving on to *Lochinvar* at Salen in 1936.

Both views by kind permission of the Mull Museum,

12.8 Captain Black Jr in the wheelhouse of *Lochinvar*. (By kind permission of the Mull Museum)

12.9 Mate Calum Robertson on the promenade deck c1950. A boy in the regulation school cap helps to date this photo. (Iain Robertson)

such days, class distinctions were abolished. The vessel then tended to run anything up to three hours late. An idea of what travel on board was like in the 1920s, as seen by holiday-makers, can be gained from the novel "The Day of Small Things" by O. Douglas (Anna Buchan), who must have used the ship herself on a holiday trip. Indeed *Lochinvar's* fame among tourists to Mull spread far and wide and in the 1950s one lady was so anxious to travel on her that she left husband and car at Tobermory, to follow later on *Claymore*, and sailed with a friend back to Oban at the end of a motoring holiday on Mull.

These particular passengers had been booked on *Claymore*, but from the 1920s cars were a regular part of *Lochinvar's* cargo and were loaded and unloaded by planks, this operation being managed in the 1950s by Calum Robertson, the Mate. Although the planks looked very shaky, the sight of this experienced officer guiding the car and giving hand signals to the driver gave even the most nervous motorist confidence. When *Lochearn* appeared on the Mull service, cars were hoisted on and off in a sling made up of ropes. A Tobermory lady, Mrs MacDonald, was in later life affected by rheumatism and found the climb up the passenger gangway very difficult. In due course her son bought a car and the crew then solved the problem by allowing her to remain in the car as it was hoisted aboard and then make for the saloon once it was safely secured on the ship. She seems to have enjoyed the experience and commended the excellent view of Tobermory which it afforded her. Present-day Health and Safety rules would not have allowed this, but it was a practical solution to the problem faced by someone who had used the ships for years and was a valued passenger.

When *Lochinvar* was first commissioned in 1908, the east side of Mull had its own thrice-weekly steamer service, latterly worked by *Dirk*, and this sailing also served Coll and Tiree. This timetable also provided for calls at Tobermory, since it was then much easier to go by sea from there to Bunessan and other villages on the east side than it was to take to the road. However, this service was suspended in 1914 and not resumed after the war. All cargo for that part of Mull had then to be shipped by *Lochinvar* and go forward from Craignure or Tobermory on the new road services. In addition much of the heavier cargo, which had formerly come direct from Glasgow on *Claymore* or *Chieftain* now came by rail or, increasingly, road to Oban, again to go forward on *Lochinvar*. More and more cars were being shipped. The result was that the vessel ended up carrying much more cargo than she had been designed to take and it was a tribute to the skill of the crew that space could still be found for it all, without encroaching too much on the passenger space. The lack of power on the crane became a definite drawback. After 1919 there was an increased demand for short cruises from Oban and, while these were normally carried out by *Mountaineer* or *Fusilier*, *Lochinvar* was pressed into service on Wednesdays and Fridays when she had a longer lay-over time in Oban. She was hardly ideal for this purpose, since deck space and saloon accommodation were both limited.

Naturally regular passengers and crew members became well acquainted over the years. Captains Black, MacLean, MacDonald and Black were familiar figures over the period from 1920 to the end of the vessel's association with Mull. The two Blacks were father and son and themselves Muileachs, hailing from Bunessan, where the father of Captain Black Sr. had owned a 40 ton sailing smack, with which he carried on a trade in general cargo and coals. The former had been master of *Lochshiel* and came to *Lochinvar* in 1921, remaining in command until his death in 1927. Malcolm Black took over from Captain MacDonald in 1947. He had been Mate of *King George V* from her first year with MacBraynes (1936) and was with her at the evacuations of Dunkirk and Boulogne. He went on to command *Lochearn* and when he retired in April 1965, he was presented by local people, in a ceremony at Bunessan, with a chiming clock and a wallet full of notes, while Mrs Black was given a Celtic brooch and a set of teaspoons. Captain MacDonald was father of Quartermaster Douglas MacDonald, mentioned later. At Oban, captains of the ship made a point of greeting returning islanders and asking after family members.

The honour of the longest continuous association with the ship belonged to the Mate, Calum Robertson, another crew member known for a genial and friendly nature. He came from a fishing family on Mull, his father, William Robertson, being a lobster fisherman and also a sail-maker. He joined MacBraynes in December 1911 and sailed first as deck-hand on *Dirk*, which at that time served the route from Tobermory to Bunessan, Coll and Tireee via Oban. During the war, in which *Dirk* was lost in 1918, he served in fleet auxiliaries and on returning to MacBraynes in 1919, transferred to *Lochinvar*, serving on her as deck-hand until 1926. This duty was followed by a year on *Grenadier* and, as stated in chapter 10, he displayed great courage on the night on which she met her end. He became Second Officer of *Loch Dunvegan* in 1930 and Mate of *Claymore* in 1931, being aboard for her last voyage to Bo'ness. He then served on *Clydesdale* and various other ships before being transferred to *Lochinvar* in 1939, remaining with her until 1954 when he became relief master. During the second world war, he was instrumental in rescuing survivors of a Sunderland flying boat which crashed near Lismore. In due course his daughter married John MacKenzie, purser on board in the 1950s. He finished work in April 1956 and enjoyed a long retirement of over twenty years. As an officer, he was known for his total imperturbability and infectious cheerfulness and, when he was absent from *Lochinvar*, she was not quite the same ship.

The work of the purser on board *Lochinvar* was very different to that on excursion ships such as *King George V*. There was a greater variety of ticket to be issued, although some passengers would hold through rail/steamer tickets to and from Glasgow and other towns. Passenger numbers were much smaller, but there was a great deal of cargo to be handled as the vessel called at four ports on her voyages between Tobermory and Oban and vice versa. To these on a Wednesday was added the call at Lismore. On board, cargo had to be carefully arranged and for the ferry ports, had to be near the opening doors in the bulwarks aft. It may have looked untidy, but it was well ordered chaos. A lady passenger for Lochaline once almost upset the system when she boarded at Oban and put her case down among some others. When she informed the baggage man of this, he asked her to move the case to the other side of the pile, mentioning that "That side of the boat does not go to Lochaline". Just after 1945, a local bus operator on Mull, Cowe by name, took delivery of his first new bus since 1939. It was a Bedford, much larger than those he had operated up till then and when *Lochinvar* rounded Calve Island, he was horrified to see that both the bonnet and the rear end of his precious bus were hanging over the ship's side. It must have been a fairly calm day and it must also have been the longest item that the ship ever carried. When car traffic became important, in the 1950s, a relief ship, often *Lochnevis* but sometimes one of the cargo ships and later *Claymore*, was provided to cater for this and *Lochinvar* and later *Lochearn* were left to concentrate on general cargo runs.

Archibald Black was *Lochinvar*'s purser for almost thirty years. He was brought up in Oban, where his father was provost for some years, and it was intended that he would make his career in banking. This was at a time when parents had to pay a bank the large sum of £5 to take on a young man. This sum was duly paid over, but not long afterwards, Archibald began to suffer from ill health – which would in fact dog him for much of his life – and it was decided that he would do better in an open air job. The company's Oban agent was sympathetic and he duly took up the post of purser on *Lochinvar*, remaining with her until his retirement.

It was a long day's work. The purser had to be on board soon after 7am to check cargo and issue tickets to the first passengers and he was seldom free until she reached Oban. After a brief pause for lunch, everything happened in reverse, but now with much more cargo. The purser's duties did not finish until after she had arrived back at Tobermory and he would be lucky to be home again by 6pm..The ticket office was small and cramped and Archibald would often bring work home with him at night. Once a week he paid out the crew's wages. It was hard work, but Archibald seems to have liked it and been happy on board the ship. He was one of the MacBrayne pursers who zealously observed the on-board notice that passengers found using the saloon "for any purpose" would be charged saloon fare and some local people, hoping for a cheap trip with some comfort, resented this. On the other hand, one of the managers in Oban dubbed him "The most honest man that ever worked for MacBraynes". That being so, it was especially hurtful that, when a general increase in wages was announced, he was not included. When he queried this,

12.10 Steward John Hogg and Chief Engineer Donald Kennedy on *Lochinvar*. (By kind permission of the Mull Museum)

the Oban manager informed him that, as he had been taken on as a favour to his father, he would not receive the new salary. It was a poor reward for years of hard work and it rankled, even although his salary was later increased to the new levels. Incidents such as this show that the firm was not always run as one big, happy family.

Despite his poor health, Archibald Black lived to enjoy some retirement, until he died in Oban hospital after an operation. He was replaced by John MacKenzie, likewise well known as a cheerful and obliging man who, in addition to his normal duties, was always willing to accept letters for posting on the mainland or to cash a cheque, in the days when cash machines were unknown and banks had restricted opening hours. John went on to become MacBrayne's agent in Oban. Most of the crew lived ashore in Tobermory.

Of the crew, one particularly well-know character was Jimmy ("Curly") Cameron, whose nickname, by the 1950s, commemorated only long-gone locks. He was from Tobermory itself and first joined the ship in 1937, to serve as stevedore, baggage man and general deckhand. John MacFarlane was known as "laughing Johnny" for his good humour and ability to see the funny side of almost any situation. From long experience, he also had a particularly good way with cattle, which were accommodated in pens on the main deck and could be awkward when in transit. Donald MacDiarmid was quartermaster and John MacCallum another well-known deckhand in the 1950s.

Douglas MacDonald was born in 1928, into a Gaelic-speaking family. However, he was brought up speaking English, this still being in the days when Gaelic was thought to be a drawback for any aspiring young man. His father was Allan MacDonald, born in 1889 in Corpach and his mother was from Stornoway. Allan MacDonald first went to sea in sailing ships and then joined MacBraynes, where he worked his way up through the ranks, to become first mate then last captain of *Chieftain*, then *Claymore* (1881). He then served as Captain on a variety of MacBrayne ships, including *Lochearn*, *Lochfyne*, *Plover*, *Clydesdale*, *Mountaineer* and finally *Lochinvar*.

Douglas first went to sea in 1944, aged 16, serving in the naval trawlers which attended to barrage balloons in Portsmouth. He then spent some time on the Clyde, on board the tugs and tenders owned or managed by the Clyde Shipping Company, particularly *Paladin* and *Romsey*. He was asked by Captain Black to work on *Lochinvar* as relief for Kenneth Graham as deck boy for two weeks one summer and ended up staying on her for twelve years. However, as some crew were with her for thirty years, he remained a comparative newcomer. Under the eye of the Mate, Calum Robertson, he learned to steer, not an easy task on a black day in the Sound of Mull, and he also became an expert on the ship's crane. The crane concerned had been part of the ship's equipment since she first entered service, when it had been supplied by Chalmers, Scott and Co. of Motherwell, and could originally handle a load of five tons. Unfortunately in 1934 *Lochinvar* acquired the dignity of a funnel located admidships (previously the exhaust was carried up through three spindly pipes on the after deck) and to clear this, a goose neck was fitted to the crane, which now had to work over the top of the funnel. Thereafter it could manage only two tons and as the volume and weight of cargo increased, this became a definite drawback. However, the post of craneman carried a certain glamour and young boys on Mull looked up to Douglas, with his skill in manipulating difficult loads on and off the ship.

Although the ship was small and the galley minute, without running water, full catering was available to cabin passengers in the dining saloon on the lower deck, which seated 32. The companionway down to this was decorated with painted scenes depicting the story of Young Lochinvar and, in the 1950s, a visiting delegation of Soviet scientists were so taken with these and the tale they told that they presented Captain Black with a medal of the permanent Soviet Agricultural Exhibition in Moscow. These paintings were removed when the ship was sold in 1960 and presented to the warship of the same name, but photographs of them can be seen in the Mull Musuem in Tobermory. Water was obtained from a pump situated on the after deck and to obtain this, the galley boy often had to negotiate a herd of cattle. Toast for breakfast was made on the range. In the galley, cooks over the years performed miracles of catering, one most fondly remembered being John MacIver, the "Wee Cook", who was from Glasgow and invariably cheerful, no matter how busy he was. He always found time too to chat to those who came to stand outside the galley, that being one of the few warm places on board on a cold day. A favourite dish at lunch time was liver and the smell of this cooking was one which commonly greeted passengers as they boarded at Oban. However, some passengers had other preferences. The local gentry often travelled on the ship, to the extent that she gained the nickname of "The Colonels' Mess". One such regular was Sir Charles MacLean, who became Lord Chamberlain. Having wined and dined on exquisite food in the best restaurants in London, he always thoroughly enjoyed a plate of mince and tatties (mashed potatoes) on board when returning home to Mull. Sir Charles was very fond of the vessel and had great respect for her crew. To show his gratitude to them for many trips to and from Oban, he invited the entire crew and their wives to Duart Castle one Sunday, providing a coach to take them from Tobermory. Refreshments were served when they arrived and later they sat down to a sumptuous buffet lunch. Another regular was Mr Forrester of Ardnacross Farm, who likewise demonstrated his high opinion of the crew in a very practical way. In 1953 television was a novelty in Mull and reception in Tobermory was in any case poor, due to the surrounding hills. When the Coronation naval review was held in June of that year, he brought the crew over to his farm to watch the event, a first time for most of them and a chance which they greatly appreciated. In the 1950s, the dining saloon was presided over by John Hogg, Chief Steward, in full steward's uniform. He was supported by Sam Berry, Steward and Euan Campbell, who had come from Tiree to join the ship as pantry boy and who was later replaced by Eddie Wilson. At a different time Messrs Johnstone and Ralph had also been stewards.

It would be assumed that *Lochinvar* did not provide any cabin accommodation for passengers and generally this would be correct. However, one regular often slept on board while travelling and had his own favourite cabin. This was Bobby MacLeod, of Scottish country dance band fame, who owned the Mishnish Hotel in Tobermory. After a hard night's playing at a late ceilidh, he would

12.11 The group photo of the crew of *Lochinvar* and their wives on the visit to Duart Castle.

They are:-

Back row (l to r): David Samson (Second Steward), Douglas MacDonald (Donkeyman), James Cameron (Deckhand), Captain Black

Second row: Eddie Wilson (Pantry Boy), Donald MacDiarmid (Quartermaster), John MacKenzie (Purser)

Third row: Donald Kennedy (Engineer), Calum Robertson (Mate), John MacCabe (Second Engineer)

Fourth row: Janet MacLean, Lady MacLean, Mrs Hogg, John Hogg (Chief Steward), Mrs MacCabe

Fifth row: Mrs MacKenzie

Front row: Mrs Black, Mrs Kennedy, Mrs MacDiarmid, Mrs Robertson

(Sir Charles MacLean, reproduced by kind permission of the Mull Museum)

12.12 *Lochinvar* in war-time grey clears Craignure bay in August 1945, while the ferry boat makes for the shore. (By kind permission of the Mull Museum)

come on board for the morning departure and make straight for the cabin normally used by one of the crew. There he would sleep peacefully, no matter the noise or the weather, until the ship was off Lismore, when he would be wakened by the steward with a cup of tea and a "jeely piece" (bread and jam sandwich). Thus refreshed, he would step ashore at Oban ready for his next venue.

It is also assumed that the ship did not see active service in either world war. While correct as far as the war of 1914-1918 is concerned, this does not quite hold good for the second war. In 1944 US commandos, inspired by the example of the British forces, had begun training in Morvern and travelled to and fro on *Lochinvar*. Unfortunately they used the fine teak railings as support for their guns during practice sessions and the marks remained for the rest of the ship's life. On one otherwise quiet Sunday they decided to "take" Tobermory as a practice for D-day and for added realism fired on the vessel while she lay at her berth.

Along with *Lochness* (*Whisky Galore*) and *Lochnevis* (*Rockets Galore* and an amateur film on Crofting in Skye, made in 1939) *Lochinvar* was one of MacBraynes' film stars. She was used in the film "*I know where I'm going*" made during the second world war and starring Wendy Hiller. Unfortunately something must have happened in the Sound of Mull, since Miss Hiller certainly left Oban on board her, but disembarked at Tobermory, in a downpour, from *Lochearn*. The day in question was in fact fine and would not have produced the desired, dreich effect required by the producer. The problem was solved by stationing two members of the WRNS on the balcony of Tobermory pier and giving them a hose connected to the fire hydrant. When the ship arrived, this was turned on at full pressure and the reputation of the west highlands as a rainy area was safely confirmed. For their part in the production, the two girls received £5 each, a fair sum for those days and no doubt much appreciated.

In December 1944 Louis MacRae joined the engine room staff at the age of 16 as Fourth Engineer. He came from a "MacBrayne" family in Skye, since his father, John MacRae, from Braes, had been a steward on *Cygnet*, in which position he met his future wife, Catherine Johnstone, the stewardess. He then went on to work on *Sheila* and finally became Chief Steward on *Lochness*, on which he remained for many years. *Lochness* at this time was part of the "Skye navy" being crewed largely by men from the Misty Isle. Captain MacArthur and the Chief Engineer John MacDonald were both from Staffin. Louis was educated at Portree Secondary School and on leaving in 1942 became a telegram messenger boy. However, he had an interest in going to sea, following in the footsteps of his older brother Lachlan (Lachie) who had gone deep-sea and who would ultimately become captain of *Loch Arkaig*. When John Noble, purser on *Lochnevis*, mentioned that a junior engineer was required on *Lochinvar*, he applied for the job, to become a lone Sgitheanach among many Muileachs. This occasioned a good deal of ribaldry, but *Lochinvar* was a happy ship and Louis enjoyed his time onboard.

To reach his new ship, he had to travel on *Lochmor* to Mallaig and then by train to Crianlaraich, for a connexion to Oban. Now it happened that the Chief Steward on that ship had also let it be known that he had a vacancy for a young lad and when Louis went down to the dining saloon for a meal, he assumed that he had come to work on board. Great was his disappointment when Louis informed him of his actual destination. In fact his first six months aboard were spent on the Clyde with Captain Graham, since *Lochinvar* was then relieving on the Lochgoil mail run, *Comet* having gone to be re-engined. Since the working day then finished at 3pm, when the ship returned to Greenock, this was a fairly relaxed life and Louis did not find out what hard work really was until the ship returned to her normal station.

Not being a local, Louis had to sleep on board, in one of the small cabins for engineers, located in the focsle. These had bunks for three, but, as most men slept ashore when the ship was on her normal run, there were seldom more than two occupants. Food on board was good and, for war time, quite plentiful. Crews were paid an additional sum for danger money and the Company retained 18/6 (92.5p) per week from their wages for their keep. The Chief Engineer had the luxury of a cabin to himself, complete with a folding wash basin and the emptying of this in the morning was another job for the most junior member of staff. In the event, due to war-time crew shortages,

Louis soon found himself working his way up the ladder to the post of Second Engineer. As long as the Chief also held a certificate for a Second post, there was no problem with this arrangement.

In the course of her long life, *Lochinvar* had three different engines. She was at this time on her second set, fitted in 1926, and was a triple-screw vessel. Generally the crew considered the third engine to be of very little use and not worth the space it occupied ; they calculated that at best it saved six minutes on the Tobermory-Oban run. The engine room at the time of Louis' arrival was in the care of first Duncan Kennedy, with David Coltart as Second, then of Duncan MacKenzie, who came from Lochaber and whose father had also been an engineer with the Company. John MacCabe was second engineer in the 1950s.

Mechanically, the most difficult thing about *Lochinvar* was to start the engines. Those in use in 1945 were started by directing a set of paraffin blow lamps on to the domes on the cylinder heads. These lamps were worked by compressed air and had to be used for about ten minutes, by which time the domes glowed red hot and the lamps could be switched off. The screws also had to be turned over for about ten minutes prior to departure. If all went well, the ship would then assume her normal service speed and set off for Oban. However, if for any reason, such as the arrival of a late passenger on the pier, the Captain returned to the berth, the engines would rapidly cool down and leave the ship without power. The entire process then had to be gone through again and the delay could become quite significant. As the most junior member of the engine room staff, it was Louis' job to see to the blow lamps each morning and to do so, he had to be in the engine room about 7am, so that she would be ready to leave on time. On dark mornings, the blow lamps had to be worked by the light of a small hand lamp, since there was no electric power until the generator was coaxed into life. The start of the return sailing was not so difficult, as the engines remained warm at Oban and could start immediately. However, a 12V heating element with plugs was sometimes used to start them at Oban in summer.

12.13 Chief engineer Duncan Kennedy. (By kind permission of the Mull Museum)

Space in the engine room was, to put it mildly, confined and headroom was just over 6ft (1.82m). Apart from the three engines, each with a compressor, there was also the generator, also with attached compressor and switchgear. This was mounted forward in the engine room and had an impulse starter which ran on petrol. It was started by cranking a handle and after running for about ten minutes, could then be controlled by a lever. Equipment for the hydraulic steering system and the control for the crane also occupied some space in the engine room, along with degaussing equipment (until 1945) and with all that gear crammed into a small space, there was not much room for the crew.

In between all the chores associated with the engines, Louis also had the task of looking after Captain Black's motor bike. He lived in Salen and rode to and from the ship each day.

Given that the ship was one of the pioneers of motor propulsion, *Lochinvar* proved to be supremely reliable and, once started, seldom caused any trouble. However, on one occasion, she stopped dead, totally without power, soon after leaving Tobermory. The cause of the failure was an airlock in all pipes, since the engineer responsible had failed to bleed these. This operation then had to be carried out manually, before the ship could be moved. Unlike some of the later MacBrayne motor vessels, she was fairly smooth-running, though until she received her third set of engines the noise level was uncomfortably high and, on her first set of engines, she had the nasty habit of spitting out particles of unburnt paraffin from the pipes that served as funnels. Passengers noticed the smell of paraffin and, later, diesel oil, which, mingled with those of frying herring, liver and sheep, gave the vessel her own unique aroma. (Others remembered it as kippers, porridge and paraffin.) In a paper presented to the MacBrayne board in 1946, the General Manager, H T Leith suggested that the vessel was overage and should be retired when *Loch Seaforth* was ready. This did not happen and instead she was very thoroughly rebuilt and re-engined in 1949, with a second-hand set of Paxman six-cylinder diesels. It was thought that this operation made her less manoeuvrable than she had been, although it did create more space in the engine room. She was also fitted with a wheelhouse, which certainly gave the helmsman some welcome shelter, but the added top weight also contributed to a lack of manoeuvrability. However, by that date Louis had left the ship, as a serious illness in February 1947 put him ashore for good and his later career was to be in land-based engineering.

Lochinvar was a good sea boat and coped well with the often confused seas which can be met off the southern tip of Lismore. She seldom missed a sailing. On 28 January 1927 she left Oban slightly late, at 1.25pm, and when she came out from the shelter of Kerrara, it became clear that a major storm was brewing. Captain MacLean decided to take her up the Firth for shelter and, in what were by now mountainous seas and driving spray, he carefully took her through the Corran Narrows, to anchor in calmer waters off Ardgour. In Mull, there was some alarm when she failed to show up, as no one knew where she actually was, but she finally reached Tobermory safely on the Saturday and a passenger, who was himself a yachtsman, was so impressed by the seamanship displayed by the Captain and crew that he penned a letter of thanks, to be published in the *Oban Times*. Lochaline pier could be difficult in a south-easterly wind and occasionally this call had to be omitted. Only storms such as that which sank *Princess Victoria* on 31 January 1953 could keep her in port and even then she would set off as soon as conditions improved and the crews would do their best to get back on schedule. Occasionally, when coming south, she had to turn back off Lochaline, when it became obvious that conditions would be really bad in the Firth of Lorne and on one such occasion she returned to Tobermory, only to find that her berth was now occupied by a cargo vessel which took most of the day to unload. Meanwhile the passengers, many within sight of their own homes, had to make themselves as comfortable as possible, to endure the long wait before they could land. When cars became relatively common from 1950 onwards, some passengers would drive to Salen and board *Lochinvar* there, thus saving themselves at least half an hour on the journey. Local passengers, homeward bound from Oban, would hope that someone with a car would be on board to offer a lift from Salen and so shorten their journey too. Unfortunately Salen pier could pose problems if the wind were from the north east and

12.14 *Lochearn* approaching Tobermory in a gale, taken during the time when Douglas MacDonald was a member of her crew. One car has been hoisted clear of the foredeck to counteract the ship's list. (Calum MacMillan, by courtesy of Douglas MacDonald and Ronald MacIntyre)

12.15 A much more peaceful scene c1960, as the ship approaches the North Pier in Oban c1960. Only an Austin car and a van occupy the foredeck. (Laird Parker, by courtesy of Frank Walton)

Lochinvar would not attempt the call, leaving the motorists then to make their way back from Tobermory simply to pick up their cars and remark that the journey had taken much longer than if they had gone by ship all the way.

Lochinvar may have been as one traveller put it, an acquired taste, but the longer she was known, the more she was appreciated. Many were sorry to lose her in 1955 when, with the arrival of *Claymore*, there was a reshuffle of ships in the fleet and she became spare vessel, being transferred to the Mallaig-Kyle-Portree route in 1959. She was not a success in this role and was looked on unfavourably by the people of Skye, the most vocal critic being Dame Flora MacLeod of MacLeod, who complained, in a letter to the press, of "utter drabness and utter miserable squalidness". She had travelled on the ship when en route to a meeting of the Scottish Tourist Board. Another correspondent then suggested that she was doing at least as much harm to the Skye tourist business as was *Lochinvar*. Muileachs were more than a little upset by the harsh things which were said about their former stalwart. The whole matter eventually reached the local MP, Neil MacLean, but the experiment of using her on what was by this date basically a cruise was not repeated and she made her last run for MacBraynes on her old service, on 28 May 1960. She was sold to English owners for use as a Thames excursion vessel.

In her place *Lochearn* came on to the Mull service in 1955. She was under the command of Captain MacInnes of Gometra and later Captains Calum Robertson and Malcolm Black. *Lochearn* was appreciated for her much more comfortable accommodation, but she nevertheless lacked something of the family atmosphere which had prevailed on *Lochinvar*. It was a great advantage that cars could now be craned aboard. However, the growth of motor traffic was such that within a short time the cargo vessel *Loch Dunvegan* had to be called on to perform a car ferry run to Salen on peak Saturdays. *Lochearn* had not been long on the service when, in August 1956, the Queen visited Oban and it occurred to the MacBrayne management that the islanders served by her would appreciate the chance to have a day trip to see the royal visitor. *Lochearn* was duly dispatched from Tobermory in the small hours to Tiree and Coll to pick up the anticipated crowds of passengers. The stewards made preparations to serve breakfasts to about one hundred diners. Unfortunately it was a foul day and only three passengers boarded at the islands. The sea was rough and by the time Tobermory was reached, two of these had had enough and disembarked, leaving one passenger to go on to Oban. The rain did not let up all day and the Queen's feet were so wet by the afternoon that a replacement pair of shoes had hurriedly to be bought for her in a local shop. It is not recorded what happened to all the material prepared for the breakfasts.

Lochearn brought a touch of feminine company to the Sound of Mull service, since she carried two stewardesses. Her chief steward, Dugald MacTavish, was very interested in making and repairing wireless sets, while Charles Hunter, the wireless operator, was an accomplished fiddler.

Lochnevis was also on the Sound of Mull service at various times in the 1950s and, with her considerably greater speed, upset the usual domestic schedule for Tobermory housewives who were married to crew members. Some of these had a good view over the Sound from their kitchen and usually began preparations for the evening meal when they saw *Lochinvar* come out from Drimnin. There was plenty of time to have everything on the table by the time the man of the house returned. In 1934 the poet J. W. had welcomed *Lochnevis* in verse as "Skye's new fairy boat" and, referring to her arrival in Portree, at 4pm, included a couplet:

"Housewives keep the kettle boiling,
  Table ready spread for tea".

The housewives of Tobermory now found that they had to get the kettle boling and the table ready spread at a rather earlier hour if all was to be ready in time. If they waited until she had left Drimnin, it was too late.

12.16 *Lochnevis* in a view taken after 1954. (Donald Hodgson Collection)

12.17 MacCallum, Orme's *Hebrides* ultimately became a member of the MacBrayne fleet, in which capacity she is seen alongside Oban's North Pier in the early 1950s. (Laird Parker, by courtesy of Frank Walton)

12.18 *Lochbuie* at speed in the Sound of Mull. (R Henderson collection)

In "*Behold the Hebrides*" (1968), Douglas Sutherland commented that the local representatives always seemed to have time for a chat and to tell visitors of people and places that they ought to see. Agents were important figures in local communities and also had to carry out some of the functions now looked after by local tourist offices.

Dick Henderson was born in the Glasgow suburb of Carntyne in 1926 and attended Whitehill senior secondary school. When he left school, he joined the office staff of MaCallum, Orme and Company in 1940 and also sailed on their vessel *Challenger* out of Kingston Dock in Glasgow. A memory of that time is of eating stew made from whale meat, but in general food was good for war time conditions. After nine years service, he became a member of the MacBrayne staff when the former firm was taken over. He was then assigned to the traffic department and his main work was to canvass for freight. The post of agent at Tobermory had been held since 1938 by F W Sutherland, who went on to become an auditor with the company and was replaced by F W MacIntosh. He was not long in the job and was succeeded on 18 December 1959 by Dick, who was to stay in Tobermory until quite some years after the creation of Caledonian MacBrayne, finally retiring in 1990. A modern bungalow was available to the agent, for rent, and when Caledonian MacBrayne took over, this was sold to him, as the new managers had no wish to become involved in the property business. Another advantage available to MacBraynes' staff at that time was that of some free travel tickets by British Railways every year and it was possible for the Henderson family to enjoy holidays in locations such as the Isle of Wight at very little cost.

When Dick was appointed to the post, Tobermory pier was busy with calls by MacBrayne steamers. *Lochearn* was the regular Sound of Mull vessel and calls were also made by *Claymore*, en route to and from Barra. In summer *King George V* called daily and on occasion yachts moored in the bay had to be moved to allow her to come alongside. When there was a second cruise ship based in Oban, she would also call on occasion.

Calls by cargo boats are detailed below. The second vessel to be based at Tobermory was *Lochbuie*, an ex-RAF rescue launch, bought in 1947 to provide a thrice-daily service to and from Kilchoan and relieve the Inner Islands steamer of the necessity to call there. Internally she was more like a bus than a ship, with bus-type double seats arranged on either side of a central gangway in the saloon, but she was comfortable enough. Until the advent of the car ferries, she also on occasion acted as an ambulance to Oban and as roads improved, it became the custom to run ambulance trips from the old pier at Craignure. As *Lochbuie* sat low in the water, a sling was commissioned to transfer stretcher cases aboard with as little trouble as possible and Dr MacIntyre, the general practitioner in Tobermory, insisted on trying this out for himself, before he would agree to its use for his patients. *Lochbuie* was later replaced by *Applecross*.

The pier hand was Alistair MacFarlane, plus temporary help in summer. Malcolm Black, son of Purser Archibald Black, spent his university vacations in the later 1950s working on the pier as an assistant. The largest load dealt with during his time there, in 1958, was another new bus, a Bedford, for Mr Cowe. (This vehicle later came into the MacBrayne fleet.) Ability to move things around was a great asset and much of this called for muscle power, but for heavier loads there was a three-axle bogie. Days when the cargo boats *Loch Carron* and *Loch Dunvegan* called were especially busy and quite often these did not arrive until about 2 or 3am, meaning that the pier staff did not have much sleep that night. Some compensation was afforded when they found an additional 4/6d in their wage packets that week. Cattle formed a large part of the consignment for the cargo boats and they received special consideration, as they were important customers. At sale times, timetables of the regular steamers could often go by the board and on 7 July 1946 two girls bound for a holiday at Torosay Castle were somewhat annoyed that, after they had dashed from Oban station to the North Pier to catch *Lochinvar*, she did not actually leave until 4pm, as there were many horses and cattle to be embarked. Farmers

12.19 The crew of *Lochbuie*. They are (l to r) Henry MacMillan (Mate), George Sproatt (Engineer), Jack Tague (Captain) and J MacFarlane (seaman). (By kind permission of the Mull Mussuem)

12.20 The same crew manning a rather smaller craft off Tobermory, possibly on the day of the local regatta. (By kind permission of the Mull Museum)

12.21 An early view of a mound of cargo at Tobermory. The identity of the ship is not certain.

12.22 *Loch Carron* at Tobermory pier on a day of high seas and a very high tide, in 1973. The Island class ferry *Coll*, which operated on the Fishnish-Lochaline service, and a fishing boat lie outside of her. (Both views by kind permission of the Mull Museum)

who had attended the sale "were chattering away in Gaelic".[1] A stock of hay was obtained from local crofts and the animals were fed on the pier before embarking. Formerly they had been herded to Salen and embarked there, but with the advent of cattle floats they were now shipped via Tobermory. Bulls could be difficult and Duncan MacTaggart, in his later MacBrayne career, had to cope with one which, on arrival at the Railway Pier at Oban, jumped over the offside of the ship and swam across the bay to the Corran Esplanade, where it was finally caught. Scallops were also important, and more docile.

Another item held on the pier was a stock of coal, not only for MacBraynes' ships (most of which were by now diesel anyway) but also to help out other sailors who ran short.

Until 1964 car traffic, which was growing apace and was by now largely handled by *Claymore*, formed a large part of the work and caused more than a proportionate share of the problems. The cars were loaded and unloaded on slings made up of nets. Spreaders and pads were put in to protect the wings of the cars. The contemporary Ford Zephyr, with its projecting wings, was by far the worst to deal with. However, once *Columba* had instituted the Mull car ferry in 1964, almost all of this traffic disappeared from Tobermory.

Four clerical staff, James Henderson (Chief Clerk), William ("Bluey") MacAllister, Ian MacKinnon, and secretary Marion MacDougall completed the Tobermory establishment. In due course Mr Henderson and Miss MacDougall married and he later suceeded Dick as agent.

Not all the work of the agent was marine-based. In 1964 MacBraynes began to operate buses on Mull and these came under his control. Three vehicles were acquired from Cowe, but most of those used on the island were bought new. Not only were services provided to and from the ferry at Craignure, but a number of vehicles were kept for tours and to provide a service across Mull to and from Fionnphort for day trips to Iona. Regular services were also operated to Dervaig and for school pupils to Gruline. In winter some

12.23/24/25 Dick Henderson's work as agent at Tobermory. Firstly he is seen catching up with the paperwork in his office, his arm resting on the safe. Next, wearing his agent's hat, he awaits passengers on the pier. In the last view, he is presenting the wheel of *Lochinvar* to Sir Charles MacLean at Duart Castle. (R Henderson)

1   Bulletin no. 19 of the Mull Museum, Spring 2009.

12.26 Unloading one of the vans on Tobermory pier, c1970. Dick Henderson is standing on the right and the crew members are Duncan MacKinnon (on the van), Alistair MacFarlane and Angus Henderson. (R Henderson)

12.27 Part of the agent's work involved meeting visiting civil servants or politicians. On 28 May 1969 Dick Henderson received Norman Buchan (right), one of the under-secretaries in William Ross's team at the Scottish Office. The creation of the Scottish Transport Group was then under consideration and the visit no doubt had much to do with that. In Caledonian MacBrayne days, civil servants of the Monopolies and Mergers Commission visited Tobermory and afterwards wrote to Dick Henderson to say that they had found the visit "very useful". (R Henderson)

12.28 A feature of the later years of MacBrayne tour operations was the running of overnight tours by rail from English cities, including either a visit to Mull with a coach tour or a sail on *King George V* . Here a group of tourists pose for the camera on the after deck of *King George V* at Tobermory pier on 17 May 1969. On the right, Bobby MacLeod, the dance band leader, presents a bottle of Old Mull to Col. G Ward, soon to be MacBraynes' representative on the Scottish Transport Group. (R Henderson)

12.29 The pens on *Claymore* could accommodate 26 head of cattle. (National Maritime Museum, Greenwich, London, neg.no.P35386)

12.30 One of the largest and most important cargoes handled by the goods services of Tobermory was that of equipment for the local distillery from the manufacturer on Speyside to Mull. In this view, Bedford L67 is about to set out from Dufftown for the journey, with a second vehicle following with smaller pieces of equipment. In front of L67 are drivers Alistair Noble (left) and John MacLean. (R Henderson)

of the coaches went back to Glasgow for use on football special services. At maximum, 15 buses were based on Mull, but this part of the road service was transferred to Highland Omnibuses in November 1971.

A small part of the road haulage fleet was also based on Mull and consisted of articulated and flat lorries and some vans. Tobermory was served by a regular van from Glasgow, driven normally by A Noble. Local delivery runs were made to Dervaig and on Thursdays to Iona. The Glasgow van brought material for the local distillery and generally took some of its produce back, a full return load being the normal for this working.

Relations with head office were good and, within the Tobermory office, very happy. It was a satisfying job.

A detailed account of the work of an agent is also given by Chris Fraser in *Christy Boy*, op. cit

Steamers and road vehicles were not the only links that MacBraynes had with Tobermory. The Western Isles Hotel was built in 1882 for Mr Caldwell of Mishnish, who also had a close interest in Tobermory pier. One of the first functions held in it was a banquet to celebrate the completion of the Tobermory waterworks, at which hopes were expressed that the town was going to become the "Scarborough of the West". In 1898 David MacBrayne decided to have his second foray into the hotel business and acquired it, but for reasons unknown failed to make a success of the venture and gave it up in 1902. Guests had at their disposal a small steam launch named *Jessie*. The hotel was then derelict until the 1930s, but is still very much in business to-day.

WESTERN-ISLES HOTEL AND PIER, TOBERMORY, ISLE OF MULL   A 9412

12.31 *King George V* alongside Tobermory pier c1950 with the hotel prominent behind. (Author's Collection)

The Craignure Ferry 1949-58.

The ferry rights at Craignure seem to have been of ancient origin and belonged to the Craignure estate. As far back as 1893 a petition was presented to Argyll County Council requesting the construction of a pier, but nothing came of this and the ferry continued to operate. The visitors of 1946 mentioned above "had to get into a little motor boat, as there was no pier for the huge MacBrayne steamer". In the post-1945 period, the owner was Mrs Miller, who leased it at an annual rental of £20. On 28 May 1949 the lease was taken over by George Clyne Sr. and his son of the same name. There were two boats used at the ferry, *Jean* and *Betty*, though only one would go out to meet the steamer when traffic was light. At busy periods one boat was used for passengers and one for cargo. The average daily number of passengers in 1949 was 42 in summer and 11 in winter and Mr Clyne estimated that in that year about 3,000 tourists had used it, many on their way to Iona.

One of Mr Clyne's first acts was to invite the surveyor from the Ministry of Transport to inspect the two boats and to his horror the latter presented a very unfavourable report on these. The larger required a thorough overhaul and the smaller would require to be fitted with an engine if she were to continue to be used in passenger service. The jetty used at Craignure was also dilapidated and in need of attention. For some time it looked as though the ferry service would have to cease while the necessary improvements were made but MacBraynes came to the rescue with the hire of a boat for £2 per week, to cover the period while the others were being overhauled. In 1951 the fare per passenger was raised to 1/- (5p) each way and it was hoped that the ferry service could now be put on a sounder and safer footing. Income in that year was £228.

For much of the 1950s, the ferry seems to have worked well enough, although, despite inflation, the fares were not raised from the level fixed in 1951. Mr Clyne was assisted by his son and, from 1955, by a young man named Jim Bennett. The two younger men divided their time between running the ferry and the local garage. On Friday 26 July 1957 the weather was bad, with driving rain and a high wind, and about 6pm, George Clyne Jr. noticed that the grey ferry boat had run aground near Minister's Point. He was concerned that, at high tide, she might float off and damage herself. As the next day marked both the end of the Glasgow Fair holidays and the start of the main English season, there might well be 200 travellers passing through Craignure and it would be impossible to deal with all of these if only one boat were in commission. Although the boat could be reached by clambering over the rocks on the shore, George decided to go out in the dinghy with Bennett to anchor the boat on the seaward side. Both were swimmers, George being particularly strong in the water and had rescued a visitor from drowning two years previously. They pushed off with George rowing, but the weather was deteriorating and both then took to the oars. Watchers onshore were then horrified to see that the boat seemed to fill and tilt over and that both men were in the water, George apparently helping Jim to climb onto the hull of the dinghy. The latter seemed to have lost consciousness. After a few minutes, both men disappeared, as did the dinghy. Visibility was now so bad that those on land – Mr MacLean of the Craignure Inn and three others – could not see exactly what had happened, but it was clear that both men were lost. Their bodies were recovered a few days later and the dinghy eventually came ashore at Easdale. The funeral was held on Tuesday 30 July and was attended by almost 500 people. A fund was set up to provide for the dependents of the two men. Ironically the ferry boat floated off the rocks at high tide, undamaged.

Mr Clyne Sr. then took over the working of the ferry by himself, saying that he looked on this act as a tribute to his dead son. However, he found it very difficult to keep the service going, despite the waiving of six months rent (£10) due to Mrs Miller for the second half of the year. For the six months from 1 August 1957 to 31 January 1958 the income generated by the ferry was £418, made up of £113 from passengers, £151 from goods and £150 subsidy from the post office for mails conveyed. Outgoings over the same period were wages £240, insurance £12, rates £3/13/4d (£3.67), paint and stores £20, fuel and oil £20 and hire of a boat from MacBraynes to cover overhaul periods £26. It is not clear if the wages mentioned covered help given by other members of the Clyne family and others. As MrClyne put it in a letter to Argyll County Council, "there is not a living in it". Normally ferry work took up six hours of the day, but at busy times this could extend to eight, not leaving much time for other occupations. Once again, it seemed that the service might have to close.

Fortunately the Council stepped in with a subsidy, in the process managing to tie itself into a legal knot over the question of whether the Craignure ferry was a ferry in the technical sense of one which connected two banks of a river or canal. It finally was decided that it was not and the

12.32 A peaceful scene at Craignure old pier, with both ferry boats awaiting the next call of the steamer.

12.33 Donald Cameron (left) and Allan Cameron, the last ferrymen at Craignure to work the service with a rowing boat.

12.34 The red ferryboat pulls away from *Lochearn*

(All three photographs by kind permission of the Mull Museum)

way was cleared for the subsidy and also an increase in fares and charges. It then remained in operation until the new pier opened in 1964 when, along with that at Drimnin, it closed and the ferry boat no longer formed part of the transport system in the Sound of Mull. It had been a part of the seascape for a very long time and had become something of an institution, a point of great interest to visitors to the area. It was also something which continued only because of the devotion and hard work of those who ran it and the willingness of its operators to continue working for earnings which were scarcely enough to maintain a basic standard of living.

The ferryboat at Drimnin was a rowing boat to the end, but was much less busy than that at Craignure.

Bibliography

Argyll CC transport papers 3/22 (Craignure ferry)

The Scots' Magazine, vol.64, no.3, December 1955. (Article "*In Praise of the Lochinvar*" by Campbell K Findlay, illustrated with excellent sketches of individual crew members. A copy of these can be seen in the Mull Museum)

Report of the accident at Craignure in the

Oban Times, 3 August 1957.

Apart from the individuals mentioned, much information for this chapter was supplied by Ms Jay MacDonald, formerly of Tobermory, now Barcaldine and Malcolm Black of Connel.

12.35 A post card view of Tobermory pier, taken between 1895 and 1904. Although the steamer is said to be *Gael*, she has a fiddle bow and is more likely to be *Chevalier*. (R Henderson Collection)

12.36 The pier, as rebuilt, on the day of Mull Highland Games, sometime in the 1950s. The Games were held on the fourth Thursday of July and on these dates, a revised timetable was offered by *Lochinvar* and other ships gave special sailings. The cattle ramp is on the right, immediately in front of the camera. (R Henderson Collection)

12.37 A view from the sea front on another Games day, with *Lochmor*, "full of flags", at the pier. (By kind permission of the Mull Museum)

12.38 On an earlier occasion, between 1947 and 1953, *King George V* makes a special call.
(By kind permission of the Mull Museum)

12.39 The coming of the car ferry brought MacBrayne buses to Mull. No.181, a Bedford CSC of 1961, with bodywork by Duple, awaits passengers from *Columba* at Craignure pier on 7 June 1969. There were now four through daily services to and from Salen and Tobermory in connexion with the car ferry, although the last evening departure from there did not run on Saturdays. The through journey time to and from Oban of two hours or less was a distinct improvement on the schedule of *Lochinvar* in former days and allowed local residents plenty of time in the big city. To-day passengers transferring from the ferry have to walk the length of the pier to catch a bus, but shelter has at last been provided for those waiting to embark. (Alastair G Gunn)

12.40 A line of Bedford SBS tour coaches with Plaxton Embassy bodywork awaiting passengers at Craignure. Nearest the camera is no.164, which was new in 1968 and had luxurious coachwork by Plaxton. The other three are identical vehicles. Day tours were run to Tobermory, Torloisk and Calgary, as well as to Fionnphort for Iona. (R L Wilson, Online Transport Archive)

12.41 MacBraynes' football team at a Coast Lines match in Liverpool c1960. Dick Henderson is standing immediately to the right of the team and Mr MacLauchlan, then manager of the Company, is on the extreme right. The names of the players have not been recorded. (R Henderson Collection)

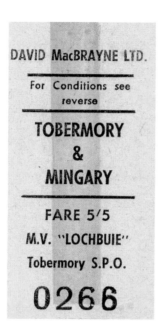

Few steamers in the fleet had the distinction of having their name on the tickets used by their passengers, but for some reason *Lochbuie* was thus honoured. (Author's Collection)

13 The End of David MacBrayne Ltd

D UE TO A LACK OF EARLY RECORDS, the financial history of David MacBrayne as a private company remains a mystery. Management techniques were clearly not sophisticated and MacBrayne Sr held tight control of all the purse strings. A purser later remembered that, when he delivered to him at head office the proceeds of a voyage, David MacBrayne carefully counted out the sovereigns on the principle of "One for the Company, one for me, two for the company, one for me, three for the Company, one for you" and so on. Only in 1902, when he was 88 years of age, did he allow his two sons, David Hope and Laurence MacBrayne to become partners in the firm, which became a private limited company in 1906 and David H MacBrayne became Chairman, assuming full control on the death of his father in January 1907. His brother had previously disposed of his share in the business. Co-directors were John Prosser WS, Edinburgh and D Campbell Brown, a banker in Oban. The latter seems to have acted as managing director, at least when Mr MacBrayne was ill in 1913. Both these gentlemen retired in 1915 and Mr MacBrayne then managed the business himself, with three heads of departments acting as directors in a supporting role. Miss MacBrayne, sister of the two brothers, was also a director in the 1920s. It was assumed by the public that the Company was highly profitable, but in fact this may not have been the case. A witness in 1928 said that there had been little profit, even in the pre-war years.

The beginning of the end of the private company that was David MacBrayne Ltd antedated the first world war. As mentioned elsewhere, the steamer service on Loch Maree had already fallen a victim to changing travel patterns and motorbus operations had become quite sophisticated by the time war broke out. Motor mail-cars, with accommodation for eight passengers, were already running on such services as Gairloch to Achnasheen. However, the motorbuses saved money for the Company and it may well have been the motor car which was responsible for the beginning of the end of its financial stability. As early as 1904 the Highland Railway had been complaining about the abstraction of first class traffic by motorists. The AA first published "Scotland for the Motorist" in 1910 and a census taken in the weeks beginning on 22 May and 7 August in the following year at various places in Argyll revealed the following traffic patterns at Connel and Tarbert:-

	Cycles	Motor cycles	Motor cars	Horse drawn vehicles
May – Connel	411	7	80	219
May – Tarbert	241	28	103	687
August – Connel	1,102	25	422	287
August – Tarbert	1,035	54	371	1,348

On Mull, where there had been two locally-owned cars in 1907, there were in1912 35, some of them quite powerful machines.[1]

According to *Motor World* of August 1913, the summer of that year "will long be remembered as an ideal season for motoring". There had been a steady stream of visitors from England and the USA to Scotland. Even the cheapest of touring cars, the Ford Touring, cost £220, which

---

1   J D Cattanach, Area Surveyor of Argyll County Council, in evidence to the Council in connexion with an application to the Roads Board for a grant.

would have been a good annual salary at the time and most cars were much dearer than that, while tyres were £20 each – and did not last very long on Highland roads. Given these costs, the tourists who now took advantage of the new mode of travel would have included many who could previously afford the longer tours offered by MacBraynes.

In 1913 the German liner *Kronprinzessin Cecilie* visited Oban with a party of 200 doctors on board and among other visitors were Prince and Princess August Wilhelm of Prussia, travelling incognito. In August of the following year, it was clear to almost everyone in the town that the doctors had come not for medical purposes nor had the couple come for a quiet holiday away from the stuffiness of the German court, but to study and map the coast with a view to a possible invasion.

The outbreak of war greatly accelerated the process of change. Foreigners departed in droves before the war actually started and it seems that the wealthier British tourists were quick to follow them. Hotels lost many from their staff, either because they were German or Austrian and were afraid of being interned, or French who wanted to join their own nation's army, while many younger Scottish men joined up. The 40 yachts which were anchored in the bay at the end of July – among them Lady Currie's *Iolaire* and H J Massey's *Myranthea* – all disappeared. By 26 September, when matters had settled down a little, the *Oban Times* was criticising the number of visitors who had unwisely interrupted their holiday in the previous month. A slight break from the tension came on 24 October when a stampede of a different kind occurred. A herd of cattle which had been landed from *Clydesdale* at the railway pier went rampaging through the streets and was not rounded up for some hours. Whereas resorts, such as those on the Clyde, which catered for middle- and working-class holidaymakers, did not immediately notice much difference in August 1914 and would in fact do quite well during the war years, those which catered for the upper end of the market immediately felt the pinch. The summer traffic of well-heeled tourists, on which the Company had depended to cross-subsidise the year-round services, vanished at a stroke. On the Clyde, *Columba* was laid up in 1915 and for the first part of the summer of 1916, and the secondary Ardrishaig sailings ended. The Oban-Gairloch cruise was cancelled, as were *Linnet*'s sailings on the Crinan Canal and the Loch Awe service, the latter not being revived in 1919. Swingeing economies were made to the services to the isles. Perhaps however, Oban did attract some of the new war-enriched holidaymakers during the conflict, since in 1916 short cruises were being advertised, despite the difficulties of the period.

Some of the economies, such as the loss of a daily steamer on the Sound of Mull, caused hardship for local people and were much resented by them. Other services were merged, originally for the duration of hostilities. The Outer Isles service was now worked by *Plover* alone, instead of by three ships and the Inner Isles run was taken on by *Cygnet*, this now being combined with the service to Coll and Tiree, much to the annoyance of the inhabitants of the latter. As *Cygnet* had been built for the Glasgow-Inveraray cargo/passenger service, she had minimal passenger accommodation and that only for short journeys in waters which were generally sheltered. She also had to be fitted with sleeping accommodation, in the dining saloon, for her new role and berths for 16 were provided on a ledge which ran round the saloon above the seats. A table occupied almost all the floor space and the accommodation was cramped and claustrophobic.

The deficiencies of *Cygnet* on this service came to crystallise all that was wrong with MacBraynes in the post-war years and it was because of her that Mr F A MacQuisten MP (Conservative and Unionist, Argyll)) first became aware of the concerns of some members of the travelling public about MacBrayne services. The travel writer and photographer Mrs M E M Donaldson castigated her as being the worst of all the horrible boats in MacBrayne's miscellaneous fleet, easily beating both *Plover* and *Sheila*. She was also "remarkably comfortless" and "a floating slum". Passengers on an outward journey from Oban might include "A few poor

S. S. Iona leaving Ardrishaig

13.1 Apparently not everyone shared in the general panic. This postcard of *Iona* was written at Cairnbaan on 7 August 1914 and posted on the next day to an address in Durban. The writer, one Polly Greenwood, makes no mention of the outbreak of war, but records that she is having a "very nice time". (Author's Collection)

13.2 *Cygnet* at Rothesay in 1921, when employed on the Loch Fyne cargo/passenger service. (Glasgow University Archives)

13.3 "One of the antiquities of the MacBrayne fleet", according to Mrs Pickworth, who sailed in *Glencoe* from Mallaig to Portree c1930. Apparently she then had a permanent list to starboard. Here, well loaded, she sets out from Kyle for Portree late in her career, by then aged 80+. To the left of the funnel can be seen the stocky figure of Captain John Gillies, whose hobby was the study of clocks and watches. It is clearly a fine day and travel on the open foredeck would have been quite pleasant, but it was another story in winter. (© Duncan Macpherson Collection, Dualchas Heritage Service, The Highland Council)

13.4 The same space could equally be used for sheep. There is a story that on one occasion, a county councillor, travelling with a steerage ticket on board *Glencoe*, sat in the saloon, from which he was soon ejected by a zealous purser. On his next trip, he took up his position on the foredeck, amid a flock of sheep, and then insisted that the same purser should make his way through the animals to check his ticket. (By courtesy of the Mitchell Library, Glasgow City Council)

folk, obviously from Glasgow, a farmer or so, two other men and a young boy."[2] MacBraynes, Mrs Donaldson considered, exercised what practically amounted to a despotic monarchy in the west highlands and treated the public as they pleased. Even those who travelled cabin found *Cygnet* wanting, as her saloon was stuffy and sleep impossible because of the constant din produced by two teapots, one coffee pot and one cruet suspended from an overhead rack. Anyone who did not want to eat had to vacate his seat or berth when meal service began, whether to passengers or officers, and go up on deck, where there was no shelter, apart from that provided by the wings of the bridge[3]. Mrs Donaldson thought the cabin fare a waste of money and preferred to travel steerage. Tiree folk disliked *Cygnet* as she had space for only four horses and that was insufficient to cater for one of the principal exports from that island. The people of Kilchoan were equally unenthusiastic about her.[4]

It seems that, after a particularly unpleasant voyage in steerage from Oban to Kilchoan, on a very wet day, Mrs Donaldson wrote a letter of complaint to Mr F A MacQuisten, who then asked a question of the Scottish Secretary, Sir John Gilmour[5], in the House of Commons on 10 June 1925.

Clearly Mr MacQuisten was not personally familiar with the ship, since he mentioned that her bridge was near her bow and that there was very little room for passengers in the remaining space. He claimed that, "in rough weather, the steerage portion . . . forward of the bridge cannot be used by anyone". His question was answered by Mr Fleming, Solicitor-General for Scotland, who did not give him much immediate satisfaction and the problem did not go away. There were times when the ship seemed not to be up to the demands of the service, when she could not make the passage to Tiree and, during one election campaign, the Labour candidate found himself marooned and frustrated on the island for ten days, while his opponents were free to roam the constituency. In the last week of January 1927, she was storm-bound at Barra for three days.

The people of Lewis were not any happier with the new level of service, which, from the beginning of October 1919, was curtailed to run thrice weekly in each direction. Complaints began in November and continued through to March 1921, when questions were asked of the Prime Minister (Lloyd George) in the House of Commons. He did not answer himself but passed the matter on to the Financial Secretary to the Treasury, Stanley Baldwin. No satisfactory answer being received from him, further questions followed, in such quantity that the Speaker suggested that they should be put as written questions, rather than hold up the business of the House of Commons. Ultimately a daily service was restored.

Two ships were lost on war service and eight other ships were sold out of the fleet. Some money was no doubt made from these sales and from the war-time chartering of steamers to maintain essential Clyde services, but the financial basis on which the Company had been operated had vanished for ever. When the war finished, it was in trouble.

While people had put up with war-time reductions in service, they were not willing to do so without complaint once peace had returned. Moreover, unlike the years after the second world war, the early 1920s were a period when it was expected that, having "won" the war, Britain would soon be in a position to return to pre-was levels of service in all fields, including transport and when this did not happen, the operators were blamed for inefficiency. The war had changed other expectations, particularly among those employed in industry and the days when stokers would happily spend hours shovelling coal into a ship's furnaces in return for a pittance had gone for good. The strike of firemen on *Columba* (and *Lord of The Isles*) for over

2   *Further Wanderings, Mainly in Argyll.* M E M Donaldson. A Gardner, Paisley, 1926.
3   *Isles of Sunset.* Walter A Mansell. D Wylie and Son, Aberdeen.
4   *Night falls on Ardnamurchan.* A MacLean. Chatto and Windus, London, 1984
5   Sir John Gilmour, bart, was Scottish secretary in Baldwin's government, from 6 November 1924 until 7 June 1929. In December 1925, he became the first Secretary of State for Scotland. His main concerns were housing and agriculture. He did little for transport and had no knowledge of shipping.

a week at Glasgow in the summer of 1919, at the height of a post-war holiday boom, showed how industrial relations were changing. Such things just did not happen pre-1914 and it took many years for people to alter their mindset. Moreover, the islanders were "part and parcel of the Empire and no more patriotic people can be found within His Majesty's realms" "Having given generously of their time and lives during the conflict", (as any memorial in the islands will testify), "they now had some expectation that His Majesty's governments would do something to alleviate their economic problems".[6]

People could not understand why the Company could not provide a better service, with fares running at virtually double those of 1914, or in some cases even more. The cost of shipping one sheep from Mull to Oban had risen from 5d (2p) to 10d (4p) (there were discount rates for large numbers of animals) and the fare for cabin passengers had risen from 7/6d (35p) to 14/6d (72.5p). It cost £5 to ship an average-size motor car. The fares from Oban to Tiree had gone up from 6/- (30p) steerage or 8/- (40p) cabin to 15/6d and 31/- (77.5p and £1.55)[7]. (On the Clyde, the day return fare from Glasgow to Ardrishaig (cabin) had increased from 6/- (30p) to 9/- (45p). At prices like these, people reasoned, the Company must be doing very well indeed and it was accused of "sucking the islands dry."

Rural depopulation was by now well under way in the Gaeltacht, where individual counties were losing population by amounts varying between 7% (Inverness-shire), 9% (Ross-shire) and 18% (islands). Argyll's population remained steady by virtue of the growth in towns on the coast, such as Oban, but this was not of much help to MacBraynes.

The Coalition government headed by Lloyd George seems to have realised that there would be problems and as early as February 1918 a committee was set up by Robert Munro, Secretary for Scotland and himself a highlander. [8] With a remit to examine the provision of rural transport throughout Scotland, it was chaired by Sir T Carlow-Martin (but with no Labour members) and went to work fairly quickly, presenting its report in mid-1919. It was a commentary on the level of steamer services in the west highlands at the time that members of this committee had to be given transport on naval ships when they went out to look at the facilities in the area, since the ordinary services were so infrequent and often already crowded. Curiously they seem not to have had any direct discussions with MacBraynes' managers, although they did speak to local authorities and also to the managers of the various Scottish railways.

The report was a curious document, in some ways backward-looking, but in others far-seeing, with recommendations which would not be put into effect until many years later; the usefulness of a breakwater at Mallaig being a case in point. The general aim of the recommendations was to improve the economy of the Gaeltacht by making it easier for the inhabitants to export their produce and to bring this about, the main instrument recommended was the narrow-gauge railway. Road transport was seen as of limited value, expensive and damaging to local roads. Many additional steamer services were recommended, such as a local service in the Sound of Sleat. The Outer Hebrides were to be made more accessible by using Dunvegan as a point of departure, it being connected to Portree and Kyleakin by one of the new railways. This would have allowed a much faster journey to and from Harris and North Uist. The Stornoway steamer should run to Ullapool or Lochinver, with onward transport being by narrow-gauge train – Lewis folk were not enthused by this proposal, despite the shortening of the sea journey. Apparently they mainly wanted to reach Glasgow and resented any proposal which would make this more difficult. The Committee was scathing about the inadequate accommodation on the Stornoway mailboat (*Sheila*) and recommended a 15 knot steamer with room for 200 passengers.

---

6   Peter Morrison, retired sub-commissioner of the Board of Agriculture, in evidence to the Select Committee of the House of Commons, 1928.

7   Evidence from the Glasgow Tiree Association to Argyll County Council, 1928.

8   Robert Munro, Secretary for Scotland, 10 December 1916 to 24 October 1922. Apart from this attempt to examine transport questions, Munro was also responsible for the Land Settlement Act (Scotland) of December 1919, under which many smallholdings were created in the Gaeltacht.

They also mentioned that steamers often had to wait for trains which ran late, having been held to await connexions from England. Their comments on MacBraynes were ambivalent. It was pointed out that theirs was a transport undertaking comparable to a fair-sized railway system, but without being in any way under parliamentary control. Given the current set-up, it would be impossible for the Company to provide a better service, but competition was not the answer and MacBraynes should be maintained as a monopoly, but under state control. In a proposal that seemed to foreshadow the road-equivalent tariff, the Committee suggested that MacBraynes should be re-organised as part of the public system of ways and communications.

In the event, these recommendations fell on very deaf ears. Too much expenditure would have been involved to allow them to pass the scrutiny of the Chancellor of the Exchequer, A J Bonar Law (Conservative/Unionist), and, even if they had passed that hurdle, it is unlikely that they would have survived the wielding of the Geddes axe.

That same government, however, had set up in many areas small holdings, for which there was a brisk demand, generally from returned servicemen, and which were successful. But there was little point in encouraging this kind of agricultural activity if the holders had insufficient means of transport to dispose of their produce. In 1928, when there was a national waiting list for such holdings, it was impossible to fill vacancies on Tiree.

With the grouping of the railways in 1923, control of another part of Scotland's transport was taken from the country and centred in London. The new Ministry of Transport meanwhile took over responsibility for trunk roads, which thus also passed out of Scottish control.

But perhaps almost as important to MacBraynes was the change in holiday patterns. The tourists, who arrived together by steamer or coach, at a more or less fixed hour (subject to weather) and who then stayed for some time were diminishing in number and a different kind of holidaymaker was coming to the area. In an editorial in 1928, the *Oban Times* neatly summed up the changes. Instead of the wealthy people who brought abundant luggage (with servants to look after it) and relied on public transport, the area was now seeing the growth of middle-class motoring. This involved tourists who, though well enough off financially to buy a car such as an Armstrong–Siddley at about £400, did not have unlimited means or unlimited time at their disposal, and also were concerned to have value for money. Unlike their predecessors, who all arrived by, say, *Chevalier* at 4.50pm, to be met by hotel porters on the North Pier, the new tourists tended to arrive at hotels in penny numbers, at almost any time of the day (and sometimes night). They took week-end breaks and sometimes even ventured north during good spells of weather in winter. They were a less hardy breed than those who had enjoyed drives through the "crisp air" on horse-drawn coaches and wanted such comforts as running hot and cold water in their rooms and a bathroom adjacent. They liked the warmth of equable (central) heating. Chambermaids with hot water cans in the morning and a fire in the bedroom were no longer the height of luxury. These tourists had an irritating habit of expecting food to be available whenever they arrived at a hotel. Hotels had to spend considerable sums updating accommodation to keep up with these demands, but found that travelling habits were now less predictable and they could not always be sure that they would recoup the rewards of their expenditure. The new Marine Hotel in Oban (now the Regent), built to cater for the new tourists, and the Lochalsh Hotel at Kyle (as rebuilt by the LMS) illustrate their expectations.

For MacBraynes, there was now less chance that people would use long-distance steamer services to reach a destination and that, while circular tours such as the Staffa and Iona cruise, with which the private car could never compete, would be as popular as ever, long single trips were not wanted. If these new tourists were tempted to take a longer sea trip, perhaps to the Outer Isles, they wanted a miniature version of the hotel comforts outlined above; communal dormitory cabins or bedding down in the saloon were no longer acceptable. In 1928, it was suggested that the tourist traffic had "practically disappeared". While this was definitely an exaggeration, there can be no doubt that the nature of the traffic had greatly changed since 1914.

Inflation was a new concept to those in Britain after 1918 and many years were to elapse before people began to understand it. For a long time the notion persisted that it would somehow be possible to go back to pre-1914 price levels, especially after Churchill returned Britain to the gold standard while he was Chancellor of the Exchequer (1925-29). But for the shipowner inflation was a very real and present condition and he had to live with it. Although the cost of new ships fell slightly from the immediate post-war years, it then stabilised at approximately double that of pre-1914. The LB&SCR had taken delivery of *Paris* from Denny's yard in 1913 at a cost of £94,856. In 1927 the Southern Railway bought the very similar *Worthing* from the same yard for £171,680 9 [9]. In the 1920s MacBraynes did enquire about a new ship for the Staffa and Iona service, but when the cost became apparent, the idea was dropped. They would have had to reckon on spending at least £45,000 per vessel, if steam propulsion were specified for a ship of about 200 ft in length, and more for a diesel vessel. In 1931 *Lochfyne* would cost £59,697 [9]. Local authorities, faced with increasing expenditure, particularly on roads and housing, looked to local rates to recoup some of this and a dispute between MacBraynes and Argyll County Council about rates on piers rumbled on from 1914 to 1920. Wage inflation had run at a similar, though slightly lower level. War losses and ships sold during or soon after the war were not replaced and by 1926 the fleet contained six veterans – *Glencoe, Glengarry, Gondolier, Linnet, Iona* and *Chevalier* – which had celebrated their diamond jubilee in the service, while *Columba* and *Claymore* were nearing their golden jubilees and *Grenadier* had turned 40, with *Fusilier* three years behind. There was only one eighteen year old "flapper"[10] in the fleet (*Mountaineer*). The Company tried to broaden its capital base in the post-war period and in 1921 the larger portion was acquired by three businessmen, Sir Hector M MacNeal, Sir Kenneth S Anderson and Lord Maclay. In total they put in £24,000 and from that date the firm was no longer purely a MacBrayne personal possession. If this move had been intended as a means of raising sufficient additional capital to allow fleet renewal, it would seem that it was not successful, since £24,000 would not have bought a ship even half the size of the 250ft (76.2m) Clyde steamer *Glen Sannox* of 1925 (cost £58,532, with a slight loss to the builders) [9]. As Mr MacQuisten put it in the debate in May 1928, there was now nothing in MacBraynes except the subsidy, the rest was scrap iron, although there were then "supposed" to be 144,00 fully paid shares in the Company, which, he added with some feeling, was not even the old MacBraynes.

In 1924, Lord Maclay approached Sir Josiah Stamp, General Manager of the newly-formed London, Midland and Scottish Railway, to suggest that it might take over the Company, on the grounds of public utility. Sir Josiah was a distinguished public servant and was at that time deeply involved with the question of German war reparations, but he knew nothing of shipping and there is nothing to suggest that he was familiar with the west coast of Scotland. He duly put the idea to his officers and it received a resounding rejection.

The response of Baldwin's Conservative/Unionist government (1924-1929) to the situation was one of complete indifference. Stornoway was, after all, a very long way from Westminster and Whitehall, where everything affecting Scotland was still decided. Despite considerable pressure from local MPs, in particular Mr MacQuisten, it was impossible to persuade any government, Conservative/ Unionist or Labour, to arrange a debate in Parliament until that of 1928. The pre-war mail contract of £18,000 per annum had ended. A new mail contract was drawn up in 1921, to run for four years from 1920, and providing for annual payments of £70,000, £60,000, £50,000 and £50,000. To these were added one-off payments £17,000 and £20,000 to settle the matter of war-time losses and chartering. An annual subsidy of £4,000 was also promised in respect of the six ships which were fitted with wireless and in the event £5,583 was paid under this heading between 1921 and 1924. This contract ran until October 1924 and was replaced by one of £36,000 per annum, running from 1 Feb 1924 until 31 October 1925, thereafter being

9   All figures taken from the Denny List.
10 A term used in the 1920s for a young society girl who had not yet been presented at court and was thought to be rather too fond of jazz music, cigarettes and night clubs.

13.5 "Tha na *Sheila* air na creagan". The first casualty of 1927, the Stornoway steamer is seen on the rocks near Applecross. (By courtesy of the Mitchell Library, Glasgow City Council)

13.6 *Chevalier* aground on Barmore Island in March 1927. (By courtesy of the Mitchell Library, Glasgow City Council)

13.7 At Oban in early 1928 *Grenadier* has been refloated and the saloon windows boarded up. Water is being pumped out of the hull prior to her being towed to Ardrossan. As can be seen, damage from the fire was fairly limited. (By courtesy of the Mitchell Library, Glasgow City Council)

extended in six-monthly periods until 31 Oct 1926, when the Company withdrew from it and it terminated. Clearly payments at these levels simply (just) maintained the status quo and made no provision for fleet replacement. Between 1920 and 1925, there was a certain amount of administrative devolution to Scotland and in the latter year a departmental committee of the Scottish Office considered the matter and suggested an approach to the railway companies, but the Scottish Office itself did not wish to take this any further, afraid that any such approach would prejudice negotiations with MacBraynes. Apart from possible residual powers devolving from the Highland Railway's operation of steamers in the 1870s, it seemed that neither of the railway companies which now served Scotland, the LMS and LNER, had powers to run shipping services on the west coast and in any case, the railways, which were not doing very well financially themselves, had shown no interest at all in assuming responsibility for west highland shipping.

However, replacement of the older ships could not be indefinitely postponed and from July 1925 discussions took place between MacBrayne managers, the Scottish Office and the Post Office. The outcome of these discussions was that, in return for a new contract with an annual subsidy of £36,000, the Company would build a new steamer of 175ft length for the Stornoway run, to be capable of maintaining a speed of 12 knots in moderately bad weather. This new ship would allow *Sheila* to be transferred to the Outer Isles service and thus free *Plover* to replace the despised *Cygnet*, but a second new ship, of 150ft length, was also proposed for the latter service. The plans were of course upset when *Sheila*, still relatively modern at 22 years of age, was lost early on New Year's Day in 1927, just south of the entrance to Loch Torridon (qv Chapter 4). This accident set off a reshuffle of ships which ultimately involved expensive chartering and a third new vessel was now proposed.

The later losses of the "annus horribilis" of 1927 – *Chevalier* and *Grenadier* – were not mentioned in the discussions, but they must have brought an increased sense of urgency to these. The former ran aground on Barmore Island, about two miles north of Tarbert, in Loch Fyne on 25 March in a south-easterly gale and blinding rain, when on passage between Tarbert and Ardrishaig. In "very trying circumstances" the 20 passengers on board were safely landed in two of the ship's boats and the mails and luggage were brought ashore. The fact that a ship of this size was carrying only 20 is a good indication of the economic problems then facing MacBraynes. *Chevalier* remained aground for a week and, her paddle boxes having been removed, was then towed to Greenock for examination in Scott's dry dock. She was found to be beyond economic repair, although one of her boilers was saved for use in *Grenadier*, and she went to the breaker's yard on 10 June. The end of the latter steamer is covered in a separate chapter (Ch.11). While *Chevalier* had not actually seen much service since 1920 and could basically be replaced by chartered Clyde steamers at peak times, this was certainly not the case with *Grenadier*. Her immediate replacement was *Fusilier*, (in turn replaced by *Iona* from the Clyde services), but she seems to have been unsatisfactory in both roles, as the Iona excursion steamer in summer and on the Clyde in winter. On three days in the winter of 1927/8, she was unable to proceed beyond Tighnbruaich, although the Loch Fyne cargo steamer, to which the passengers were ultimately transferred, managed to complete the voyage around Ardlamont "without difficulty" on at least one of those occasions. There had been great alarm and excitement among passengers and people were literally afraid to travel by *Fusilier* in stormy weather. She was deficient in both power and stability. Her lack of speed would do a great deal to hamper the tourist traffic to Iona in the summer months.[11]

Despite these various problems, the discussions went ahead in a fairly constructive way. Lewis people were pleased with the first proposal, but islanders on Coll and Tiree reacted furiously to the idea of being served by *Plover*, which was "old and slow" and asked for a new ship of their own. MacBraynes were not now willing to commit themselves to the immediate construction

11   Evidence presented to Argyll County Council by Donald Blair, JP, grocer, Tarbert and by Mr I MacKenzie, manager of the Columba Hotel, Iona, and correspondence in the Langmuir collection.

of a third ship and this was accepted by the authorities, the draft contract being accordingly reduced in length from ten to five years. There was also agreement on minor matters, such as the proposed alteration of the time-table of the Stornoway steamer to allow her to connect with the early train from Kyle, and the discontinuation of local calls by excursion steamers at piers such as Salen (Mull), in the interests of tourists, who might otherwise be tempted to take a motor coach drive. All through the discussions, MacBraynes had refused to disclose details of their financial position but assured the authorities that the figure of £36,000 per annum was the minimum required to keep services going. The final version of the new contract was presented to parliament on 1 December 1927, but due to pressure of business could not be ratified before the Christmas recess. Without this, MacBraynes were unwilling to go ahead with firm orders for the two new ships, although they did continue work on their specifications.

Unfortunately, this delay allowed the opposition to MacBraynes time to rally their forces. As mentioned in a letter from the Company to the Scottish Office on 6 December 1927, a committee of Conservative/Unionist MPs had been formed and began to wage a vigorous campaign against the award of the new contract to the Company. It is not recorded who was the moving spirit behind this committee, but it may well have been Mr MacQuisten. The result of this agitation was that Baldwin's government listened to its own supporters and agreed to hold a debate on the subject in the House of Commons.

This duly took place on 18 May 1928 and did little to progress matters. Agreement was at once reached that the sailors and officers of MacBrayne vessels displayed at all times a very high standard of seamanship but beyond this there was no agreement at all. Most Conservative/ Unionist and Liberal speakers suggested either competition or involvement of the railway companies as a solution, while the Labour speakers preferred outright nationalisation. Mr MacQuisten suggested that there was a suspicion that part of the subsidy was used to prevent rivals from getting in to serious competition with the Company. (It is not clear which rivals he had in mind.) He also seemed to think that MacBraynes owned all the piers and ferries and so could "choke off" these rivals. A full-scale enquiry was suggested, but this was quashed when a Labour speaker pointed out that there had been one in 1919 (see above) and that another enquiry was not likely to yield any new information. Another Labour speaker, T Johnston[12], drew gales of laughter from Members when he detailed the age of some of the ships such as *Glencoe*. His mention of the "old" *Sheila* (built in 1904) "and now lying, praise be, at the bottom of the Minch", showed how little he understood of the structure of the MacBrayne fleet or the actual location of her accident. *Mountaineer* was "the flapper of the fleet". He went on to make the remarkable assertion that the average age of the fleet was over 68 years and no one bothered to challenge this figure – it was in fact 37 years 4 months – and he had a good deal to say about *Cygnet*. "If he (a passenger from Coll to Tiree) goes steerage, he will find that there are no seats on the steamer and he either stands or lies among the cattle. If he does lie about among the cattle and it is a stormy day, he gets mixed up with cattle excrement and so on before he is finished". Sir John Gilmour said little beyond indicating that the government was thinking of a new five-year contract. Baldwin himself modestly put it that the government did not have the competence to run a shipping company. Various speakers also questioned the competence of the civil servants in the Scottish Office. Mr David Kirkwood (Labour) put in a good word for the herring girls, suggesting that only sturdy Scottish lassies could cope with the travelling conditions that they had to endure. Less romantically, but very accurately, he went on to suggest that a debate on a mail contract was far too limited a way to consider the area's transport needs as a whole. Only Mr E Shinwell (Labour) thought to mention the matter of the accommodation provided for crews on board MacBrayne ships. It was, he said, "vile". He did not go on to add that, on some ships, there was no crew accommodation as such, the men having to camp out in the saloons for the night (See accounts of *Grenadier* in Ch.11 and *Gondolier* in Ch.1). The debate became

---

12   Thomas Johnston was then Labour MP for Dundee and would later become Secretary of State for Scotland in Churchill's war time coalition government.

quite bad-tempered, with Mr Kirkwood unfairly calling Sir John "stupid" and Mr MacQuisten, with reference to the war lords then rampaging through China, alleging that awarding the new contract to MacBraynes would amount to giving them a machine gun with which to shoot up the west highlands. However, just before the end of the debate, he proposed the setting up of a select committee of the House to consider the matter further, with powers to take evidence in Scotland, and Baldwin's government agreed at once to the suggestion.

In fact, although the Hon. Members no doubt appreciated the chance to air their prejudices, in defence of their constituents, they could well have spared themselves the bother of the debate. Clearly rumours and ill-natured gossip had begun to circulate after the Conservative/Unionist committee was set up in December, and on 9 February, D H MacBrayne had written to the Secretary to the Post Office to say that the Company had decided to withdraw completely from the new contract. The Company would carry on for the present and were willing to dispose of their fleet on terms which would make "no difficulty". In a cry which clearly came from the heart, he added, "We object and are tired of the constant criticism of the Service, and do not think that anything we could do would satisfy the critics". It would seem that he had simply had enough. It would also seem that this letter had not been made public when the debate took place.

Under the chairmanship of Roy Wilson MP for Lichfield (Conservative/Unionist), this committee was immediately convened, to report before Parliament went into recess in July. Its time was therefore very limited. It consisted of eleven members, seven representing Scottish constituencies, but of course none from the areas affected. The first meeting, on Thursday 21 June, took evidence from Messrs P R Laird of the Scottish Office and A R Kidner of the Post Office, and was initially held in public. However, when it became evident, on a question from Sir R Hamilton (Liberal, Orkney and Shetland), that there was no question of MacBraynes going on with the contract, the Chairman announced that the hearing would be held in private and the public were turned out. He promised that there would be further public hearings in Scotland and advised local authorities and others to gather evidence of their needs. Meanwhile the Committee would continue to consider written and oral evidence in private.

Argyll County Council had already, on 16 December 1926, set up its first transport committee and its report on transport facilities by land and sea was accepted by the full Council on 12 October 1927. Headed by John MacLachlan of MacLachlan, Convener of the Council, with Lt Col T O Lloyd as Vice-Convener and other members including Sir John Lorne MacLeod, a former Lord Provost of Edinburgh, it would hardly be considered a left-wing body, but nonetheless its main recommendation was that shipping services would have to be subsidised, with suitable controls on the operators. The Committee had made contact with the British Legation in Oslo and had procured much evidence on the operation of supported shipping services in Norwegian coastal waters. The Council was therefore in a very good position to reply to the parliamentary committee. They now energetically set about gathering further evidence to submit to Westminster.

A meeting in Tiree called for a 30% reduction in fares and the Glasgow Tiree Association submitted a good deal of evidence which shed much light on the actual operation of MacBrayne's services. (Appendix 3) The County's Medical Officer, who was a member of the transport committee, reported on the increase in malnutrition among children since before the recent war. This had risen from 8% in 1914 to 12% at the present time. He attributed the increase to the fact that local people had to sell produce such as eggs and milk at a loss due to high transport costs and only gained enough from this exercise to buy tinned milk and processed foods. Mr R Mair, Managing Director of T Corson and Co (1922) Ltd of Oban mentioned that his company alone shipped 7,500 cattle, 30,000 sheep and 170 horses annually by MacBrayne ships. If island farmers at mainland markets did not get the price they wanted for their animals, they preferred to sell at a loss, rather than incur the cost of taking them home again. He complained about the lack of sufficient cattle boats and the use of ships which were not designed for this trade. (It was common to use passenger ships at times of peak cattle movements, a practice which continued long after 1928.)

Other local authorities were less well prepared than Argyll, but nevertheless gathered a good deal of background information to place before the Select Committee. Lewis was then administered by Ross and Cromarty Council and its evidence recorded the hardship faced by itinerant workers in the fishing industry, mainly herring girls but also including coopers and carpenters. In all, these people made 8,000 single crossings per annum to and from Lewis, at a fare of 11/7d ((58p) single, and sometimes had to stand throughout the entire passage. This contrasted with 15,000 crossings by passengers in cabin class, fares 38/- (£1.90) single. In 1914 these fares had been 4/- (20p) and 18/- (90p) respectively. The people of Lewis were, however, afraid to say anything which would damage their chances of obtaining the new ship already promised and their MP, Mr Livingston, who could not be present for the debate, had sent a desperate telegram to Mr Runciman, MP, saying "Don't, for Heaven's sake, do anything which will make us lose our new ship". The people of Skye, rather unrealistically, wanted two mail services and a weekly cargo sailing from Glasgow. They also asked that the Inner Isles steamer should call at Staffin and Kilmalug.

The South Uist and Barra District Committee, on 11 June, recorded that the type of steamer used was unsuitable, being slow and having poor accommodation in the steerage, that fares and freight rates were too high – they claimed that these were between 500% and 800% above 1914 levels, but this is not borne out by printed tables – and that an improved service would be of benefit to the fishing industry. The people of Kilchoan contented themselves with asking for an improved mail service.

Local people and their political representatives might as well have saved themselves the trouble of gathering and submitting evidence, since on 28 July, long before the Select Committee's report had been received it, it was announced that it was recommending the creation of a new company, with a capital of £350,000, to be owned jointly by the LMS and Coast Lines. The background to this development seems to have been that, as early as 24 May, Sir Josiah Stamp, now President of the executive council of the LMS Railway, had written to Sir Alfred Read, Chairman of Coast Lines to suggest a possible joint take-over of MacBraynes, perhaps also including the LNER. News of this had clearly leaked back to the Committee. The immediate result was that the LMS and LNER companies were asked to discuss the matter with Coast Lines Ltd and Sir Josiah was asked to prepare a report on west highland shipping. This company would have a new mail contract and either a fixed subsidy of £50,000 per annum for ten years or one varying between £25,000 and £75,000. Four new vessels would be ordered and there would be a 10% reduction in rates for goods traffic. There would be eight directors, three each from the operating companies and two representing the British government. The LNER, though very prepared to co-ordinate services with the steamers, did not wish to become involved financially, which, in view of its own uncertain position during the next few years, was just as well. If anyone thought that the arrangement was a little odd, they were too polite to say so in public.

Sir Josiah, not given to bursts of enthusiasm at the best of times, positively exuded pessimism on this occasion. The new company was "not a promising or profitable commercial enterprise" and the LMS had become involved only on the grounds of public necessity and with considerable reluctance. To him, the whole matter was clearly peripheral. His biographer makes no mention of it, nor did he himself allude to it when addressing a meeting of LMS staff in Glasgow in March 1929. It would seem that he was not popular with railway staff in Scotland, one of whom referred to him as "That old sod, Sir Josiah"[13]. Fortunately he was content to leave the matter of ordering new vessels to Sir Alfred Read who took a more positive approach. The new arrangements were approved by Parliament after a debate in November and thus David MacBrayne (1928) Ltd was born. According to the centenary history, there were in fact only five directors. Sir Alfred became Chairman, with Sir Josiah as Vice-chairman and Sir Alexander Gracie, who was already

13   *The LMS – A Railway in Retrospect.* C Hamilton Ellis, Ian Allan Ltd

a member of the LMS Scottish steam vessels committee, also represented that company. Lt-Col Norman MacLeod represented the British government and the quintet was completed by Mr J W Ratledge, presumably also a shipping representative.

It had all been very curious and was an excellent example of what Sir William Lithgow would, much later, call the "patronising and neo-colonial thinking of central authorities".[14] The arrangements were made in great haste, with no thought of their long-term significance, and with no public scrutiny in Scotland, and it seems clear that Baldwin's government did not want to have to listen to a Select Committee, which would sit for months, take much evidence from local authorities and local people and perhaps then produce a report recommending the expenditure of a good deal of money. They simply wanted to be rid of the problem as quickly as possible, without leaving the west of Scotland bereft of steamer services and without losing the support of local Unionist MPs. The MacBrayne centenary history (1951) probably got it right when it used the phrase "Sir Alfred Read and the late Lord Stamp[15] "came to the rescue and relieved the government by acquiring the fleet". It was a very English solution, decided in London and implemented from London, with minimal Scottish input, but at least the government did not listen to the wilder free marketeers in its own party, such as Captain G Fanshawe (Conservative/ Unionist, Stirling and Clackmananshire and a member of the 1928 committee) and try to bring in some form of competition. That particular idiocy had to wait for forty years before it would receive another airing. It must also be said that the formula adopted allowed the injection of new capital into the Company and thus provided for new building, to bring the fleet nearer to being up-to-date. The chance to consider the overall transport picture had once again been lost.

The first of the new ships, *Lochness*, was built by Harland and Wolff at Govan, that firm having built many ships for the Royal Mail Lines group, of which both it and Coast Lines were then a part. She was completed very quickly, possibly because a good deal of the preparatory work had already been done before the changes. The second and third of the new ships, *Lochearn* and *Lochmor*, were built in 1930 by the Ardrossan Dockyard Company, then owned by Coast Lines. That yard had little experience in building passenger/cargo ships of this type and other firms might have made a better job of them. The fourth new vessel was *Lochfyne*, delivered by Dennys of Dumbarton in 1931. She was launched by Lady Stamp and Sir Alfred Read, in a speech at the luncheon which followed, commented adversely on the state of many of the piers in the islands and expressed a hope that they would be "somewhat modernised". Lady Stamp received a diamond and platinum brooch, but Sir Josiah apparently took no part in the proceedings. Two further ships of the same type, *Lochnevis* and *Lochiel*, came out in 1934 and 1939.

The (1928) was dropped from the title in 1934 and nationalisation in 1948 saw the share owned by the LMS being assumed by British Railways. This passed to the Scottish Transport Group in 1969 and the share owned by Coast Lines Ltd was purchased by the STG on 1 July of the same year. Outwardly there was no change through all these developments, apart from a very brief experiment with grey hulls in 1929/30, and probably most passengers were unaware that there was anything different about MacBraynes after 1928, 1948 or even 1969. The Company went on looking and behaving very much like its old self until it was subsumed into Caledonian MacBrayne in 1973.

---

14   He was speaking at the commissioning of *Sound Of Jura*.
15   Sir Josiah became Baron Stamp of Shortlands in 1938. He died in an air raid in 1941.

Sources –

Biographical Dictionary of the House of Commons, vol III, 1911-1945

Report of the Committee on Rural Transport, 1919. National Archives of Scotland APU6/41

Material in the archives of Argyll and Bute Council

260 Committee on Transport – Schedules received in reply to Circular as to MacBrayne's contract 1928

261 Committee on Transport – Report on Special Services 1927

262 Committee on Transport, general file 1926 – 1928

263 Committee on Transport, general file 1928

264. Committee on Transport, general file 1928 – 1929

265 Statements of Evidence as to Mail and Transport Services in The West Highlands, submitted by the County Council of Argyll to the Select Committee on the Western Highlands and Islands (Bound vol.) 1928

266 Official Report on Parliamentary Debate on Western Highlands And Islands (Print) May 1928

267 Official Report on Parliamentary Debate on Western Highlands And Islands (Print) Nov. 1928

268 Contract between the Postmaster General and David MacBrayne Ltd. (Print)

269 Contract between the Minster of Transport and the Postmaster General, and David MacBrayne Ltd. (Print), November 1928

270 Report from the Select Committee on the Western Highlands and Islands (Print)

The Bailie no. 1803 (Mr MacQuisten)

The Scottish Secretaries. David Torrance. Birlinn Ltd, Edinburgh, 2006.

Josiah Stamp, public servant. J H Jones. Sir Isaac Pitman, London, 1964

Appendix 1. Services to Mull in 1914 and 1928

1914 Winter service to Tobermory from Oban
MWF at 5am in winter (To Coll, Tiree and Bunessan)
Daily at 6am (Outer Hebrides)
Daily at 1pm. Sound of Mull service

1914 Summer service as above with following alterations
TThSO at 7am (To Lochinver)
MWFO at 8.30am (To Staffa and Iona)
Daily at 10am (Outer Hebrides)

From Glasgow
Monday, Thursday and Friday – times subject to cargo
1928 Winter service
MWFO at 8am (Outer Hebrides)
Daily 1.15pm (Sound of Mull)

Summer service as above, plus
MWF 9am (Staffa and Iona)
Sound of Mull steamer had a later departure on Wednesday.
Mails from Tobermory no longer carried on steamer returning from Iona and Staffa at 4.5pm

From Glasgow
Winter once weekly, summer twice weekly

Appendix 2. Traffic to and from Tiree 1927-28

Passengers   3,192.
Livestock   1,063 cattle, 29 horses, 4,373 sheep, 251 pigs.
Cargo   1,470 cases of eggs (30 dozen per case), value £3,442/10/- (£3,442.50)
             283 crates of herring, value £566. (1927 was a bad year for herring)

Single fares from Oban 1914: 6/- (30p) steerage, 8/- (40p) cabin. 1928 77.5p and 31/- (£1.55) respectively

Appendix 3 "The Storm roared its loudest…"

It is not clear who wrote the poem, dated June 1928, of which this is only the second part, the first part being missing. It has not been possible to trace the individuals who are referred to by first names only and it is probably purely coincidence that these names – Tom, Freddie and Davie – are those of MPs Johnston, MacQuisten and Kirkwood, all of whom spoke against MacBraynes in the debate. "Winnie" is of course Winston Churchill, Chancellor of the Exchequer. It clearly has something to do with the proceedings of the Select Committee and is worth reproducing here, if only to repeat the message that politicians and civil servants sometimes see things differently when away from London, Edinburgh or (now) Brussels. There have been more recent examples …

The storm roared its loudest and the vessel rolled and pitched,
The Mail Boys thought the end had come, the Steamer was bewitched,
The Skipper went below to dine, remarked the breeze was grand,
Said Freddie, Captain I would like once more to see the land.

When Tom had fed the Fishes Twice, he felt a little better,
And to the Steward he said, he'd like to send a friend a letter;
So to his "Good Pal Winnie" who keeps his "Brother's Purse"
He told the story of the Mails, but made it so much worse.

Arrived at last in Castlebay, three men went quiet ashore,
And waited in the best Hotel, their heads still very sore:
They wired for a battleship, some great *Barham* or *Renown*[16],
That they be safely carried back to Dear Old London Town.

No more we'll hear Bold Davie's voice, or Tommy shouting loud,
Big Fred has no recovered yet, feels no reason to be proud;
In London they will hide their heads, as quiet as any mouse,
Just slip in for a coffee, to the Great Strand Corner House.

Don't ridicule those gallant men, who sail the Western Seas,
To carry Foodstuffs and the Mails, their Fellow Men to please;
Theirs is a Noble calling, manning ships so stout and Small,
Built for the narrow harbours, into which they're forced to call.

Though you are highly recompensed, for all the part you play,
How much more should the sailors be, who daily find their way;
From the Mainland to the Islands, their tortuous course to find,
While you recline in luxury, not trouble on your mind.

---

16 *Barham* was a Dreadnought battleship of the *Queen Elizabeth* class of 1915 and *Renown* was actually a battle cruiser.

With the Cooper at his Barrel and the Lawyer at the Bar,
Put the Parson in the Pulpit, let the Chauffeur mind his Car;
No idle talk will e'er remove those "Gems from off the Sea",
The natives like Good Postie's Knock the same as you and me.

Then join in all ye "Hefty Sons" who from the Islands come,
From Stornoway, from Harris, Fairest Islay and from Rhum;
 Your thanks are due to "Fred and Co" who to the world proved,
The Mails they must be carried, for your Islands can't be moved.

When Freddie to his Partners said, we'll make a great mistake,
If from this Good Old Firm now, these Mails away we take;
It's easy in the summer time, but through winter's storm and rain-
The only Folks to do the job are Good Old D. MacBrayne.

The Routes lie through the Islands, four Hundred Miles and more,
Through waters deep and narrow, past many a Rock Bound Shore;
The Harbours and the Piers are small, no scenery could be finer,
We grant this trade could not be done, by Motor, Plane or Liner.

Reproduced by kind permission of Miss I Robertson.

Appendix 4. Frederick Alexander MacQuisten

This gentleman who did so much to change west highland shipping in the 1920s was born on 23 July 1870 at Inverkip, in Renfrewshire. He was a son of the manse, his father, Alexander MacQuisten, being minister at Inverkip for over 40 years. In due course he went on to the University of Glasgow to take a degree in Law, graduating in 1891. He then worked for various legal firms in Glasgow and later became a partner in that of Dunlop and MacQuisten, his special interest being company law. He seems also to have had an interest in firms trading in fuels, since he was involved with the Burmah Oil Company and later with the Campbeltown Colliery Company. He went on to become a KC (Scotland) in 1919 and a KC (England) in 1932. In 1901 he married Margaret Reid, from Muir of Ord.

Mr MacQuisten's first entry to politics came in 1907, when he stood for Glasgow City Council as a Tory-Democrat and was elected to the Townhead ward by a large majority. In that same year, there were fierce debates about the licensing of public houses and he won his first taste of fame by speeches defending licence holders in the Licensing Court. Thus encouraged, he stood for Parliament as a Liberal Unionist in Leith in December 1910 but failed to be elected. The same happened when he fought Glasgow St Rollox at a by-election in 1912, but he was successful at his third attempt in 1918 and became member for Glasgow Springburn. He failed to hold the seat in 1922 but was selected for Argyllshire, then usually a safe Unionist seat. However he did not succeed in taking it in the election of December 1923 but did win it with a majority of over 3,000 in the following October. He retained that seat for the rest of his political career, being returned unopposed in 1935, and according to Mrs Donaldson, became "a most keen and persistent champion of all highland interests". He died on 29 February 1940.

Mr MacQuisten is probably best remembered now not for his contribution to the end of David MacBrayne Ltd but for a rather bizarre attempt he made in 1921, during a debate on moral topics, to have lesbian relationships criminalised. It is not clear why he wanted to take this step, but the Lord Chancellor, Lord Birkenhead, managed to dissuade him on the grounds that "Only one woman in a thousand has even heard of the condition" and that it was not worth while wasting parliamentary time on such a motion.

Frederick A MacQuisten was certainly no friend to MacBraynes and he clearly played a large part in the downfall of the old Company. However, unlike some more recent critics, he was at least consistent in his attitude to it.

13.8 An unwelcome sign of the new order. *Claymore* at Kyle, wearing the short-lived livery of grey hull. (© Duncan Macpherson Collection, Dualchas Heritage Service, The Highland Council))

13.9 *Lochness* when new, with grey hull. (Author's Collection)

13.10 *Lochmor*, with grey hull, at Loch Scavaig. One of her boats has been lowered to ferry passengers ashore. (Miss I Robertson collection)

13.11 The observation lounge of *Lochfyne*, as built, looking aft. Although the Lloyd Loom chairs grouped around small tables looked very attractive, they did not maximise seating capacity and, for her summer services, this was too limited. Matters improved in the 1950s, when less elegant bus type seating was fitted. The soda fountain, which dispensed ice cream, can be seen on the right. The large radiators made this a comfortable haven when she was on winter service. (National Maritime Museum, neg. no.G11584)

13.12 The rather cluttered upper deck of *Lochfyne*. (By courtesy of the Mitchell Library, Glasgow City Council)

13.13 Captain C Cameron, Master of *Lochfyne* in the 1930s, having transferred from *Iona*. (By courtesy of the Mitchell Library, Glasgow City Council)

13.14 Although not covered in the 1928 agreement, the hint dropped by Sir Alfred Read at the launch of *Lochfyne* was taken up by the Company itself and money was found to modernise some piers, with Tobermory and Fort William receiving new buildings in an attractive Art Deco style. Post-1945, *Lochfyne* brings a fair crowd to the latter, at which five Maudslay buses await tour passengers. (Author's Collection)

13.15 *Lochnevis* at Kyle in 1934. Judging by the interest that is being shown, this may have been her first call. She is en route to Raasay and Portree. Motor traffic has appeared but most cargo handling is still done by hand and is very labour-intensive. Beyond the saloon car can be seen one of the large lamps used (ineffectually) to illuminate the pier by acetylene gas and castigated by Chris Fraser as being dirty and distinctly smelly. (Duncan Macpherson Collection, Dualchas Heritage Service, the Highland Council)

13.16 As stated, the Company's title reverted to its traditional form in 1934 and in this view of bus 65 outside the Coast Lines' Office in Inverness, the "1928" has been scored out. New in 1934, this was a Bedford WLB with Duple coachwork, seating 14 passengers, and is working on the replacement service for the Loch Ness local steamer. Behind the lady in the fashionable fur stole is a branch of the National Bank of Scotland. (The Omnibus Society)

13.17 Until 1933 the Company was fairly conservative in its vehicle-buying policy, but in that year it made a radical change and bought two buses of new AEC Q type, with side engines. MacBraynes must have liked the design, since in 1945 they acquired a third, second-hand from Edinburgh Corporation. It became no.53 and is seen at Fort William in the late 1940s. (The Omnibus Society)

13.18 *Lochiel*, last of the class of motorships. This view shows her as sailing after 1954. (Laird Parker, by courtesy of Frank Walton)

Tailpiece. A motor ferry boat tendering one of the steamers. Although these launches were an improvement on the former rowing boats, passengers and goods still faced a soaking when using them, while goods could be ruined if not properly covered. In this case, the main cargo seems to be a large box of Gold Flake cigarettes. (By courtesy of the Mitchell Library, Glasgow City Council)

By 1936 the Company seemed to have recovered something of its old élan and the cover of the timetable projected a positive image. (Author's Collection)

14 MacBraynes' Last Battle

A S MENTIONED AT VARIOUS POINTS in preceding chapters, Hutchesons and MacBraynes were able to carry on their business by peaceful co-existence with other companies, without any great fear of competition. It was therefore ironic that the Company's greatest battle with a competitor should come in the last few years of its independent existence.

For very many years the basic timetable for the Islay service did not change. While there was a distinct improvement in comfort when *Lochiel* replaced *Pioneer* just at the start of the second world war, there was little actual change in the service. When MacBrayne took over MacCallum, Orme and Company in 1948, the task of serving Colonsay was added to the Islay steamer's roster. Curiously, in view of what was later to happen, in October 1946 the General Manager, Mr Leith, had suggested that MacBraynes should give up serving Port Askaig, as it was "too dangerous". Local passengers would have to pay their own bus fares to Port Ellen, but nothing was said about cargo. The proposal was not published and was soon dropped.

In 1959, *Lochiel* gave a single sailing in each direction daily (except Sunday), to and from each Islay pier on alternate days. She sailed from Port Ellen on Monday, Wednesday and Friday and from Port Askaig on other days, leaving the Islay pier at 8.50am and arriving at Tarbert at 11.40 or 11.50am. The ship returned to Islay at 1.30pm, going to the opposite port to that which she had left in the morning. Gigha was served on all Port Ellen sailings, Jura on all those to Port Askaig and Colonsay in summer had calls on four days per week. Departure from Glasgow by train to Gourock was at 8.29 and passengers arrived in Islay in the evening at 5.50pm, the through time to Port Ellen being eight hours and twenty minutes. Gigha was also served by a passenger-only ferry from Tayinloan on the Kintyre peninsula.

Vehicle rates were then calculated by weight and drivers were asked to produce a certificate at time of shipment, though in practice this was seldom requested by crews. In 1959 a small car (10cwt) (509kg) cost £3/10/- (£3.50) single but a three-monthly return could be had for £5/3/10d (£5.19). Despite these relatively high fares, the demand for car space grew and by 1965 *Lochiel* had been transferred to a car ferry roster, while *Lochnevis* took the normal mail and passenger sailing. There was also a direct cargo service from Glasgow, normally in post-war years provided by *Lochbroom* or *Loch Ard*.

Ileachs had been disappointed that their island had not been included in the plans for the first batch of MacBrayne car ferries and were therefore pleased to learn in 1965 that the Company had formulated plans to run a car ferry service from a new terminal at Redhouse, at the mouth of the West Loch to Port Askaig and, on some sailings, to Colonsay. These plans had been discussed at a meeting held on 3 November 1964, attended by C B Leith of MacBraynes, officials of Argyll County Council and civil servants of the Board of Agriculture for Scotland. (As the country did not then have a department of transport, that Board had to function as a de facto transport authority for rural areas.) A drive-through ship was proposed. Popular opinion in the south of Islay, fearing the loss of calls at Port Ellen, was hostile. Some mention was also made of the possibility of creating an overland route via Jura, but the people of that island were not in favour of this, preferring to be served by the existing route to Craighouse. The matter of serving Gigha was also a difficulty. The County Council set up a special sub-committee to take the matter further and in due course appointed A M Robertson of Helensburgh as consulting engineer. On 21 November 1966 he submitted his estimates. A new terminal at Port Askaig would cost £257,000 and one at Port Ellen

14.1 *Lochiel* at Port Askaig about 1950. A fair crowd is on the pier and there are a number of pre-war cars in attendance, but it would appear that none of these is for shipment. (Author's collection)

14.2 *Loch Ard* with what looks like a complete flitting on board in a Pickford's crate. (Laird Parker, courtesy of Frank Walton)

14.3 Looking forward from the bridge of *Loch Ard* in Kingston Dock, Glasgow. This view gives an idea of the many and varied items conveyed by the cargo vessels. Her two derricks could lift five and ten tons respectively, a considerable advance on the maximum of seven tons on previous vessels. She could accommodate 130 head of fat cattle and could also carry buses, lorries and, as seen here, cars. Two attractively furnished two-berth cabins also allowed passengers to recreate the cruises of former years, but this facility was not widely advertised. (Glasgow University Archives)

either £85,000 or £150,000, depending on the form of construction adopted. That at the West Loch would cost £285,000, while the total for an overland route would be over £600,000, exclusive of the upgrading of roads which it would entail. On Islay, a committee of transport users was set up. Initially its members favoured an overland route, but later became very determined advocates of the maintenance of a service via Port Ellen. There were some suggestions that hovercraft should be adopted in place of conventional ships and Cdr J R C.Montgomery, RN (retd), wrote an article in the magazine "*Hovering craft and Hydrofoils*" outlining plans for a service of 50 knot hovercraft between Port Ellen and Ardrossan via the Mull of Kintyre. Few shared his enthusiasm for this.

In the meantime other developments had taken place. The first suggestion of competition came in 1966, when John Rose, an ex-sailor, combined with two haulage contractors, Gavin Hamilton and Christopher Pollok, to set up Eileann Sea Services (Island Sea Services), to run a vessel of the landing craft type to Islay. With the help of a loan or grant from the Highlands and Islands Development Board (sources are not clear on this point), they commissioned *Isle of Gigha* from Thames Launch Works, though she was actually built in Bideford in Devon. She began the service in May 1966 and by October was carrying 180 tons of goods per week, out of a total of 250 tons to and from Islay. Unfortunately the methods of operation were open to question and, on 11 November of that year, she capsized while on passage from Gigha to Port Ellen. The captain and the driver of one lorry were rescued by *Lochiel*, which fortunately was on passage from Port Ellen at the time, but two others were drowned and that was the end of Eileann Sea Services. However, the vessel was salvaged and overhauled by Ferguson Brothers of Port Glasgow, before being offered for sale. In July 1967 a group of businessmen with interests in road haulage founded Western Ferries Ltd, with a capital of £100,000 and ordered a vessel from Fergusons. The directors were G B Clapham, L J Gilchrist, I V R Harrison, Sir W Lithgow, G T Wordie and P J Wordie. *Sound of Islay* entered service on 7 April 1968 between new and very basic terminals at Kennacraig, about eight miles down the West Loch from Tarbert, and Port Askaig. A grant of £4,500 was received for the former. The ship could carry 20 cars or a mixture of cars and commercial vehicles on her open afterdeck, these being loaded and unloaded by a stern ramp. Twin rudders and a bow thrust unit gave her excellent manoeuvrability. She had very basic accommodation for 93 passengers and her crew numbered only five. Catering was limited to a vending machine. A twice-daily service in each direction was offered and Sunday sailings were also provided. The charge for an 11ft car was £2/15/- (£2.75) single and the new service got off to a good start, so much so that there was clearly a need for a larger and better ship. Public opinion in Islay was largely favourable, as many prices, such as that of petrol, had been considerably reduced. However, one "satisfied islander" (who was in fact now dissatisfied) wrote to the *Oban Times* on 19 September 1968 to point out that, while rates from Tarbert had indeed gone down, he was now paying £8 per ton for cattle feed from Glasgow compared to £3/10- (£3.50) when it had been brought all the way by MacBraynes' cargo vessel *Loch Ard*. The rates for grocery items showed similar increases.

Western Ferries, having increased their capital to £250,000, then went on to publish plans for an overland route to Islay via Jura, using a new, larger vessel and, given all that had been said about the virtues of private enterprise, surprised many by hinting that this might require a subsidy, at least in its initial stages. William Ross[1], Secretary for Scotland in Harold Wilson's government, did not think much of this idea and rejected it on 25 July 1968. It was therefore not taken any further, though the rebuilt *Isle of Gigha*, now renamed *Sound of Gigha*, was acquired and on 1 March 1969 opened a new service between Port Askaig and Feolin on Jura. The loss of traffic on MacBrayne's service to Port Askaig was serious. In 1968 the Company landed 5,161 passengers there and embarked 5,412. In the next year, these figures declined to 3,507 and 3,951 respectively. For Jura it was much the same story. The 1968 figures were 2,082 and 2,273, but in 1969 these fell to 1,491 and 1,301. Figures for Colonsay were almost identical in both years, while those for Gigha actually showed an increase in 1969. *Sound of Gigha* remained on the inter-island link until 1998

---

1 William Ross, Secretary of State for Scotland from 18 October 1964 to 19 June 1970 and again from 5 March 1974 to 8 April 1976. He was then MP for the Kilmarnock division of Ayrshire.

and from 1973 onwards the service was subsidised by the local authority. It is now run by Argyll and Bute Council, using the ferry *Eilean Dhiura*.

Peter Wordie, Managing Director of Western Ferries, was very aware of the methods of low-cost ferry operation in Norway and in 1969 *Sound of Jura*, a sister ship to the Norwegian vessel *Smola*, was acquired from shipbuilders in that country. She was thoroughly up to date, with variable pitch propellers, a totally-enclosed bridge and a bow thrust unit and, having a greater speed than her predecessor's 10 knots, was able to give a thrice-daily service on the route. She was the first drive-through ship to operate in Scottish waters. With two saloons, one of which was rather claustrophobic, and a small tea bar, her passenger appeal was also much improved and at her commissioning Mr Wordie admitted that the accommodation on *Sound of Islay* had been somewhat spartan. Her passenger capacity on the Islay service was 250 in summer and 74 in winter. The latter figure would certainly have caused problems had she been the only ship operating at winter holiday times. There was no suggestion of any service for foot passengers, of whom MacBraynes sometimes carried 2,000 in one week, although the Glasgow-Campbeltown buses did pass near the terminal. Western Ferries made a very small profit in 1967/8 (£4,000) but, with *Sound of Jura* in service and scooping most of the traffic, this increased to £43,000 in 1969/70. It dropped back to £17,000 in the following year, when they faced real competition. These figures were not enough to maintain interest payments on borrowed capital and those who had put money into the Company received no dividends at this time. On its own, even a profitable Islay service could not sustain the Company.

Meanwhile, in December 1968, MacBraynes had at last been given permission to order a new, drive-through ship for the route, from the Ailsa Company of Troon. Argyll County Council could now go ahead with an application for financial assistance for its new terminal at Redhouse, near Kennacraig in March 1969. It also progressed to the stage of negotiating the purchase of the foreshore from the Crown Estates, but there the matter stalled. It was obvious that the new facilities could not be ready by the time the new vessel would enter service, leaving the Company with the prospect of having a new ship which would be unable to operate from the existing terminal, as her draught would be too deep to allow her to come right up the West Loch. Help was at hand with the transfer of the Company to the control of the Scottish Transport Group in 1969, the process being completed when Coast Lines' share was acquired on 1 July of that year. The Islay problem was solved by the transfer of the side-loading car ferry *Arran* from the Clyde in the following November. The direct Glasgow-Islay cargo vessel was withdrawn and when the new ship (*Iona*) finally entered service in 1970, it was on the Gourock-Dunoon run on the Clyde.

On 17 January 1970, despite complaints which had been made in the past, there was considerable local sorrow when *Lochiel* made her final sailing. She had served the islands well for just on thirty years and during all that time passengers had appreciated the service provided by her Chief Steward, D Sinclair. Captain D MacLeod had also become well known, having commanded the vessel since late 1960. However, with *Arran* in service, using side loading and hoist operation, the timetable had improved considerably. There was now an early morning sailing from Tarbert at 6am every day, to Port Ellen on Monday, Wednesday and Friday and to Port Askaig on other days. The second sailing of the day from Tarbert was at 11.50am, except on Thursdays and Saturday when it was at 2.15pm. This went to the opposite Islay pier to the morning sailling. Jura was served on all Port Askaig sailings and Gigha on the second Port Ellen sailing on Tuesday, Thursday and Saturday. *Arran* and her crew were being worked fairly hard and, while half an hour was allowed at the Islay piers, there was only 15 minutes at Colonsay and no special time allowance at all at Gigha and Jura. The single fare for a car of 11ft (3.35m) length from Tarbert to Islay was £2.15/- (£2.75), a return being double that amount. An excursion return, valid for a day trip or from Friday or Saturday to Monday or Tuesday, for this length of vehicle, could be had for £3/14/- (£3.70). By 1972, the single fare for the same length of car had come down to £2.50 and the excursion return had increased to £5, but this applied to cars of any length and represented a reduction for those over 14ft 6in (4.42m). It was now also valid on any three consecutive days during the week. To

14.4 The cover of the timetable for Western Ferries' services for summer 1972, showing *Sound Of Gigha* (above) and *Sound of Jura*. (Author's collection)

14.5 There seems to be plenty of business for both *Sound of Islay* (left) and *Sound of Jura* at Kennacraig in 1969. (By courtesy of the Mitchell Library, Glasgow City Council)

14.6 *Sound of Jura* demonstrates her sea-going qualities. (By courtesy of the Mitchell Library, Glasgow City Council)

compare these fares with those of 1959 it is necessary to increase the latter by about 150% to allow for inflation and it can be seen that, as well as the small reduction in cash costs, there was also a considerable reduction in real terms. Cars had to be at the pier 30 minutes before departure. For foot passengers travelling from and to Glasgow there was little improvement. The service was now by coach, leaving the city at 07.40 (MTWF) or 09.00 (ThS). The best time was by the early departure on Tuesday, this giving an arrival at Port Ellen at 2.20pm, a through time of six hours 40 minutes. The later departure required a through journey time to Port Ellen of seven hours 45 minutes, very little better than in the old days.

A good deal of the traffic which had been lost to Western Ferries now reverted to the MacBrayne service, although the former retained the lion's share. In the first week of February 1971 *Arran* carried 25 cars and 67 passengers outbound from Tarbert, with 19 cars and 88 passengers inbound. In the same week Western Ferries carried 43 cars outbound and 204 passengers. By the end of the week on 3 July, the difference was less marked. Western Ferries carried 961 passengers and 204 vehicles outbound, while MacBraynes took 70 cars and 608 passengers out and 68 cars and 706 passengers inbound. Of these inbound passengers and cars on *Arran*, exactly half the cars (35) and just over half he passengers (358) embarked at Port Ellen.

In 1972 Western Ferries offered three daily services to Port Askaig from Monday to Saturday, with two on Sunday. These left Kennacraig at 6am, 11am and either 4pm or 6.30pm. The single fare to Islay for an 11ft (3.35m) car was £2.90, return being double that amount, but an excursion return cost only £5 for any length of car and was available on the same terms as those on MacBraynes' service. It seemed that the two operators were co-existing in a classic example of perfect competition. Western Ferries, however, did not serve Port Ellen, made no provision for foot passengers and were not interested in catering for small cargoes.

This external calm concealed the battle which had meanwhile raged behind the scenes. In London there was now a Conservative government in office, with Edward Heath as Prime Minister, and privatisation was in the air. Negotiations were begun between the Scottish Office and Western Ferries, with a view to that company becoming the sole operator to Islay and its neighbouring islands. In November 1971 Gordon Campbell[2], Secretary of State for Scotland, announced that the subsidy to MacBraynes for their Islay/Colonsay service would be withdrawn and that Western Ferries would receive a subsidy for a service to Colonsay. The STG announced that in these circumstances the Islay service would cease from 31 March 1972, *Arran* being moved to Tobermory to provide a service to Coll and Tiree. This provoked an explosion of public anger in the south end of Islay, the Ileachs having now had time to realise just how much they valued MacBraynes' service. Under the auspices of the Scottish Transport Users' Consultative Committee (STUCC), which was involved because of MacBraynes' former railway connexion, a public enquiry was held in February 1972, at which Mr I MacFarlane represented the Company and the Scottish Transport Group. A total of 587 written objections to the proposal was received, of which 498 were from people in Port Ellen and other places in the south end of Islay. Various public bodies, such as Social Services, Argyll and Bute NHS, the local tourist organisation and the Islay presbytery also objected, while both Argyll County Council and the local District Committee submitted written evidence against the plan. A somewhat stormy public meeting was held in Port Ellen on 3 February 1972 and there were storms of another sort when STUCC members came to try *Sound of Jura*, a good sea boat but a notorious roller, as the trip had to be cut short due to bad weather.

In the course of the meeting and in the evidence to the Committee, a number of hard things were said about Western Ferries in general and *Sound of Jura* in particular. One objector wrote that he had yet to meet a satisfied customer who had used Western Ferries, which he described as a "cheap, under-funded little company". The ship was quite unsuited for passengers with disabilities, due to the steep companionways from the car deck and a gentleman in a wheelchair had been obliged to remain in his car throughout the passage, despite this being against regulations. The toilet accommodation was inadequate and in bad weather became unspeakably awful. There

2 Qv Ch 4.

was no service of hot meals and the drinks machine often broke down. There was no steward or stewardess to look after children travelling unaccompanied and no provision for the carriage of stretcher cases. The people of Colonsay doubted that the ship could serve that island in bad weather, bearing in mind that in winter there were times, as in April 1964, when even *Lochiel* could not make the passage for eight days. In any case, the linkspan which would be necessary to allow *Sound of Jura* to berth at Colonsay had not been delivered and the islanders faced the prospect of having to live for several months without any service at all. The almost total lack of accommodation at Western Ferries' terminals came in for much criticism. The Company had no agency on Islay and passengers wanting to book a passage had to telephone to Kennacraig, on a line which seemed to be engaged for much of the day. MacBraynes had, however, kindly acted as an unofficial local enquiry office for their rivals.

Some objectors had noticed that, should Western Ferries take over as sole provider, their services would not be covered by the STUCC and there could be no chance of future enquiries such as the present one, should the public be dissatisfied with any further changes proposed to the service. *Sound of Islay* would be totally unacceptable as a spare ship to cover overhaul periods of *Sound of Jura*.

The more detailed objections from individuals give a good idea of the variety of cargo which was then handled by MacBraynes' vessels. Many focussed on the likely loss of the service for the carriage of small parcels, especially important in the case of medicines. Five hundred small parcels had been dispatched by Tarbert traders in three months in 1971 and, although Western Ferries later offered to make arrangements with contractors to carry this traffic, objectors feared that this would lead to a steep increase in rates. Those from Gigha supported this point, instancing that sugar cost £11 per ton on a MacBrayne ship and £15 per ton on that of Western Ferries. Farmers and crofters in the south of Islay, who normally walked their livestock to Port Ellen pier and then had it carried by MacBraynes at £2 per head, would have to hire a road lorry at a charge of £1.50 per animal just to take these to Port Askaig. They also raised questions of feeding and watering the animals. In any case, they feared that Western Ferries were not interested in the livestock traffic, although this was denied and the Company mentioned the special non-slip surface ("Intergrip") which had been applied to the car deck of *Sound of Jura* to help the animals keep their feet in rough weather. One of their supporters suggested that cattle, transported all the way in lorries, were now much less agitated than when they had been herded onto a MacBrayne vessel, but this interesting point of animal psychology was not pursued. A bank manager in Port Ellen raised the matter of carriage of coin in bulk. Local fishermen feared that they would no longer be able to export their catches in boxes. The seafood industry had successfully been established in Port Ellen, employing up to 50 people, with almost all the produce going for export abroad, and the proprietor was concerned that the delay involved in shipping via Port Askaig would lead to loss of quality in his products. Hoteliers worried that tourism, which was increasing by about 10% per annum would suffer and that the uncertainty surrounding the services was harming bookings for the coming summer.

The questions raised did not all relate to the alleged shortcomings of Western Ferries or their vessels. It seemed that (as always) no one in authority had any clear over-view of the whole situation and some hard things were said about the failure of Argyll County Council even to begin planning the repairs and development of local roads, especially on Jura, which would be necessary to cope with new travel patterns. However, it did seem that the newcomers had not really grasped the intricacies of providing a shipping service in the west of Scotland.

The outcome of the enquiry, announced with commendable speed on 3 March, was that there would be serious hardship to Port Ellen passengers and shippers if the MacBrayne service were withdrawn, particularly with regard to the additional costs which they would incur and the extra time they would have to spend on their journeys. Their subsidy was confirmed, *Arran* continuing on her usual run, with the prospect of an even better service to Port Ellen at some date in the future. Colonsay was to be served by MacBraynes from Oban. Given that a TUCC was allowed to consider only the question of "hardship" in the event of withdrawal of a service, this represented a notable victory for this Committee and MacBraynes and was in fact one of the very few occasions on which a decision by a Committee led to a complete change in official policy. It also said a great deal about the concern shown by Gordon Campbell, for the people of the isles. Perhaps his willingness to listen to their views and to be prepared to subsidise a state-owned undertaking was one of the reasons why Mrs Thatcher did not hold him in very high esteem. It was also thanks to him that the Western Isles was given its own local authority when local government reform came in 1974; no longer would the islands be simply an off-shore part of mainland authorities.

In due course the MacBrayne services passed into the control of Caledonian MacBrayne in January 1973. Western Ferries had almost conceded defeat and were negotiating the sale of their business to the Scottish Transport Group, on a figure of £2.25 for each share, when the Clyde shipbuilder Sir Willaim Lithgow stepped in and the business was reconstructed under the auspices of Dornoch Shipping Ltd as Western Ferries (Argyll) Ltd. This was not quite the end of the matter and there were negotiations between the County Council and Western Ferries for the purchase of their terminals at Port Askaig and Kennacraig, for which the Company asked a total of £800,000. (The terminals on Islay and Jura plus Kennacraig had cost about £200,000). This matter dragged on for some years, until the terminals were finally taken over and the Islay service transferred to Kennacraig on 25 June 1978. Western Ferries soldiered on in competition with first a rebuilt *Arran*, converted to drive-on operation, then from 1974 with the new *Pioneer*, but on 19 July 1976, without any warning, sold *Sound of Jura* to Mexican owners. *Sound of Islay* continued on what was virtually a freight-only service until 30 September 1981, when Western Ferries withdrew from this route and the vessel was sold to owners in Newfoundland.

Iona, which proved to be a most versatile vessel, was not destined to serve Islay until 1979, but did have a brief spell as a MacBrayne ship in 1972, when she donned a red funnel and took over the Stornoway mail service from *Loch Seaforth*.

Once again, though not for the last time, it had been demonstrated that there was no room for competing services on a route to the western isles. Western Ferries resented the subsidy paid to MacBraynes and said so loudly and clearly, although they themselves had hinted at times that they would like to receive some form of public assistance, especially after *Sound of Jura* was commissioned. They had been brave enough to pioneer a new form of ferry operation in Scottish waters and Caledonian MacBrayne later paid them the compliment of copying the basic design of *Sound of Islay* in their new Clyde ferries *Juno*, *Jupiter* and *Saturn* and in the later *Pioneer* and *Claymore*. They had brought down fares perhaps rather sooner than would otherwise have been the case, but it is likely that these would have come down under MacBrayne auspices when the planned new ship had entered service. They had neglected foot passengers, who still form a significant proportion of Islay passengers, and, more importantly, had neglected public opinion in the south end of the island. They had not realised just how much travellers appreciated the high standard of on-board facilities of MacBrayne ships and perhaps these same passengers had not appreciated these either until it seemed that they were about to lose them. Nor did anyone realise at the time that the traditional services, which generated far less CO_2 emissions per passenger- or ton-mile were much more friendly to the environment than were fleets of lorries pounding the A83 to connect with roll-on ferries, no matter who operated these.

In the long term, the only permanent beneficiaries of Western Ferries' arrival on Islay were the people of Jura, who from 1969 were able to enjoy a frequent service to and from Port Askaig instead of only three calls per week by *Lochiel*. In providing this short crossing, Western Ferries showed the viability of this type of service to a Scottish island and thus paved the way for its adoption by Caledonian MacBrayne in the 1970s. It was on this type of operation, rather than on the traditional steam packet routes that they were to find their niche.

Bibliography

The Sound of Silence. Subsidy and Competition in West Coast Shipping. Andew Wilson. Published by the author, c1975

The Sound of the Clam. Andrew Wilson. Published by the author, c1977

Western Ferries roll on to Success. Stewart Hunter. Ships Monthly, March 1976

From Burma to Barra. The life and times of a Marine Superintendent. Sandy Ferguson. Ardminish Press, Gigha, 2008

West Coast Tales. Walter Weyndling. Birlinn Ltd, Edinburhg, 2005.

Hovering Craft and Hydrofoils, vol.4 no.3, 1965

Argyll County Council papers:-

338 Islay etc steamer services. Includes reports by A M Robertson, Consulting Engineer, and by the County Clerk on transport services to Islay, Lismore and Iona

340 Vehicular Ferry Services to Islay, Jura etc. Includes preliminary report by A M Robertson on terminals and memorandum by Islay Transport Users' Committee on overland route.

468 Islay mail service 1969-71

469 Steamer services to Islay, Gigha and Jura, 1968

Evidence submitted to the STUCC and its report of March 1972 on shipping services to Islay, Gigha, Jura and Colonsay, papers RCC 7/15/1 and 7/15/3 in National Archives of Scotland

14.7 *Iona* was to be the last ship built for MacBraynes, although she served them for only a few months. As built she was disfigured by a ridiculous little funnel, perched atop her bridge, and for most of the time that she carried this, it was painted yellow. However, for a few months in 1972, she carried the traditional red funnel, as seen here. In 1974 she was rebuilt and the offending item removed. She has had a long and successful career and was back on charter to Caledonian MacBrayne for a few weeks as this book was being prepared for publication (Author's Collection)

14.8 *Arran*, after conversion to end loading, and *Pioneer* off Mallaig in May 1979. The former was then on the service to the Small Isles in place of *Loch Arkaig*, while the latter was working the Armadale ferry service. *Iona* was by this time on the Islay route. (Author)

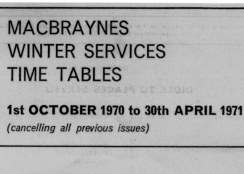

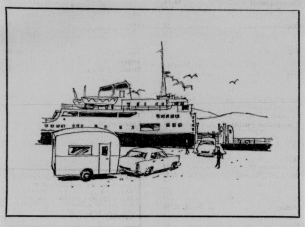

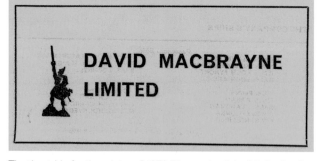

The timetable for the winter of 1970-71 contained the full details of the revised Islay service. (Author's Collection)

Postcript – The Hutchesons and The MacBraynes

L ITTLE IS KNOWN ABOUT ALEXANDER HUTCHESON but contemporary sources give a fair picture of his older brother David. David was born in Inverkeithing in 1799 and the family soon afterwards moved to Port Glasgow, where his father worked in a cooperage. Mr Hutcheson died not long after the move and his widow had a struggle to bring up a young family on a limited income. She succeeded in this, however, and also found time to give her children a good education. David became a clerk on leaving school and in 1817 joined the firm of the Glasgow and Leith Shipping Company, as a clerk in their office in Port Dundas, Glasgow. He then moved to work for a Mr Kid, agent for Mather and Thixton, shipowners of Liverpool. Mr Kid died quite soon afterwards and Messrs Burns succeeded to the agency, promoting David Hutcheson to manage it, with a share of the profits. He and his brother clearly did well, since both became heads of department and when, in 1850, Messrs Burns decided to divest themselves of their interest in west highland shipping, the Hutchesons took over, along with David MacBrayne, the new firm officially coming into existence on 10 February 1851.

There is not much detailed information about the running of the Company by the Hutchesons, but they clearly showed some enterprise in developing the tourist business, with the building of successive new vessels for the Ardrishaig service, culminating in the splendid *Iona* of 1863. She was not the first steamer with deck saloons, but she set the pattern for all subsequent paddle excursion steamers, on the Clyde and elsewhere, right up to the building of *Maid of the Loch* in 1953. Although she served on the Clyde for only one season, her successor inherited the saloons and much of her furniture and she herself was improved in 1873 when fitted with steam steering gear and engine room telegraphs. The facilities for tourists were further improved in 1866 with the construction of *Chevalier* and *Linnet*. The Hutchesons also had the foresight to take a lease on Staffa, to ensure that any profits from this Victorian tourist mecca did not accrue to anyone else. They certainly laid very sound foundations for MacBrayne's later expansion of the Company. David Hutcheson was variously described as shrewd and persevering, brisk and energetic and full of "go". In private life he was affable and of a warm disposition. He was fond of music and poetry and was a gifted singer, delighting many with renderings of Scottish songs such as "The wee German Lairdie", a ribald ballad about George I. He married a Miss Dawson, but, if they had children it would seem that none survived into adult life. He gave up his interest in the Company in 1876 and died at the age of 81. Alexander, about whom much less is known, also gave up his share in 1878.

David MacBrayne thus succeeded to the business in 1878 and ran it under his own name from 1879. He was clearly a successful businessman, typical of the mid-Victorian period in Scotland, and fully committed to the concept of Great Britain. Yet his career can be summed up in a few lines and little is known, or has survived, about the man David MacBrayne.

Although the family came from Argyll, David was born in Glasgow, whither his grandfather Donald MacBrayne had migrated early in the 18th century. His father, David, was registrar of the Barony parish in the city and in due course he married Elizabeth, daughter of Dr John Burns, minister of that parish and sister of George and James Burns, who were soon to become well known in shipping circles in the west of Scotland. The couple had three sons, of whom David, born in 1817, was the middle one. He was initially apprenticed to a printer, then became a clerk in a shipping firm, most likely to have been that of his two Burns uncles. When the Hutcheson brothers acquired the Burns' interest in west coast shipping, David came into their firm and ultimately became a partner in it. In 1860 he married Robina Robertson, daughter of an Edinburgh banker. They had three children, two sons, David Hope and Laurence and one daughter. The family lived latterly at 11 Park Circus, Glasgow, where David died on 26 January 1907. When in Oban on business, David MacBrayne initially stayed in the Great Western Hotel, but latterly acquired his own property in the town.

David MacBrayne inherited a sound business from the Hutcheson brothers in 1878, though it is likely that much of the success of at least their later years was due to his efforts. As a man of affairs, he was clearly astute and generally successful, although not all his ventures turned out as he had probably hoped. His two attempts to enter the hotel trade seem to have ended in failure and his brief venture into deep-sea shipping was likewise short-lived. Throughout his life, he took a close personal interest in the business and it was well known that he was intimately involved in the planning and design of *Columba*. The use of steel in her construction and the many new features incorporated into her design suggest that he was not afraid to innovate. It is said, however, that his favourite ship was *Claymore* and that he always made a point of going down to the quay to see her off, when he was in Glasgow. It has also been recounted, though this cannot now be verified, that he personally received and counted the cash brought to the head office, at 119 Hope Street, by the pursers of the various ships which came into Glasgow. He certainly remained very much in sole charge until almost the end of his long life and his sons were not taken into partnership until 1905, the firm becoming David MacBrayne Ltd on 1 January 1906. He served for some years on the Clyde Trust and was also a JP. For many years he was a member of the Volunteers, predecessors of the Territorial Army, and rose to the rank of major. Of his temperament, little is recorded, although he was referred to as "the genial Mr MacBrayne" in the journal Mercantile Age, c1880. He seems to have had an excellent retentive memory and this is borne out by the deckhand Neil MacArthur who, in the "Isles of Youth" broadcast in 1936, said that MacBrayne knew most of the crews by their Christian (first) name. He also had a keen insight into character, which no doubt stood him in good stead in running a firm which employed 755 members of ships' crews and 696 agents and office staff. His "perfect delight for detail" was apparent in the internal arrangements of *Columba*, for which he received much credit, particularly in the manner in which limited space was used, with not an inch wasted. Of his private interests, nothing is known, but somehow it is difficult to imagine him singing comic songs about the royal family. If indeed it was he who wrote the first version of "Summer Tours", he clearly had an interest in geology and was also something of a North Briton.

David Hope MacBrayne was born in 1862 and educated at Merchiston School, Edinburgh, then Glasgow University and Trinity College, Cambridge. He was well-travelled, having visited Algeria, the Sahara, New Zealand, Canada. His main hobby was collecting ferns and he brought back many specimens from his travels to Scotland. He had a good knowledge of practical seamanship and sailed his 9-ton cutter *Arab* around the west coast of Scotland for many years. Possibly he felt some frustration at his father's prolonged holding of the reins and there was certainly a flurry of innovation after he became head of the Company, with the building of three motorships – *Comet* (1907), *Scout* (1907) and *Lochinvar* (1908) – of which the first and last had long and successful careers, and the construction of the magnificent *Chieftain*. Road motor services were also energetically developed. It was to be the misfortune of David H MacBrayne to take over at a time when the basis on which the Company's prosperity had been built was changing, a process greatly accelerated by the first world war. Frustration may have set in again after 1918, when he found himself charged with making exorbitant profits, at a time when there was only just enough in the coffers to keep matters ticking over and nothing at all to allow modernisation and development. It would seem that he was glad to give up in 1928, when he had in any case reached normal retirement age.

Laurence MacBrayne was born in 1867 and, following the example of many Victorian business men in Scotland, his father sent him to school in England, at Cheltenham College. He was an able scholar, winning a Maths scholarship to Pembroke College, Cambridge, from which he graduated with a First in that subject. He was also Captain of the college's first XV rugby team. He had a brief period in the legal office of McGrigor, Donald in Glasgow, then went on successively to a shipping office and a marine insurance office. During this time he followed a course in marine architecture and marine engineering at what was then the Royal Technical College. In due course he became AIME and a member of the Institute of Shipbuilders and Engineers in Scotland. Like his older brother, he was fond of travel and visited many overseas countries. However, he seems to have had little interest in the running of David MacBrayne Ltd and in 1907 gave up his share in the partnership, although some accounts say that he was a director in the 1920s, as was his sister, Miss F MacBrayne.

Laurence in due course married and the couple had one son, John Burns MacBrayne, who was killed in the Battle of the Somme in 1916. His father endowed a bed in Glasgow's Royal Infirmary in his memory. In 1923 Laurence gave his father's old house at 11, Park Circus, to the University of Glasgow to serve as MacBrayne hall of residence "with a preference for students from the western highlands and islands". He followed this up in 1930 by an endowment to allow extension and proper upkeep of the building. He also, in 1925, founded three scholarships of £50 per annum each, in Engineering, Medicine and Pure science, awarded in rotation and each tenable for three years by students from the west highlands at Glasgow. Holders were required to live in MacBrayne Hall. Laurence also bequeathed his own home at 8 Park Circus for another hall of residence and it opened as Kelvin Lodge in 1947. He died in January 1941 by falling from a window of his house.

This summary is based on information supplied by the University of Glasgow and on that contained in issues of *The Bailie*, as follows:-

D Hutcheson, no.40. D MacBrayne, nos.303 and 819. David H MacBrayne nos.1448 and 1970. Laurence MacBrayne no.1448 and no.112 of the new series.

Bibliography

The following books have been used generally in the preparation of this present work. Those which have been consulted in a more limited context are listed at the end of the appropriate chapter and individual references are given as footnotes in the text.

Across Hebridean Seas. Iain F Anderson. Chatto and Windus, London, 1937

An t-Aiseag an Iar. Dòmhnall E Meek. Clò Beag, Glaschu, 1977

Christy Boy. Chris Fraser. Fraser and Son, Glasgow, 1994

Island Going. R Atkinson. Collins, London, 1949

MacBrayne Centenary – one hundred years of progress. David MacBrayne Ltd, Glasgow, 1951

Steamers of the Highlands and Islands. Ian McCrorie. Orr, Pollock, Greenock, 1987.

MacBraynes for the Highlands. Iain A MacGregor. Turntable Publications, Sheffield, 1977.

Na Nuadh Bhàtaichean. Ailean Boyud. Acair Earranta, Steòrnobhagh, 2006.

Royal Road to the Isles. Ian McCrorie. Caledonian MacBrayne Ltd, Gourock. 2001.

Scotland for the Holidays; tourism in Scotland, c1780-1939. A Durie. John Donald, Edinburgh, 2003

Speed Bonny Boat. J Whittle. Saltire Communications, Edinburgh, 1990.

The MacBraynes Book: Their Highlands and Islands by Bus. Stuart Bell. Scottish Borders Press, Sunderland, 1999.

In fair weather and foul. Colin J Smith. Ferry Publications, Narberth, 1999.

Road to the Isles – travellers in the Hebrides, 1770-1914. D Cooper. MacMillan, London, 2002.

Scottish Coastal Steamers. Brian Patton. Silver Link Publishing, Kettering, 2nd edition, 1999.

The Denny List. David J Lyon (ed). National Maritime Museum, Greenwich, 1975.

The Kingdom of MacBrayne. Nicholas S Robins and Donald E Meek. Birlinn Ltd, Edinburgh, 2006.

To Western Scottish Waters. Robert N Forsyth. Tempus Publishing Ltd, Stroud, 2000.

West Highalnd Steamers. C L D Duckworth and G E Langmuir. Brown, Son and Ferguson, Glasgow, 4th edition, 1987.

Summer Tours in Scotland. David MacBrayne/David MacBrayne Ltd. 1881-1939.

Clyde Passenger Steamers 1812-1901. Captain James Williamson. 1904, reprinted by SPA books, Stevenage, 1987.

Oban – Past and Present. Charles Hunter. *The Oban Times,* Oban, 2nd edition, 1995.

Video. *West Highland Steamer Memories,* Colin M Liddell, Film Sound and Video Services, Alexandria, 1991

This video includes films of pre-1939 trips on board *Fusilier, Gondolier, Lochmor* and *Lochfyne,* in addition to much post-war material. A recent DVD from the same producer gives coverage of the fleet in the post-war years.

Indices

Persons and firms

Organisations

Places

Ships

The ships change, the weather does not. Even with all modern aids, there are still times when all the traditional skills of seamanship are needed to cope with the storms of the Minch. On 25 October 2008 *Hebrides* made a slightly-delayed arrival at Tarbert, while the gale raged at forces up to 11. Despite the atrocious conditions, she completed all her scheduled calls on that day. (Donald Hodgson)